GAME ART:
CREATION, DIRECTION, AND CAREERS

RICCARD LINDE

CHARLES RIVER MEDIA, INC.

Hingham, Massachusetts

Publisher: Jenifer Niles
Cover Design: The Printed Image
Cover Image: © Riccard Linde, or Digital Illusions CE AB 2004. Reprinted with permission.

CHARLES RIVER MEDIA, INC.
10 Downer Avenue
Hingham, Massachusetts 02043
781-740-0400
781-740-8816 (FAX)
info@charlesriver.com
www.charlesriver.com

This book is printed on acid-free paper.

Riccard Linde. *Game Art: Creation, Direction, and Careers.*
ISBN: 1-58450-395-5

Library of Congress Cataloging-in-Publication Data

Linde, Riccard, 1976-
  Game art : creation, direction, and careers / Riccard Linde.
      p. cm.
  Includes bibliographical references and index.
  ISBN 1-58450-395-5 (pbk. with cd-rom : alk. paper)
  1. Computer games—Programming—Vocational guidance. 2. Computer games—Design—Vocational guidance. I. Title.
  QA76.76.C672L55 2005
  794.8'1526'023—dc22
                                    2004029759

Printed in the United States of America
05 7 6 5 4 3 2 First Edition

CHARLES RIVER MEDIA titles are available for site license or bulk purchase by institutions, user groups, corporations, etc. For additional information, please contact the Special Sales Department at 781-740-0400.

This book is for all of us who have, with dedication and sacrifice, given our lives to art, with the hope that we will never stop evolving as artists.

CONTENTS

FOREWORD

The future of gaming is exciting. The gap between content creation for film and game development has nearly closed, and it is becoming more important than ever for an artist to understand the technical challenges that will be faced in creating the next generation of games.

Once upon a time, there were low-polygon artists and film artists—not anymore. In the upcoming generation of game platforms, you will see characters rendered with hundreds of thousands of polygons, and levels with over 5 million polygons in a single field of view by normal maps and displacement. Finding talent to produce the level of quality needed for next-generation game development is getting increasingly difficult. Not only are the aspects of model complexity increasing, everything else is, too. Both shaders and animation are exploding into new realms, from facial animation to full-blown programmable shaders that previously could only be done with software renders. Now, shaders previously seen only in movies can all be done in real-time. What this means is, if you want to make it into the games industry, you have to be ready. Being ready is going to take time, hard work, and a passion for the industry. You have to be ready to learn as much as you can about game development, because the more you know, the better you can be at your job. This does not mean that, to be an artist, you need to know how to program. However, it does mean that it will help you a lot if you understand the technical challenges of the rest of your team. This will help you do your job better with greater efficiency. An example of this is normal mapping. This technique allows you to use a high-resolution model and map it to a lower polygon version with an associated normal map texture. The result is a low-polygon model that looks nearly the same as a model many times its polygon density—all through the use of shaders and textures. Knowing this technique as an artist will help you increase the quality of the game content, and allow you to understand the best workflow to get you there. One method that helped me learn new methods was *modding*. A mod is a modification to an existing game that alters content or gameplay. Mods are usually made by the community of game players to alter the game the way they want to play it. These gamers usually allow these mods to be downloaded for free. Before jumping into developing my first game, I created a mod called *Desert Combat* for *Battlefield 1942* (*DesertCombat.com*). It was an excellent process for me because I was an artist and designer, but I did not know all the miscellaneous items that went into the pipeline to get it into the game engine. Creating a mod is a great way to learn, and allows you to try new ideas and iterations quickly. One reason is that you are starting from a stable platform on which to iterate your ideas and try new approaches. It can quickly teach you about the process of exporting your data into special formats; special image formats used for memory allocation, and even different ways to UV your models for texture quality, normal map approaches, and performance. The simple process of creating a building and importing it into a mod can teach you a lot about workflow and how to improve it. Alternatively, even to learn how other titles do it differently. Most mod tools these days are the same tools that developers use to create the game itself. Therefore, it is a valuable approach if you want to try new ideas or just to learn.

As game development teams become increasingly larger to meet the content needs of, many small developers will soon need to find a home with larger developers to stay alive. Large developers often have the option of moving talent around between multiple titles as needed. While the amount of content increases for new titles, the budgets barely move. This means that companies are increasingly outsourcing content and only hiring a very talented core of individuals. This is where you come in, making it is more important than ever for you as an artist to increase your worth by improving your workflow, become more efficient, and to learn how to work together as a team to get the job done. This doesn't mean you have to work 12-hour shifts, it means that you have to learn more about how games are made outside of just creating art so you can help your team achieve the goals with greater efficiency. This book is designed to help you learn more about the game development pipeline and to understand the challenges that lie ahead. It will definitely get you up and going, but it is going to take passion and eagerness to work as a team to keep you there.

Frank DeLise, General Manager
Digital Illusions

ACKNOWLEDGMENTS

Time flies by. It seems like only yesterday I was sitting in my parents' home learning 3D on my own, far from the high-tech world and others who shared the same interests. A special thank you goes to those friends and loved ones who still support, after all these years in the industry, my dedication to art and my traveling throughout the world.

With deepest gratitude, I tip my hat to Jeremy Price and Yvette Marcoux for taking their time to help me with my English grammar along the way, and for helping to edit this book many late nights.

I also want to thank *all* the people I know within the industry—no one mentioned, so no one forgotten! To the people with whom I spent late *Battlefield* nights, thank you for good development and for getting me through the crunch times. Finally, to all of those who took time from their lives to help with this book:

Contributed Art: Tommie Löfqvist, Julio Ceron, and Ryan Love
Technical 3D: Törbjorn Söderman
Foreword: Frank DeLise
Companies: Digital Illusions, Alias|Wavefront, Charles River Media, Discreet, and Rt/Zen

I thank you all.

PREFACE

G ames are one of the most unpredictable media in today's enter-tainment business. Programmers, artists, and designers as a team are creating virtual playgrounds where players are able to escape and enjoy themselves, with a brief break from their real lives. Different from movies, a game is highly interactive and gives players the possibility to do what they feel is right at any particular moment. With the capabilities of today's games, there are millions of unforeseen actions the player can do in this virtual playground, making it difficult to control and predict for the developers. This is why I say it is a wonderful experience and an amazing challenge to be part of a game production team. It will definitely keep you engaged and alert at all times.

The intention of this book is to give aspiring game artists an overview of what it is like to work in the games industry—methods for those working in the field, and techniques to help you gain speed and knowledge about various technical aspects. This includes how and what you should do to evolve as a game artist to be successful in your game career. This guidance will be useful for those who are taking formal 3D courses, and for those who are self-taught. With this book, I hope to give you the knowledge and drive needed to take the first step into the games industry, or to help you hone your current skills.

The games industry is moving at a fast pace on the hardware/graphics card side, and the bridge between the GFX programmers and the artists is widening. Game productions are now more technical than ever, which can create problems for the artistic people who love to create art but do not want to be bothered with the technical aspects of a program. There is no escape; game artists need to understand what and why certain things are being done, and learn why they are used within a game development, so that they can be a fully functioning part of the team.

This book explores the games industry from my perspective as an Art Director. It will teach you to explore and think the way I do, and guide you to take the same path, if so desired. I will guide you through what is important for an artist to know from an Art Director's point of view, so that you know how to work in the industry, both from an artistic and technical perspective. The techniques covered will and have been used in top-line PC games today, and will be the foundation for the graphics that will be used in the next-generation consoles.

BENEFITS OF READING THIS BOOK

This book is written to teach any artist the standard production process for game art. It provides you with the knowledge, tools, and techniques needed to create quality game art efficiently. It also gives you tips and tricks that solve several common problems with which many artists have difficulty, and techniques that can help you produce the portfolio you need to apply for your next big dream project or to start your career in the industry.

The games industry uses a lot of terminology and technology of which the artist needs to be aware. With all the different things that happen within the PC/game consoles and the game engines you'll be working on, the better prepared you are, the better you'll be able to handle the limitations of creating art for the different gaming consoles. As this book is aimed at artists, not programmers, terms and expressions are simplified and explained as they apply to the artist. Many technical "terms" are included to help close the gap between the artist and programmer, without going into too much detail—just enough so you'll understand. Personally, I have only worked in the games industry for four years, but I have worked with low-polygon production and 3D art since the age of 12. This book shows you the techniques I used to learn and gain my knowledge without formal training. I'll provide you with plenty of tips on what I've learned and show you how to use these ideas in your own work. To gain the most from this book, keep an open mind, question each subject, and do not hesitate to try new ways to create computer art. The book is neither an A to Z tutorial walkthrough nor a bible; its purpose is to give you a deeper understanding of the techniques and tools used in the industry, so you can apply them to the variety of projects you will encounter.

WHAT TO EXPECT FROM THIS BOOK

Using my experience as an Art Director and my research in the areas of game production, I guide you through the latest technologies and the several ways there are to produce high-quality art effectively for the consoles of today and tomorrow.

The content in this book is professional, and in some cases might seem complicated at first. However, mastering the aspects presented here will give you a solid foundation on which to build and hone your skills as an artist in the games industry.

The book is divided into four parts. The first two parts define the artistic process involved in creating art for games, including the basic knowledge you will need. The last two parts of the book include technical in-depth information about performance and more advanced techniques of game art creation. This book was not designed to be a start-to-finish game process; rather, it is a basic-to-advanced course, through which you will advance step by step until you are ready to learn more about game technology.

Part I: The Industry and the Artist

Part I gives you insight into what the games industry is about for an artist, how it is to work with games, the process and where artists fit into it, and the career opportunities available. It also gives a structure and advice for interviews, ideas for salary discussions, and how to create your portfolio for highest impact.

Part II: Game Art Creation

Part II contains the artistic chapters. It discusses how you can gain further personal knowledge in your art creation, and covers subjects such as light/darkness, color, emotional content, how to read reference images, personal workflow, and different ways to work together in a production team. Part II is also the main creation part where you'll learn all the basics needed to start creating game models through modeling, UV mapping, texturing, effects, animations, and collision. To keep things as simple as possible, these chapters only discuss what is necessary for creating art for games, and introduce you to many terms that we discuss in-depth in Part III.

Part III: Technical Knowledge

Games are all about technology—the machines, the programs, techniques, and performance. To get to know it all, Part III explains in-depth the technical parts of creating art for games. It covers technical game-related information, including texture formats, L.O.Ds, vertex costs, fill rate, mipmaps, Tri-stripping, polygon cost, and lighting per-pixel and per-vertex. Part III concentrates on teaching you about gaining performance and understanding platform-dependent techniques.

Part IV: Advanced Game Art Production

The most recent game engines, the nicest graphics cards, and the upcoming game consoles will support some amazing features. Part IV discusses more advanced techniques that are mostly PC dominant now, and will be part of the next-generation gaming consoles. We cover techniques such as multiple UV-texturing, normal maps, high-resolution sculpting, and how shaders work. Throughout these more complex tutorials, you will be challenged to use the knowledge learned from the earlier parts of the book and apply that knowledge to modeling, mapping, and so forth, all with in-production examples.

WHAT YOU NEED TO KNOW

This book is written to teach as many specific methods used in the games industry as possible from a non-program-specific perspective. Because 3D packages are becoming more similar, it becomes less important which one you know. Different studios are using different tools, so it is important that you are open to using available tools. Therefore, it is assumed that you have a working knowledge of at least one major 3D program (3ds max or Maya) and Photoshop. In this book, we will switch between them frequently for different tutorials. I recommend reading the manuals for these programs and perhaps some related books before starting this book. Remember, *you* create the 3D art, not the program. It is merely a tool to let you exercise your creative side.

PROGRAMS USED IN THE BOOK

Being a game developer, you will get used to learning several unique tools for special situations. This book will introduce you to several of these, tools that will help you to create or to do your job. You might not be familiar with all of these programs so remember to use the manual if extra help is required.

Alias|Wavefront Maya 6, Discreet 3ds max 7, and Photoshop CS will be used on several occasions throughout the book.

> **Maya 6 PLE limited version:**   (*www.Alias.com*) (*www.alias.com/eng/ products-services/maya/maya_ple/index.shtml*)
>
> **Discreet 3ds max 7:**   30-day trial (*www.discreet.com*)
>
> **Photoshop CS:**   30-day trial (*www.adobe.com*) (*www.adobe.com/ support/downloads/main.html*)

Chapter 13 and 19

> **Adobe Photoshop Normal Map/DDS Authoring Plug-ins:** *developer.nvidia.com*
>
> **Texture Atlas Tools:**   *http://developer.nvidia.com/object/nv_texture_ tools.html*

Chapter 18

> **Nevercenter Silo 1.3:**   *www.silo3d.com*
>
> **Pixologic ZBrush 1.55 Demo (ZBrush 2):**   *www.Zbrush.com*

Chapter 20

This chapter requires Microsoft® Direct X 9.0c together with NVIDIA® GeForce™FX or an ATI™ 9700PRO graphics card and Microsoft Windows XP.

Included on the companion CD-ROM under RtShaderGinza\Setup.exe:

> **RT/shader:** Ginza, trial version, *www.rtzen.com*

INDUSTRY AND THE ARTIST

As a game artist, you are facing an amazing, booming industry. The games industry is like nothing else—the people, the games, laughter, friendship, overtime, milestones, and pizza. This industry has it all, all the stereotypes.

Part I concentrates on what is important for an artist in the world of game development. We cover what you need to do to become an artist in the industry—what is expected of you, the different job positions, your portfolio, salaries—and explain the process of game creation and its production cycle.

The goal here is to understand what artists are involved with in game production. In addition, you should come away with a basic understanding of what you need to do to enter the games industry, and move on to the next step in your career. May you have many entertaining moments ahead, both with this book and within the industry.

1

THE GAMES INDUSTRY

GAME HISTORY

In 1972, Magnavox released the first at-home computer game (see Figure 1.1). The game had two vertical rectangles that the player would maneuver to hit a "ball" across the screen akin to ping-pong or tennis, an idea invented by Ralph Baer. Magnavox was one of the few companies dealing with games at that time, and employed notable game pioneers such as Nolan Bushnell, who later resigned from Magnavox and, with Ted Dabney, started Atari. After a few years in development, Atari released a home video game system based on the same ping-pong type games.

FIGURE 1.1   Ping-pong game.

This was the start of the commercial games industry. For a number of years, Atari had a strong hold on the market, and licensed the rights to build Pong consoles to Coleco. Sega then entered the gaming industry and also licensed Atari's products. About this time, Namco and Nintendo also entered the arcade gaming market.

During the early 1980s, Atari's success inspired new people to start up companies to produce games on their own consoles, including Electronic Arts, LucasFilm Games, and Activision.

Nintendo released its NES console nationwide in 1986 with *Super Mario Brothers*, which became an instant success. With strong brand names and loveable characters, Nintendo's games gained wide popularity. Sega entered the hardware scene after being a third-party game developer to create its own console, and released the Sega Master system. Although Sega's machine was superior to the NES, Nintendo's gameplay and strong characters won over the market. In the mid-1980s, Atari lost its monopoly to Nintendo. Atari's former third-party developers moved over to create their main titles for Nintendo's NES console, and today, even Atari is following in these same footsteps. At that time, Nintendo was outselling Sega and Atari by 10 to 1 in the United States.

Commodore had been a strong competitor with its C-64, and released the Amiga in 1985. With the Amiga came easily accessible computer paint programs, and the platform for which many of today's 3D programs such as NewTek LightWave® 3D and Maxon™ Cinema 4D released their first versions. The Amiga made it possible to create art and 3D at an affordable price, thereby offering many hobbyists the ability to explore and create art on their own home computers.

At the time, PC computers were mainly aimed at business and office use, and did not have the graphical power or the affordable prices to compete with the Amiga, Nintendo, or Sega. However, even with the lack of graphical power, the market opened for PC text-based adventure games. Later, when graphics cards evolved, these games turned into graphical adventures that we today call "point-n-click." At this time, LucasFilm Games became LucasArts.

The Windows PC breakthrough into the gaming industry came when Id software developed the first 3D engine for the game *Wolfenstein 3D*, and later the earth-shattering game *DOOM* in 1993. This changed the way we create art for games and brought us into the 3D era for which most of today's games are created.

Sony Electronics, which worked with Nintendo for several years creating their CD drives, music chips, and so forth, discontinued their partnership in the early 1990s. Nintendo by this time had full control of the game console industry, but Sony Interactive Entertainment developed and released its PlayStation in 1994 in Japan and in 1995 in the United States. It was an instant success with players and an easily accessible platform for third-party developers. In 1999, the Sega Dreamcast system was released based on Microsoft® Windows® CE to support easier game production. During 2000–2002, Sony released the hugely popular PlayStation 2. Later, both Microsoft and Nintendo released the Xbox and Nintendo Game Cube, respectively.

Today, the PC is a major part of the gaming industry in the game playing where the most advanced technology is developed, and the boundaries are pushed for every new graphics card released. The PC technology is constantly upgrading, and the gaming titles are larger and more open. One example of this is *Battlefield Vietnam* as seen in Figure 1.2, which with its memory requirements makes it impossible to create on any of the same period consoles. The PC with Windows® is also the most common development environment. Both Photoshop® and the major 3D programs have migrated to Windows and are adopting their workflow toward game production. The Xbox, PlayStation, and Game Cube have been in the market for four+ years. The next-generation gaming consoles are in development, and so are the games that will be available at release date.

FIGURE 1.2   *Battlefield Vietnam.* © Digital Illusions CE AB. 2004 Reprinted with permission.

THE PEOPLE AND THE INDUSTRY TODAY

Many of us who work in the games industry have the same experiences—the love for the games we grew up with, the games we are playing today, and a spirit of community among the people involved.

As constructive as this work is, many of us gave it a chance because we wanted to do what we love—create games and make it our career, with or without university education in art, music, programming, design, or production. With a common goal, we have joined together to create something we find inspiring, something we strive for, whether for the love of the games, design, music, programming, or just being an artist who loves to model and get paid for it. This sense of community and friendship is what will keep you in the office late when things need to be done. Even if you start out not loving games, they and the industry you are about to enter will probably draw you in.

Of course, not everything is gold and glorious—everything in life comes at a price. The games industry has many issues in its process that we all hope will be handled better in the near future. However, as with any industry that grows so fast, it needs to catch up with itself.

The International Game Development Association (IGDA) concentrates on the subject, *Quality of Life within the Game Development Industry.*

They provide the industry with an open forum, and their research shows that it's a tough industry.

The games industry is less than 30 years old, and the people working in it are young, with an average age of 27. Seventy-five percent have been in the industry less than eight years, with two to five years being the most common level of experience. Compared to many other industries, these numbers are very low.

The games industry is suffering from the long hours and hard crunch times required to meet deadlines. Stories of people working 80-hour weeks to create the quality art needed to meet the deadlines before the final shipment are not uncommon. Working such long hours every week is difficult both personally and physically.

The IGDA article *Quality of Life* also tells us that the yearly salaries do *not* include overtime, which in many cases is expected without compensation. In fact, IGDA research shows that one-third of the companies have people working as many as 65 to 80 hours a week for crunch, and 50% of the companies see this as a normal part of doing business in the games industry. The IGDA data also shows that 50% of the workers are uncompensated for this extra time spent on the product.

With the overtime and social disadvantages that come with the job—and the insecurity that many studios suffer while waiting for the next project—it is very common for people to resign from the gaming industry and move on to a more stable income, or to the movie industry, making the gaming industry lose many of its best talents and most experienced people.

AN INDUSTRY ON THE MOVE

The games industry began with only a few hundred people, and games were created with "teams" of one or two persons. Today, the games industry is a multibillion-dollar industry with teams of hundreds and multimillion-dollar budgets. It's an industry that has seen, and will continue to see, exponential growth. Due to this growth, smaller studios are having a harder time surviving because of a lack of funding, failure, or being consumed by bigger companies. There are, however, smaller independent studios opening up, so people within the industry should have a wider base of selection with time. Games are always created at a hectic pace, but the goal is always to include the best possible content and to make the games more stimulating to satisfy today's consumers. These consumers expect more content from every new release, so a new game needs to come with huge improvements over its predecessor. This requires us as developers to keep up to date and learn new things. This demand to always innovate and be creative creates stress and pushes us to the technology limits, which of course is a trend on which the games industry is built and why is it so stimulating and interesting.

However, with all this overtime and demands from the public, is there a future within computer/console games? Yes!

Statistics and revenue dollars show that people spend more time playing games than they do in theaters watching the new blockbusters. This game playing results in the games industry today generating more revenue each year than Hollywood movies do, and more people are being hired within the games industry every day. It is definitively a growing industry.

With higher market demands, companies demand more from their employees today than ever before, and they have raised the bar for the applicant, which in turn means that the expertise within the studios will also increase over time. With more highly educated people entering the industry from other industries, the acceptance of extremely long hours may tend to fade, and perhaps some of the glow between the people that exists in the current game development studios may be lost. However, the industry will also be taken more seriously, become more organized, and mature with these changes. Many studios have started to require that the applicant have an education within the subject and a university diploma. You still have a chance to start in the industry without one, if you are a good artist or developer. This industry relies heavily on creative, young, eager people of whom there are many ready to get started. And, if you are qualified and can do the job, companies will hire you.

REFERENCES

Doteaters: *www.emuunlim.com/doteaters/*
Gamespot: *www.gamespot.com/gamespot/features/video/hov/index.html*
IGDA: *www.idga.org*

SUMMARY

1. The games industry has released many interesting machines and games through the years, but it is just beginning. The industry expects to see new next-generation gaming consoles released within two years.
2. The average age of people in the games industry is still young.
3. Many of the developers grew up with games, and share special memories and joy of the games they love to play and create.
4. Working in the industry can become a struggle for a normal life, with stress and insecurity for an unsafe project always looming overhead.

GAME ARTISTS

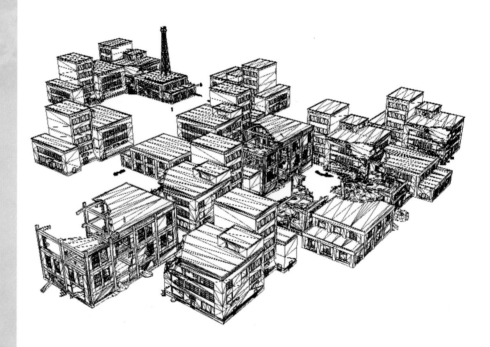

The games industry offers artists a wide range of opportunities and the chance to work with animators, modelers, texture artists, designers, and special effects people. However, becoming a game artist requires much more than artistic talent.

Creating art for videogames requires a wide range of knowledge and skills. This chapter examines the types of jobs and possibilities available for artists in game development, and what you'll need to do to qualify for those positions.

ARTISTS IN THE GAME INDUSTRY

Do you need to love the games that you create the art for as an artist? No! It is more important that you know how to make a beautiful, clean object, animation, or texture and be able to follow the production guidelines with which the team works. Will you enjoy the industry more if you like games, thereby perhaps being even better at what you do? Most likely, yes!

For some studios, your love for games can be more important than your skill in creating games. So, do you love games?

My personal belief is that as an artist, you should try to avoid being blinded by games. Play them, but be aware that you are probably missing the art content. Games are addictive because of the gameplay, not the art. From a professional perspective you should try to play games as an artist rather than as a gamer. Take a step back, look at the game, and learn from what you see. Analyze it. Look at it as you would look at a painting in an art gallery. Ask yourself, "What does the art in the game tell me?" Does this game teach you something about art production or its processes? Enjoy games, but do not forget to be an artist, especially if you want to work in this industry. In the end, a company will benefit more from your artistic knowledge, than your joy of playing games. Spending your spare time evolving as an artist is far more rewarding professionally than playing games.

 Many of the best artists in the industry do not play games in their spare time; they are too busy creating art, expanding their knowledge, and bending the rules.

HOW TO BECOME A GAME ARTIST

In this industry, it currently makes very little difference if your education comes from learning at home or going to school. In the end, all that matters is that you are dedicated to what you do and are able to produce what the studio is looking for. The following sections discuss some important points when it comes to learning software, and developing as an artist.

"Home School"

If you plan to advance your 3D skills at home by yourself, we recommend splitting the process into several parts.

First, what do you want to achieve? Whether it's learning program features, doing animations, creating 3D art, or developing your artistic skills, knowing what you need to learn will help you succeed. Concentrating on one task or subject at a time will help you focus, learn quicker, and retain the knowledge easier.

In this industry, repetition is your friend; work with the task at hand until it becomes second nature.

It is also very important to read the program manual (yes, it is there for a reason). Start with one task, read about its purpose and functions, and then do the tutorials. If your manual does not have a tutorial for each subject, create your own small tests, and do not advance until you know and understand the specific function completely. Repeat this process throughout the entire manual, and in the end, you will have a solid understanding of the entire program.

Knowing how everything works technically inside the program will give you an understanding of how different aspects of the software connect and work together within the program. Play around and try things not covered in the tutorial; for example, see what happens when you merge different commands. Doing so will help you to learn and develop your personal workflow and speed, which will benefit you in a production cycle.

Again, break the learning process into small tasks. Trying to create a full scene from scratch, thinking you can learn along the way, will only lead to discouragement, frustration, and more than a little angst. Not understanding certain aspects of the program, or not getting the results you want because you did not know the process, translates into wasted time and effort. Even worse, if you are in production, you might end up having to redo a lot of work if it was done incorrectly.

When we know the limitations, we can see the possibilities.

You might think that the learning process just described is too structured and boring. You might struggle with one task for days until you really understand how it works. Remember, however, that we learn through trial and error. The more time you spend on a task, the more accustomed you will become with the processes involved. When creating something in a production environment, it is better to know what you can and cannot do.

Explore each feature and find workflows that get you the results you want. Then, find other ways to accomplish the same task. Doing so will make you learn and evolve as an artist. Accept the notion that to succeed, you have to fail. That is how you learn, understand, and remember.

If your goal is to learn about classical art, use the same basic learning process. What is your goal? Is it to expand your art experience? Make sure you shut the computer off and pick up the pencil. The 3D program will not teach you how real lighting works, how a pencil is used, or how composition and balance are achieved from a given area (frame). Try motion kinematics and timing with a real camera doing short films, or just take photos. Forget the computer for a while.

Of course, the ideas presented here could be applied to everything, even this book. If you do not understand a topic, read it again, research it on the Internet, and conduct your own small tests until you truly understand the concepts discussed here. Then, move on, be open to all suggestions and processes, and try to find the best method for a given task.

We live in a time filled with free information. The Internet is an amazing resource teeming with references, open discussions, and forums. It has videos and instructions on how to create classical and 3D art. You have a far greater opportunity to learn faster and get a deeper understanding on your own than many of us who started in the industry several years ago. With focus, time, and dedication, you will most likely succeed.

Time and dedication will help get you anywhere you want, and help you learn everything you want to know.

In School

Many schools now offer courses on the tools necessary for game artists. The biggest benefit of attending a school is that you will always have a teacher close by to answer your questions. It is important to choose your school carefully, and base your decision on your interests, the curriculum, and the reputation of the teachers. With the right school and the right teacher, you have the opportunity to learn quickly and efficiently. Learning at home and doing your own tutorials can be much more difficult, and at times frustrating, even if you have a structured schedule and strong will.

Whether you need to take classical art or computer art lessons depends on your knowledge and skill in these disciplines. You should look at the computer as a tool, just like a pencil. The computer should be used to help you create your artistic ideas, not serve as a media around which to base your art. If you do this, computers will limit you as an artist.

Attend the courses you think are most suitable for you to reach your goals. However, if you plan to become a game artist and do not have a solid base in classical art, we recommend that you consider taking those classes before you take computer art lessons. Doing so will teach you how to be more creative and express ideas and concepts that you will be able to apply to the computer software later.

Schools can be very informative, exciting, and interesting. However, if you find that a particular subject is not fun or stimulating, you might lose focus. Remember, however, that concentration and dedication will get you through. Moreover, if the school is supportive, ask if you can create your own tasks—which should be possible, especially if you paid for the class. Then, with the teacher's help, create something based on your own ideas. However, if the curriculum does not match your own interests or bring you closer to your own goals, use your time more productively.

The school should be teaching you what you need to learn to become a game artist. Even though the classes and resources are great, the main problem with most schools is that they teach uniformity. Everyone does the same tasks with the same software. Haven't we all seen the same portfolio at the end of the year?

The same animation test done by 20 people will show who is a better animator, but it will not display creativity. You should never use an assigned animation test on your final demo reel. Rather, use something unique that you have done yourself based on your knowledge from the same class.

 If we experience something as fun, we get stimulated and learn faster. And, remember: however stupid the question might sound; it is always better to ask than to sit in silence.

While attending school, ask as many questions as you can and gain as much information as possible from your teacher. Put in the effort and make the best use of the time you have in the classes, even if you have to follow a certain curriculum and some of the tasks are boring. It will always teach you something in the end, so keep your concentration and dedication high.

 Think outside the box. If you follow the flow, you will end up competing with people with the exact same knowledge—and no one will be unique.

EXPECTATIONS FROM THE STUDIO

Being in the industry today demands a lot from you as an artist, both in your ability to be creative, and in your technical skills and understanding of programs and techniques. This said, you will still be expected to be fast and accurate while creating consistently beautiful art.

You can never be sure what program you will be using in a project, and processes and software might change depending on the project. Moreover, the studio would like you to know the program they are using when you start.

We personally think it's better to know one 3D program thoroughly than have a weak knowledge in, for example, three. Programs are very similar nowadays, and if master one, you should be able to easily transfer to another. Therefore, make sure you know everything that is needed and know your way around at least one program. The major programs used for today's game production are Maya®, 3ds max™, Softimage™, LightWave®, and Photoshop®. Knowing at least one of these will get you in a good starting position.

Artistically, studios will expect you to be able to take directions from the management team and to adapt to specific styles and processes during the asset creation. They also expect you to work well together with a team, and Art Directors will expect you to be interested in art and hopefully games. It is also important to have an interest in and sense of art, and know and understand composition, colors, and lighting. You must be able to follow schedules, be productive, and make your own valid decisions based on your knowledge and direction from the leads. The studio expects a lot from you as an artist.

A Career as an Artist

Some artists enter the industry today without a solid classical art background, and for some, being an artist in the game industry is their first profession in life.

The game industry has evolved a lot since the first games were released. Today, the industry requires roles that are more specific for the artists, and the most suitable person for the job should fill this position. In yesterday's game development, developers might have had 1 to 10 artists on a project. Everyone could get an opportunity to do a bit of everything in the process from start to finish in case someone were bored or wanted to try something else. The industry and the games created today require much more structure and planning. The assets created for them are both technical and time consuming to produce. The time for creating a game remains the same, but the titles require much more human resources.

The AAA titles of tomorrow will therefore consist of even larger teams. Art teams of up to 50 people will be common in the near future. Big teams like these are a lot of responsibility to manage, and build up a lot of stress on the leads. With these big teams, it will become more common to divide large groups into subteams where a subleader has specific responsibilities delegated to him.

During this type of game developing, chances are that an artist is stuck in his expertise and creates a single type of asset over the lifespan of a game; for example, creating only vehicles for a game that has a two-year production time.

With these larger teams of the future, we should see more career-specific positions become available. With that said, it is important to understand that the best chance for you to be hired and grow with a company is to keep a solid general skill set. Mastering one single area makes you valuable for the studio if they need that information, but not if they don't. By keeping your knowledge of the other areas within the development up to date as well, you develop a very wide base to stand on if you need to assist another artist in his task.

Let's divide artists in a studio into two groups, management artists and production artists. Management positions within the game industry include the people who supervise and overview/follow up the process, rather than being in the art production. Examples of these positions include Lead Artist, Art Director, or Technical Art Director. For some people, the lack of creative input in management positions drove them to return to production.

Technical Art Director

Games as products are based on techniques and complicated game engines. The bigger the teams become, and the more advanced the art creation becomes, the more people are needed who have a high understanding of how things work inside the game engine and to act as the bridge between the programmers and the artists. This person researches new methods, and creates methods for the artists to follow, so that artists can concentrate on creating the art and not on the technical side of game creation. A Technical Art Director would create and customize the tools and features that the art team needs to work effectively and efficiently.

The Technical Art Director works closely with the programmers and the Lead Artist/Art Director to create processes and programs that will assist the artists and programmers in their work.

To become a Technical Art Director, you would need to know how to read and understand one of the major programming languages and 3D programming scripts (e.g., C++, Mel script, 3ds script), and have the artistic understanding to act as the link between the artists and the programmers. You should have a deep understanding of how the tools and processes work within a game engine. You will need to communicate with the leads, artists, and the programmers to get everyone up to speed with the new techniques and processes.

Art Director

FIGURE 2.1   Direct-light, camera, and action.

Each production should have a person with the final responsibility and the final call for how the art in the game looks. The Art Director (AD) brings the artists' quality together and sets the visual standard. In addition to the creative vision for the game, he also needs to assure the product's quality standard and that the game is shipped with the quality on which the team has agreed. In today's game industry, many people want to express their opinion of how things should look within a game, which can make the AD's job more difficult. He should have his mindset, and not cater to individual wants. Doing so will put the project in jeopardy or culminate in a project that is unbalanced or different from what was agreed on at the beginning of the process.

The AD might not be the most talented artist in every task, but he needs to have a good understanding of what can be done with art, a good sense for the feeling and perfection, and the knowledge of prioritizing quality versus time.

It is very important that the AD knows how to give creative and accurate feedback to the artists; this will help them develop ideas and creativity.

As AD, your main responsibly would be to create the vision for the game, while overseeing the quality of the assets. The AD also makes sure that the feeling of the textures, animations, and models suits the game. The AD also works together with the Lead Artists and Technical R&D to create processes, and writes the Style Guide, a descriptive documentation of all required game assets and production processes.

As an AD, your vision can be unreachable because of the producer's production schedule. This makes it hard to put in the changes that are required to achieve the highest quality. An AD should always be aware of what is going on, be flexible, and be able to change things quickly if necessary so the schedule doesn't slip.

To become an AD, your artistic senses should be top notch. You should know how the world works and have a sense for what makes good composition. It is your job to make the game visually interesting and the art appealing. A prospective AD would benefit from classical art lessons, photography, and traveling. He must explore variations of the art creation process. A good AD would be a person who can use words and images to explain his ideas to the team and help the artists achieve his goals.

Lead Artist

The Lead Artist is at the top of the art food chain. He is the artist with the final responsibility over the project's art production. The Lead Artist is the project administrator, and the main communication link between the artists and the producer. Among other tasks, he is responsible for setting up the project's art schedule, predicting the time needed, and ensuring that the assets are completed and the schedule is followed throughout the project. The Lead Artist ensures that timeframes and milestones are met and delivered with the content and quality as promised. While overseeing the artists in the studio, the Lead Artist also handles the personnel development, discussions, applicant interviews, time reports, vacation requests, and even at some places, salary discussions. The Lead Artist works together with the Art Director and the Technical Art Director to work out the processes needed for the artists within production and maintaining the Style Guide.

Programs that would be beneficial to know would be Microsoft® Project® or similar task project program.

To become a Lead Artist, you should be a good leader, a good organizer, tolerant to stress and decision-making, and understand the time needed for content creation. A Lead Artist requires good personal communicating skills. It is important that you understand the people you are supervising. As an art lead, you also need to have good technical skills to educate people about game creation processes and be able to predict the time needed for different tasks.

People in the position of Lead Artist usually have a wide experience in many areas of game art creation, and are considered experts in several of the processes.

Modeler

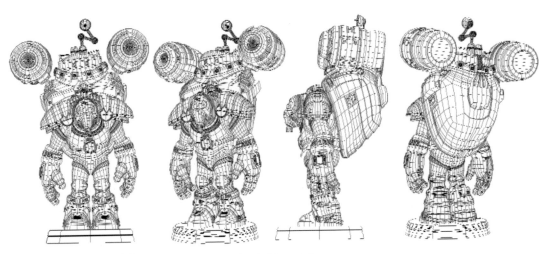

FIGURE 2.2 Ceative Modeling. © 2004 Ryan Love. Reprinted with permission.

All 3D games need objects, and some of today's 2D games have 3D background sets. This makes the position of *modeler* very common among artists entering the industry. Working as a modeler can mean many things, depending on the project on which you are working. Some of the asset types required for modelers to build include:

- Characters/creatures
- Vehicles
- Weapons
- Construction/buildings
- Vegetation

Different assets require different modeling skills and methods. Due to the complexity of game assets, many modelers will become specialists in certain areas. Being a fast modeler is always beneficial, but if the person's haste through the objects only results in the need for revisions to meet the expected quality level, it's better to spend extra time to make sure the model is right the first time.

For modeling, Maya and 3ds max are the two most commonly used programs in the business, so it would behoove you to know these programs inside and out.

To master the methods of modeling, consider starting with clay modeling. Shape the material with your fingers. Once you have mastered how something looks, feels, and works in real life, you will most likely be able to do it much easier on the computer with the knowledge of measurements and symmetry. Modeling 3D objects comes with several other responsibilities. You need to know and understand the principles of the UV mapping process, since in many studios you will also be texturing the objects you model. With the newer graphical engines, we have the ability to add details on meshes through texture render passes. Modelers should know these techniques so they adapt their model techniques to maximize the benefits of the texturing tools on their low poly models.

Texturer

Texturing is the second biggest production task for artists in the game industry. Unless your game is based on some specific shader systems such as toon-shading or procedural textures, each object in the game needs to have a texture. The Texture Artist will often also model objects. Today's game industry is going through a huge change in how textures are being rendered. This presents the texturer with great challenges, both visually and technically. The game consoles of today have a limited amount of memory, which reflects greatly on how textures are being created regarding the number and sizes. The latest texture techniques available require more time and skill to get quality results. This, in turn, demands even more from the Texture Artist.

Photoshop maintains its dominance as the most common program in the business, so knowing how to use it will benefit you tremendously.

A Texturer would profit from artistic understanding and knowledge of colors and compositions. Investment in a good camera will allow you to study the world and its details. Learn how age, use, wear, light, and dirt react with an object and its surrounding environment. If you are working in a team, it is important to work together in order to mimic a specific style and attain a consistent quality for the game.

Level Designer

Many games now have huge interactive environments, and there are positions where an artist will work solely on creating the different levels for the game. The Level Designer/Artist is more likely to construct the level by using art assets that have been created by the other artists. A level editor program will commonly be an in-house editor where the level designer has full control over the art and gameplay aspects. Depending on the Lead Game Designer and the product, the Level Artist will be allowed a certain amount of creativity in how the gameplay should be within the level.

Level Designers are artists who love to play games and have a good analytical understanding of what makes a level work. This involves being able to note what is fun and interesting in the different gameplays that you encounter. We recommend playing a variety of games to get ideas. To practice and become more familiar with the process, you could also use any of the free level editors that come with many games today to create your own levels for practice.

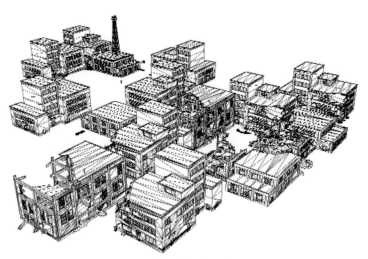

FIGURE 2.3   Placing objects and building levels. © Digital Illusions CE AB.
2004 Reprinted with permission.

Environment Artist

Every level needs a unique look and feel. An Environment Artist must influence the mood and feeling within the game's levels. Environment Artists can expect to texture the ground and/or sky, set lighting, and create the overall artistic feeling and mood to make the level come alive.

Full knowledge of Photoshop will give you a definite advantage.

To truly become a skilled Environment Artist, you should invest in a camera and study how light and shadows react in different times during the day or night. You will benefit by having a thorough understanding of colors and the ability to balance worlds of grass, ground, and sky. Make sure you closely examine your surroundings to learn as much as possible about the world's color indoors and outdoors, during the day and night.

Animator

Compared to the movie industry, where characters and their movements are closer to reality, the game industry is filled with performance restrictions that limit the way characters and animations can be done. Consequently, being an animator within the game industry is a challenging task. Animating characters and creatures in a game environment means creating many animations that must sync together through different blending systems—a very technical process. Many special programs and in-house software have been developed to help the animators and the game reach a higher esthetic and a more realistic quality.

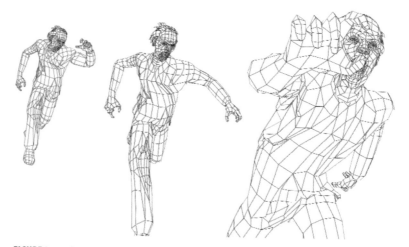

FIGURE 2.4   Strong pose animation. © Digital Illusions CE AB. 2004 Reprinted with permission.

Depending on the studio, the most common programs used are Maya, 3ds max, character studio™, Softimage XSI, Alias Motion Builder™, or LightWave3D.

Animation is a skilled art, and it takes a lifetime to master it. To become proficient, good timing is extremely important as well as knowing how to show emotional expressions within the characters' movements.

To achieve a greater understanding of timing and movement, consider investing in a video camera to record yourself and others doing specific movements. An alternative is to buy a full-size mirror to look in while you try out the movements. Mimic different styles and learn how to act out the movement that you are about to animate.

Effects Artist

Effects for games today are often an underestimated task. Effects are hugely representative and contribute to the mood of the gameplay. Very few game artists in the industry concentrate and dedicate themselves solely to game effects. An Effects Artist should be technically skilled with a strong artistic sense. Game effects involve knowledge of physics and require close interaction with the programmers involved in effect creation.

Often, the effects programs are created in-house to support the company's engine.

To create believable effects, we recommend researching physics and weight, and studying how things react in real life. Analyze explosions, water, fire, and smoke, and then use any of the 3D programs that contain a good particle engine to simulate and set up different possibilities of what you see in the real world.

Concept Artist

FIGURE 2.5   Concept Art. © Digital Illusions
CE AB. 2004 Reprinted with permission.

There is great need for concept art within the game industry. Scenes, characters, and objects are all conceptualized before production begins, and more detailed concepts and visualizations are needed during a production. This allows everyone a common vision of the title based on the AD's directions.

Although there is a need, the positions for full-time Concept Artists are limited in many studios, and might be nonexistent in smaller ones. Therefore, many of these job positions are outsourced or contracted by a Concept Artist with the required skills and style for the task.

If your goal is to become a Concept Artist within the game industry, you would benefit from excellent drawing skills in both environment and characters. Practice to visualize other people's ideas. When drawing characters, posing and expression are very important to add distinctive qualities so the creator can quickly read the image and what it is trying to portray.

For environments and objects, you would benefit from a background in illustration, with practice in perspective and scale. Improve your skills of capturing the mood inside the image.

Cut Scene Artist

Some studios have specific people dedicated to creating the movielike cut scenes and the promotional movies for their games. This may be the closest a game artist will get to the movie industry. Many of today's latest games have fantastic graphical content that you will be able to direct and storyboard for in-game cut scenes, that later render within the game engine. Other times, high-resolution assets will be created for pre-rendered FMVs (full motion video).

Cut Scene artists should be proficient in storyboarding, camera angles, directing, animation skills, hi-res modeling, texturing, rendering, and lighting. Knowledge of post-production processes and software such as Final Cut Pro™, Premiere™, After Effects, or combustion™ is also beneficial.

Keep Up or Give In

In the process of becoming a specialist in your work, you could be assigned the same task for the entire project. This could make you a guru in that area. This is important, but solely modeling 25 cars in two years will not keep you up to date with your artistic skills. With employment in this industry comes competition, not only between the studios and among the people, but also from the hardware manufacturers (better graphics cards, and more functions, features, etc.). This makes us strive to improve the way we create the art and the game. We all need to advance alongside the latest programs and techniques; otherwise, we do not stand a chance on our next title.

You are never better than "your next finished product."

To advance within the industry, you will need to stand out among the crowd. Make yourself indispensable; learn something that no one else knows, and make sure the company will continue to need you in the future. This may be harder than you think, since many people are capable of creating good art. We recommend that you learn and understand both the technical side and the processes involved in the creation of the game. Continue to develop your skills in production speed. This includes modeling, texturing, effects, concepts, and animation. Equally important is to continue learning as an artist. All of these skills will greatly benefit you. There will always be a need for artists who are technical problem solvers, and you will probably be requested to touch up or take over someone else's tasks during your time in the industry.

If your goal is to succeed and advance as an artist in this industry, you need to extend your range of knowledge and become "the best" in something. Therefore, concentrate on what you really like to do and what you can truly master. Listen to yourself; perhaps what you are most talented at is not what you want to do. Is it worth sacrificing your happiness for something you will be appreciated for and hopefully have a chance to advance in? The company wants to use you for what you are most efficient and best at. Game developing, after all, is the same as any other workplace—it strives for productivity. You will often do things that you might not find stimulating, but the studio knows you do those tasks best. To get out of a bad cycle, you might have to struggle alone in your spare time to show that you are able to do other things as well.

Therefore, as soon as you decide what you are really good at, concentrate and dedicate your soul to it. That will be your ticket into the industry or to the next level in your career.

 Never compete against anyone other than yourself. Your goal should be to improve yourself and your own artistic ability. Accept failure; it is through our mistakes that we really learn and grow.

SUMMARY

To become a game artist requires hard work and dedication.

1. Playing games is important to stay in touch with the industry and your work, but do not be blinded by them; view them as a painting in an art gallery.
2. Learning from home or school does not matter; dedication does—which you should have, even after some years within the industry.
3. Choose a school carefully, and let the reputations of the teacher and examinees speak for themselves.
4. Get to know yourself and learn what position might suit you best. Set a goal and work toward it; it will make it easier for you to succeed.
5. Being in the management team, organizing the game and artists, means that you do not create art. If this is not why you entered the industry, this position will probably bore you.
6. The business is still young. As the teams and studios become larger, they create new positions. It is always good to try to get into the industry as soon as you can decide what you want to do.
7. It is important to stay up-to-date with the most current technology and art creation. If you move on to a new position or you need to change your job, you won't have to spend months catching up.

3

YOUR PORTFOLIO—
INTERVIEW—CONTRACT

fetus : 2003

WHAT TO INCLUDE IN YOUR PORTFOLIO

When you are putting together a portfolio for the games industry, or to help you move to the next company, what should you include, or perhaps leave out?

Knowing what job you are applying for will help determine what to put together in your demo reel and portfolio to best illustrate your skills. You want the people who look at the work, and those who will be hiring you, to be "wowed" when they see your portfolio, so it's very important to only include your very best work. If you have the slightest doubt of the quality of one of your images, animations, or creations, do not include it. Concentrate on the parts that are specific for the position for which you are applying. If your expertise is modeling, concentrate on including modeling/texturing that can convince people that this is your main priority and where you will add strength to their studio. Submit clear and well-done models, both visually and technically, and include information about polygon amounts, placements, and the techniques used. (See Figure 3.1.)

Quality over quantity is a good rule when it comes to your portfolio.

FIGURE 3.1   For highest impact, make sure your portfolio includes quality art, even if the art is not directly game related. ©2004 Ryan Love. Reprinted with permission.

One should pay attention to several criteria when sending in a job application. An employer will tend to look for the following things:

Skills in the field of work: Does the applicant know how to model/texture/animate, and know the basics of 3D art?

Creativity and originality: Does the applicant understand the basics of traditional art—weighting and timing in animations, feeling in images, composition, drawing, sketching, color, and lighting?

Potential to grow: Will the applicant be easy to teach, learn easily, can he work independently and as a team player, does the portfolio show evolution, and does the person have technical knowledge?

Shipped titles: What titles has the applicant worked on and what specific skills did he use on those titles? (While former experience can mean a lot, it cannot be relied on; you are never better than your next product or the team with which you are working.)

If you have experience within the industry, the studio will expect you to know and understand the processes of how to create a game, and have experience in its technical structure. You should be used to working with a team of artists, and know what it means when deadlines are looming.

Even if you don't have any prior title experience, if you are a good and eager modeler, animator, or concept artist, (just to name a few positions) you will be able to catch up quickly in the production phase, with the right guidance. Most potential employers' main questions tend to be, "How long will it take to get the new employee up to full production speed producing high-quality artwork, and what can he add to the team?" A person with former production experience could at this point have an advantage, but all new employees have to learn the specific studio procedures. If the person is eager to learn the technical aspects of game production and work with the team, he should have an easy time getting into the process.

ART TEST

Many times, the studio will request an art test, which should represent the average quality that the studio can expect from you in the position for which you are applying. This can include anything from modeling a car, drawing concepts, or animating a walk cycle. It is an important test for the management team of the company to use in assessing your abilities and making sure that you are the right person for the job. Make sure to put your best effort into this test. Make it accurate and do what they ask for, since it is likely that you are also being tested on your ability to follow instructions. If the test is unclear or the studio does not give enough information, ask them to explain the parts you do not understand. In a production environment, you will usually have very clear directions, and it is rare that you will have to create something from your imagination alone. The same is usually true with an art test. The studio should be able to give you complete guidelines for the test, unless their intention is for you to show what you can come up with on your own. In that case, be as creative as possible, but still realistic in what you think they expect you to do.

THE FIRST INTERVIEW

One attractive feature of the game industry is that it is a relaxed environment. People generally do not have to attend formal business meetings or wear suits when creating art, so you don't necessarily have to wear one to an interview. However, make sure your appearance is clean and neat, and a good smile can never hurt. The impression you make in the interview will be how you are remembered when the company is assessing the applicants. Remember to be relaxed, listen, and learn, and do not try to educate the people interviewing you. You do not want them to think you are a potential troublemaker or that you have a big ego. They are more interested in finding a team player, someone with whom they will feel comfortable working long hours and late nights. People like people who are energetic, so show your enthusiasm by asking relevant questions, and do some research on the company so you can show an interest in its products.

ART SALARY

With the industry maturing and more funding becoming available for each product, companies will have larger budgets to pay their employees. Of course, having more money also means selecting and paying for the best people to secure the future products.

An employee's salary can greatly vary depending on the studio location, employee experience, age, skills, and if he receives other compensation. It is hard to say how much you can make or what you are worth since it depends on the company's needs and the deal you can make with them.

For a fresh-out-of-school artist, a feasible starting salary could be $25k to $50k a year. On the other hand, an established, Art Lead/AD/Technical Manager who is vital to the outcome of the product can be paid between $50k to $110k a year. Many times companies offer a lower entering salary but compensate you with better bonuses, more vacation, overtime pay, royalties, insurance, special health plans, or company stock option plans.

Little research has been done about what is considered a normal salary within this business. In 2003 Gamasutra surveyed various international developers, and although the information was slimmed down to only represent the American game developers, it shows us some interesting numbers. A salary for an artist, depending on the years and position in the industry would range between $40k to $75k, and among the artists over 70% got compensated in other ways on top of their salaries.

When you are ready for your salary discussions it is important to take all this into consideration, in order to be able to estimate how much you are worth to your future employer. If you are fresh out of school, you should be aware of that there might be another person ready to undercut himself to be able to get his foot inside the industry, get experience, and start creating his favorite game for a living. This makes it easy for studios to view their first-year artists as disposable personnel who will probably move on for the first better offer. Never undercut yourself; it hurts not just you but also the industry. Rather ask for what you are worth and then let the company negotiate to what they can afford. If you undercut yourself it is also harder to get the raise to where you wanted to be in the first place. This forces you to move on for a new interview where you don't undercut yourself, but still compete with people that do.

A good way to deal with an interview is to understand the situation of the company. Many times, studios need to hire people at the last minute, or they may be looking for a really good artist to fill a gap. It would help a lot if you know how eager they are to hire you. However, if you have made it as far as salary discussions, they most likely want you, but at what price?

Try to evaluate your skills for the position for which you apply. Make a list of your strong points and things that you think will justify the salary you are requesting. In the worst case, they will say no and propose a lower amount. Repeat your qualifications to help validate the amount you asked for, and then, if needed, try to meet them halfway. Remember that they have already chosen you, so now it's your turn to say yes or no. Do not fear the silence or jump too quickly for on-the-spot suggestions. Take your time and use it to your advantage—it gives you time to think of what to say. Make sure that you do not walk out of the meeting unsatisfied, so try to agree on the amount that feels comfortable for them (and you). Keep in mind that game developing is a business and that employees' salaries are the largest expense for the studio, so in the end if they do not give you what you think you are worth, you can always say no and wait for the next opportunity.

THE CONTRACT AND THE FIRST SIX MONTHS

Be sure to read the contract thoroughly. It might seem to be the most boring, legalistic piece of paper you have ever seen, and you might just be itching to get in there and show them what you are made of. However, be patient—there will be lots of time for that (your whole career in fact) if everything goes well. Be sure you read the small print and fully comprehend what you are signing. If you don't understand, ask questions. Several companies have different "restrictions" on what you are legally allowed to do if you quit or leave the company. So be careful, and if the contract limits you in any way, ask what it means and try to get it changed to suit your needs. Remember, they want you.

Some things are frequently included in contracts; for example, they often include a "trial period" or "probation period" as a safety precaution. This is done for the sake of the company to see how well you work with the team and to determine whether you are suited for the job. The length of this trial period varies, but three to six months is standard. Does this mean that you need to work 24/7 for six months to show your dedication? Hopefully not! The company should want you to succeed and understand that you will be working with the team for a long time, so they won't want you to burn out in the first couple of months.

Once you start in a position, be sure to ask questions. If you are given a task you are not familiar with, ask for help or instructions so you aren't blamed if something goes wrong that the leads thought you knew. Your lead will be much happier to show you the proper method up front, rather than have you do the work incorrectly and have to do it again. There are many unique studio-specific procedures, which will take you time to learn and comprehend. Remember that it is through failure that we learn, so do not blame yourself if you don't get it right the first time. With so many experienced artists working with you in the team, there is sure to be help close by.

SUMMARY

1. Never include anything in your portfolio that does not reflect your best work. You want to make a good first impression, so include *quality*, not quantity.
2. Include what is important and relevant for the application, and have a clear and understandable portfolio.
3. Skills are most valuable, so if you have skills that no one else has and if the studio needs these skills, highlight them and they will be more likely to hire you.
4. Dress properly for an interview and approach everyone with a smile.
5. At salary discussions, research how important your knowledge is to the company and how your skills relate to other people in the industry and their salaries. Be realistic.
6. Make a list of your strong points that would justify a salary above the average. Do not undercut yourself.
7. Read the entire contract carefully. Do not let anything or anyone push you to sign something that you do not understand or with which you are uncomfortable. If you have any questions, do not hesitate to ask them—better before than after you've signed.
8. You will work in this industry for a long time, hopefully, so do not let the company, or yourself, burn you out in the first six months.
9. Work, learn, and communicate with the team around you, because no one knows the specific workflows for the studio better than they do.

GAME CREATION

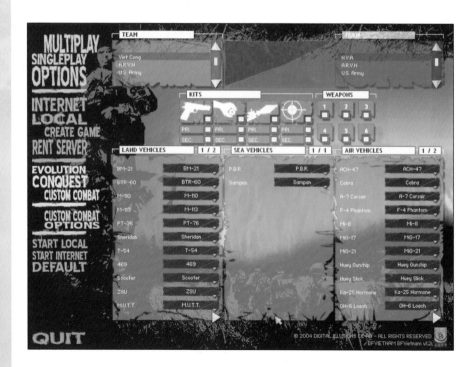

THE TEAM

Working in a big studio will give you the opportunity to learn fast because you will have access to the knowledge and experiences of a big team. In the next few years, teams will grow larger to meet the demands of creating more content for the advanced techniques.

Currently, a typical game development team consists of:

- Producer
- Lead Designer/Lead Programmer/Lead Artist/Art Director
- Programmers—Rendering, AI, Sound, Physics, Tools, HUD UI
- Artists—Concept Artists, Modelers, Texturers, Animators, Effects Artists, and User Interface Creators
- Designers—Game Designers, Level Designers

These people are all necessary to complete a game, and for larger teams, depending on the size of the project and workload, there may also be assistants and associate positions for the producer and the leads. Most smaller studios will have fewer people or combined positions, so each person performs a wider range of tasks.

PREPRODUCTION

Before a new game concept is approved and the studio puts the whole team into production, the game core mechanics and major focus need to be defined, and then refined. The developers and publishers need to ask, "Will the public play this game?" Gone are the days when studios could create a game that was not widely appealing or catered to the customers' wants. With today's big teams and big budgets comes a lot of financial risk, causing publishers and developers to rely more and more on franchises, proven concepts, and consumer demands.

From an Idea to a Game

A videogame concept can come from many sources. They can be licensed from a movie, book, established entertainment franchise, or be ideas that the development team believes would make a good and interesting game design. The key feature is that there is no "rule" to the process, so how a new concept is developed will vary from studio to studio.

Concept and Pitch to the Publisher

Once the designers determine the main idea, it is time for them to sell the product to the rest of the group. Both the team and the publishers need to believe in the product.

Here is where the artist first works on the project to create appealing and believable concepts for the publisher, or in some cases, render an *emotional preview*, a video that presents the mood and features of how the game should play and be experienced in motion. The idea is for the publisher to understand the game design, get a sense of the emotional feeling within the game, and see how the game should be played. At this point, it is very important to make the publisher understand what the designers are trying to do with the game, since they need to believe the game will return the money they will be investing, and generate a profit.

Scheduling/Production

When organizing today's productions, we use scheduling programs such as Microsoft Project. The bigger a project becomes, the more structure it needs to have, and the processes of creating the assets within a game need to be clearly organized from the very beginning. There are many miscalculations still within today's game creation schedules, and it needs to be every studio's goal to become increasingly efficient and match the projected time needed to create titles. One can say that game production has developed from a few hardcore team members who worked really hard, to a large production structure where everyone works together to reach the goals and deadlines.

Proof of Concept

Some publishers require a preproduction phase, which is similar to the creation of a mini game. This means that you have a deadline to deliver one playable version that should be representative of the actual game. The time allocated to do this can be as much as 50% of the entire project. This is the time to iron out faults in gameplay, give everyone a general idea of the game, and define what needs to be created for the rest of the production cycle. Through this method, the publisher is able to forecast the sales numbers and assess whether the game is going to be what they expected. After this, the developer knows what they did in this first level, and they can just repeat the process to complete the project.

PRODUCTION

Throughout preproduction, assets and information are collected to complete the full game. When, or if, the product is accepted by the publisher in the preproduction phase, and the idea has proven successful, real production is started based on the project's budget and schedule. The following sections briefly outline the production process.

Milestones/Deadlines/Crunch Times

Every studio handles each project differently, and is dependent on the Producer who oversees the production. If you are working as a third-party developer, you will probably have both internal and external milestones. A *milestone* is a deadline requiring certain deliverables that need to be 100% complete before anyone can proceed to the next stage. In this way, the producer is able to see that the production is going in the right direction. If the deliverables are not ready by the due date, it can mean a lot of overtime work (crunch time). The game needs to be playable and representative while work is in progress, which can take up a lot of production time, so people try to keep the builds as stable and good-looking as possible. Unforeseen problems, however, can result in last-minute changes to huge parts of the game, and add unexpected overtime hours in order to meet a milestone.

Alpha

Alpha is the first major milestone in the production. Many companies define Alpha as *code complete*, meaning no new code features should be added to the game. This allows the necessary time to make the code stable and fix code-related problems. Alpha can also mean that some studios stop the art development as well, and it is time to touchup the art. Oftentimes, 3D engines are being created at the same time as the product is in development, so it is good for artists to have a solid and relatively stable game engine from which to tweak the final game. Locking the code makes it possible to understand and test the performance, and determine how far the game is from completion. If the game is in development for the PC and needs to meet certain hardware specifications, you might need to cut art or specific features to gain performance and frame rate at this point.

Bug Testing/Fixing

Before the game is delivered to the customer, it needs to be tested to find bugs and errors. A bug within a game is a malfunction of any of the game assets or functionality.

Bug fixing is a very time-consuming phase that starts soon after delivering the Alpha build. During this phase, game testers play the game to find and reproduce errors. The testers go over the entire game from start to finish, and test all of its functions to make sure that it works as planned. Bugs have their own classifications, depending on how serious they are for the product. The more risk the bug poses for possibly delaying the game being published, the higher the priority of the bug. Bugs are usually rated in importance from A to F. The presence of bugs means that the game will not ship and they need to get fixed as soon as possible.

One of the biggest problems with fixing bugs is that you have to go in and change things that might be working fine. By repairing one hole, you might open several new ones, and even start a chain reaction that creates problems in other parts of the game. Bug types are also highly dependant on the type of the game you are creating, and the game's construction can make the list seemingly endless. *Battlefield 1942* is a large open area playground filled with objects where the player is free to do whatever he wants. Its very nature introduces a huge opportunity for many types of bugs, since it is hard to predict all of the player's potential actions. Conversely, a car game (tunnel racer) where the player goes forward and has a limited area to play on makes it easy to predict what will happen during gameplay, and so there are fewer types of bugs.

Art Freeze

Art freeze is the most important deadline for the artists. At this point in production, no new art can be added, and any placeholders (art that was just temporary) should have been replaced. After art freeze, the artists will spend the majority of their time fixing bugs.

During this phase, the art is reviewed one last time to make sure that everything is as good as it can be. If a project is scheduled well, and has had a successful development period, there should be time for any changes that need to be done based on priority.

Beta

Just as with Alpha, the definition of Beta depends on the studio and the publisher but in general, all assets should be locked before entering the Beta stage. At this point, the game enters a final testing phase to enhance performance and correct any final bugs and glitches. At this point, the game should be fully functional with no known bugs. After this part of production, the assets for the game are completed. If plans for a new game are in production, the majority of the team transfers to the new project, or starts creating concepts for new ideas. Only a small team will be required at this stage to oversee the final product in case any bugs appear that might affect the final delivery date. At this point, game developers are often pressed for time, trying to squeeze in extra assets and touching up quality before Beta reaches its end. And again, depending on the publisher, reaching Beta can be as close as three weeks before the product is to ship to stores, if everything goes well in the final stages.

Quality Control/Game Localization

After reaching a stable and optimized game at the end of Beta, the game will go through a final test with the publisher to verify that everything works as it should. This includes menus, functionality, localization, and the overall quality. The purpose of this review is to answer the question, "Are the consumers getting what they're paying for?"

Can a player finish all the levels? Are there any crashes? If there are, the production team needs to fix these things immediately and then go through the entire process again. The final check is to make sure that nothing detrimental happened during the bug-testing process and that everything is 100% ready for shipment. If the game is multilingual, it also needs to go through a localization process to test the quality and verify that the text in the game is correctly translated, appears at the right spot, and the game can be understood in each language. The localization teams are also responsible for different cultural issues within certain locations, and this can require that the game be adapted to the customs of that language/country by changing specific sensitive content, art, or language. This is done at an earlier stage, but is something that will be checked during the final test.

Gold

After going through the entire production phase and passing all quality control tests, the game is finally ready to "go Gold." This means that the approved content CD-ROM goes into the replication process to make the actual CD-ROMs that will be sold to the consumer. The phrase "going Gold" comes from when the studio delivers the final game data on a gold-colored CD-ROM. Today, final master game discs are far from golden; they rely more on security and use a special protected CD-ROM technique.

If your final game was delivered within the projected timeframe and the content was what you had envisioned, your team should be proud and happy that you succeeded—hopefully without too much overtime. The game will soon be on store shelves and you will have your first, or another title, in your portfolio.

IN BETWEEN PROJECTS

Going from "crunch mode" to "business as usual" can be a strange turnover. One day, you are up to your ears with work and everyone is stressing to get everything done. Then suddenly, there is nothing left to do; it's like turning off a light switch. This is when everything can feel very empty and boring, but it is a time commonly used to research new technologies and learn new things before the next project begins. It's also a good time for team members to take time off and recuperate from the all-consuming process of "getting it out the door."

SUMMARY

1. Artists are not the only people involved in game development. Each person on the team has his own responsibilities, but everyone needs to work together as a team to meet the deadlines.
2. Coming up with a game and getting the publisher to finance it is not an easy task. The process of selling the product internally and externally can be long and intense. Then once you have approval, you begin work on the actual game, so be prepared.
3. The different areas of game production create a dynamic progression, one that takes many turns, both good and bad.
4. Each milestone has deliverables that usually require some crunch time to reach top-notch quality on time.

GENERAL ART CREATION

As artists, we experience new things each day. Life is a continual journey of gaining new knowledge and deeper understanding. To become a game artist requires hard work and dedication. There is much to learn—techniques, unique programs, and workflows. As a game artist, it is a challenge to be both creative and technical at the same time.

Part II of this book guides you toward newer and higher goals, both in your personal artistic evolvement and to extend your knowledge as a game artist. It teaches you the basic knowledge needed and how to think when you are creating art for games. With techniques such as modeling, UV, texturing, collision, animation, and effects, we'll guide you through a typical game-in-production processes. The goal of this part of the book is that you learn and gain the knowledge of how artists create art for games, both technically and artistically. This knowledge will be a good start for what you need to know to succeed in today's and tomorrow's, game development team.

CHAPTER
5

GROWING AS AN ARTIST

You are an artist, not an assembly line, although it can feel like this sometimes. As artists, we should always try to achieve the best we can by pushing our technical and personal limits to produce the best content. In the game industry, we would all like to work with the latest graphical technology so that we could push the limitations of the graphics even further, while creating that new, beautiful game. It is important as game artists, however, to be open to new art styles, to widen our knowledge, and learn more ways to create art. You will need to adapt your skills to different projects and styles. To create a beautiful game, the team needs to include a few highly competent artists with knowledge in various areas to help those newer to the field. The wider the knowledge base, the more likely it will be that someone will know how to solve the problems that arise.

Working together toward a common goal requires a well-planned schedule. Throughout the schedule, high-quality art is expected for the timeline of the product. The publisher needs the product shipped at a certain date, and the stores are waiting from the day the contract was signed. It is up to the team to make the game as good as possible and deliver by the deadline. Having extra room in the schedule for unanticipated events, or for artists who need extra time to reach the bar of quality, is a safe way to secure the schedule.

For the graphics to be the best quality, the schedule needs to be followed and the team needs to be taught. Everyone needs to understand where the quality bar is, and the timeframe in which it needs to be met. They also need to be able to make fast decisions if something unexpected arises. This book shows you ways to create high-quality art within game production, and presents ideas on how to reach a higher level in your own personal development as an artist. To succeed as an artist in this industry, you need to be creative and innovative as often as possible.

 Do not wait for creativity to come to you! Through experimenting, you will discover more, new, and better ideas.

EVOLVE AND EXPAND

As individuals, we all evolve differently, but without the proper guidance, can we control our own evolution? Being a game artist can be very frustrating at times. When you started with 3D graphics, your time was filled with hours of learning and testing features to master the different programs. You were as eager as a child with a new toy, and time had no meaning. With the new ability to replicate the real world within a computer, you most likely started modeling 3D objects based on details of all kinds, in an attempt to replicate your favorite objects, and to see characters spring to life within the program.

The first step for you to evolve further as an artist and expand your knowledge is to stop what you have been doing. Try to move on to things that you have never done before. If science fiction, cars, or fantasy creatures have been your objects of choice to model, draw, and paint, it is probably time to learn something new.

One way to do this is to look beyond what everyone else is doing in 3D. Pick up books about classical artists, or better yet, research modern art installations and abstract art. These people are very creative and open-minded. In your evolution, try to visualize and understand all different aspects of art—not only 3D—so you can expand as an artist as much as possible. What is modern art? What can it teach you? What is its message and purpose? Some people see abstract art as uninteresting or even repulsive, perhaps because they have difficulty relating to it or an inability to understand it. Think of abstract art as reading a book—the viewers have the option to create their own emotional connection to the image, which can be completely different for each person. This personal connection will attract the viewer to the image for a long time. To take a completely different example: many classical painters were very skilled artists who in the beginning of their careers studied the very basics in art, animals, human anatomy, color, and image composition. They learned how to read, draw, and create an image in perfect detail. Many of these same painters started to create art in a different way later in life, concentrating more on the emotions within the image. The first rule when creating art is that art has no rules. By throwing out all the old knowledge you have and starting fresh, you can test and draw your own conclusions for what works and what doesn't. Do not be judgmental—break all those old rules and feel free to explore. In the end, when it comes to your personal evolution, it is the knowledge you gain while doing the art that matters. Regardless of how you ended up with the result, you should always look at your art as a temporary creation.

Working in a game development studio is the total opposite, however. Here, it is all about structure and following development procedures. The team has the responsibility of unifying the style for the game. People are more or less making a large painting together. We would not want the left corner to mismatch the right corner of a big painting when it represents a game with unbalanced content. To reach the same goal, we need to use processes that have been evaluated and streamlined for the best result and speed, and are well tested and understood by everyone. Remember to add charisma and character to your art; it will catch the viewer's attention. Let's now look at several processes that we think will help any artist evolve and learn new creative methods.

Emotional Images

Take a moment, relax, and look at Figures 5.1 and 5.2.

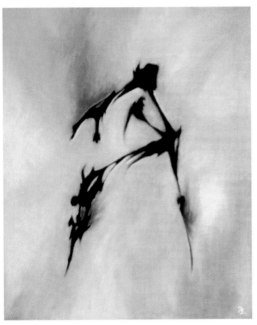

FIGURE 5.1   Thoughts.

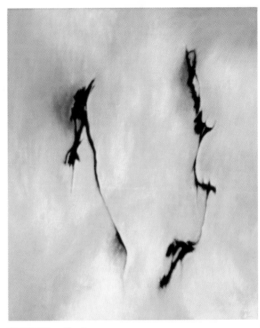

FIGURE 5.2   Illusions.

Figures 5.1 and 5.2 are quite similar—yet different!

Consider the saying, "a picture is worth a thousand words." For us to be able to create real art, we need to learn to read the message created within the image. Then, we can learn how to express ourselves and put emotional impact in our creations. While studying images, we should look for the emotional feeling in each—the message or thought that the creator directly or indirectly wanted to communicate to the viewer. This content gives the image its history and a story to tell, even if it is done with just a single word, as in Figure 5.3.

Emotional content within an image can be expressed in various ways such as composition, shapes, light, and color. It is important that we make sure the viewer grasps what is important in the image. This does not mean that he needs to understand the entire image immediately, but it should catch his attention. Now, let's go back to Figures 5.1 and 5.2. Do these images now mean anything to you, and do you view them as two

FIGURE 5.3   What does this image tell you? Describe it in one word.

different things, even though they are very much alike? Take a moment to think about it. If we look at today's 3D art, we can see occasions where a single object is located in an empty world, with a fast and simple light setup. The object shows no sign of expression or feeling. There is no personality or history, and no composition or emotional content. How can we find interest in the subject, and relate to the image? Should we even call this art, as these images become rather uninteresting to look at after some time no matter how detailed and wonderfully created they are. Many times, the only reason a modeler will spend all his time creating an object is just for the recognition of how skillful and accurate he is, just as the classical painters mentioned earlier. 3D as a media is very young, and so are the people using it. As mentioned previously, classical artists evolved over time. Is this something that we will see happen with 3D? Photography was originally invented for the idea of replication and documentation, but it has become art for many. Perhaps 3D media were never meant to be more than a tool to create replicas of reality, and move them within the binary world. We still wonder why so many 3D artists model and texture an entire object, if the plan is to use only the front side of the object in a final image. Are 3D artists creating single images because of the fun of modeling and texturing, or is it for the freedom of expressing themselves in 3D? How are you modeling your objects, building up your scenes, and creating your animations?

 Be creative and different, borrow ideas, and be inventive. Do what no one else has done before.

Photographing/Composition

As you probably already know, it's a good idea to buy a camera and start taking reference photos to create a library of images to use for your texturing. Today's digital cameras are so affordable that there is really no excuse not to own one. The functionality of a camera stretches so much further than just taking reference photos and collecting textures, however. Artistically, we can use it to learn about composition and the relationship between light and darkness in an image. (See Figures 5.4 and 5.5.)

FIGURE 5.4   Scene photographing.

Taking photos gives you the opportunity to decide angle and content and how to crop images in real-time. Compared to 3D and concept drawings, the camera is an extremely fast way to determine what works and how it can look good. This makes the camera an excellent way to practice different variations of composition based on real-world environments. This is especially true if you force yourself to take your photos in black and white, which will make the image easier to view since color can have an impact on how you choose your composition and layout. The knowledge you gain through setting up interesting scenarios in photographs will help you be more precise when composing your 3D scenes, and thereby help you avoid unnecessary test renders.

FIGURE 5.5   Scene photographing.

Another technique to use to get interesting scenarios and learn composition is to cut out an area of paper representing a frame that you can
look through. This way, wherever you are, you can experiment with the
position and composition of your images without a computer. This
method also works well with the computer, where you can create a
frame and change composition and size to cut and concentrate your
image on the message similar to Figure 5.6, where the dark area shows
the frame and the part cut out.

Digital cameras can also be used with great results for character reference and poses. Today's cameras are great for fast photos of yourself or a
friend to capture the pose that you need to illustrate in your drawings.
Again, "a picture is worth a thousand words"—and that's what photography is all about. Nice tourist photos and arranged group photos in which
everyone is lined up in a row smiling have their place—fond remem-
brances of special times. However, artistically, what do they give us? A
photo that is unpredictable and unarranged will contain and reveal information that is more interesting; something the viewer can look at for a
longer time. Imagine that same group photo if it were shot *after* everyone
thought you had taken it. The whole image is alive and shows not only

FIGURE 5.6   Cut out the area to make a more interesting composition.

the people, but their personalities and a brief moment in their lives—the photo has become more interesting.

As an artist, ask yourself how you can make an image interesting and unique. Consider the composition, angle, light, story, and its meaning.

With all the possibilities that a camera can give you in your artistic development, it could become one of your best investments.

Research and Reference

Life is the best reference you will ever get. It is time to open your eyes and pay attention to things that happen around you! Every second of your life counts as reference in what you learn and do.

Consider:

- Character emotional expressions
- Character movement and reactions
- Character characteristics, clothing, and acting

- Construction, design, and materials
- Physics, weight, and power
- Time, aging, and anatomy
- Earth, wind, fire, and water

These are just a few areas where there is much to discover, so get ready to study and get a deeper understanding of how everything works. Finding a logical explanation as to why a thing is created the way it is, will make it easier to explain. Be aware of how you read people and how you present yourself. All things in real life are constructed for a purpose—aerodynamics for airplanes, trains, and cars; designed shapes to help sell a product; and tall buildings to symbolize power and house large companies. Study how people live, the way they speak, eat, walk, and act in their everyday life. Learn how to read people's feelings and see how they react to commercials, family, and the unknown. Ask yourself, "Why is it like this," and "How would I create art that relates to these ideas?" Also study yourself and how you react to these different things in life. With an open mind and eyes, you will gain more experience from the world, which will reflect on how you see and create art.

Traditional reference is important as well, so before you create any art, do a deep analysis of the specific task at hand; doing so will result in a better outcome. The Internet is a great place to start your search for reference material; it is a fast and easy way to find all kinds of information. As an example, if you are going to create a cave or an old Indian temple, you don't have to go to India. There are travelers and explorers who have been all over the world with cameras in hand, and there are Internet sites where these people meet and share their photographs. When used correctly, these images can be a great source of reference. Other great resources to collect as reference and to get inspiration for your work could be games—to see what has been done and strive to create something even better. Movies are good resources as well. Movies catch the mood, environment, and characters of which game creators can take advantage. Whatever you do, do not stop exploring for reference material in life. Open your eyes and see how people react to different occasions, and when they do react, memorize the feeling that you got from them and understand why they reacted the way they did.

Light and Darkness

Light, the source of all life! Without light, we would not be able to see what our creation looks like. Understanding how to apply light will improve both your art and artistic development immensely. Painting with light is like sculpting the objects with visibility. Think of light as what shapes the object. The light determines the shape of the object surface, not its material. Without light, all materials look the same.

By knowing how to use light in your scene to build up contrast and composition, you can guide a person to the main interest from the first moment he sees your creation. Before building up your scene, start thinking of the message that you want to give the viewer through your image, and how this would be presented with lighting. Is it dramatic, happy, mysterious, or perhaps dangerous? Creating realistic scenes and environments is dependent on your ability to achieve the correct lighting. A bright day with no clouds has hard, dark shadows. A dark room with a single hand-held flashlight has low visibility, but strong hard shadows from the single light. A cloudy day will have very soft shadows, if any. Light helps us read the types of different materials and the shapes of the objects. How does strong sunlight look on a plastic object compared to a metallic object? Does it change when the sun is behind a cloud? How does a lit-up round edge look compared to a sharp edge on similar material? All materials and shapes react differently to light.

Compared to Figure 5.7, the colors added to Figure 5.8 do not solve its composition (see the results in Figure 5.8). When working with light and deciding which parts of the image are important, try using grayscales to help you find balance within the image. Having a good light setup is vital if you are going to show a model. Spend time on the lighting to get the most out of your modeled shapes. Showing off your wonderful model in bad lighting could have a worse impact than showing a simple model with interesting lighting.

FIGURE 5.7   Gray colors set the value and create the intensity of the image.

FIGURE 5.8   Same intensity, same image, but with colors added.

Color Schemes

Colors are just not beautiful, they are highly important in how we see the world. We see more colors than shapes or details. Our eyes' central vision is just 2% of the total field of view; what we see in the outer areas are just colors. Colors are also critical in determining the mood of a scene or an image, so it is important that we know how to use them well when creating art.

We associate each color in life with a different occasion and feeling. A yellow rose means friendship, while red roses mean love. Stronger love depends on the deepness of the color. Colors also have different associations and meaning in different cultures, so you should keep this in mind when creating.

Let's look at Figure 5.3 again, and then at Figure 5.9, but this time in blue color tone. The powerful contrast between the red color and the white eyes has disappeared. A bit of the image's power is gone. Why? The red in this image was helping us to visualize the feeling of fear and terror.

We want the images we create to be interesting. They should stimulate the person viewing them. If you look outside, you will notice that the colors in the world blend; nothing really stands out in saturation, and in general, the colors are very desaturated and dull. One idea to create beautiful images is to let people escape the everyday gray by adding more saturation and contrast so that the image becomes more intense and draws more attention.

FIGURE 5.9   Without the red color, does the image carry the same message?

As we can see in Figures 5.10 and 5.11, by applying contrast and saturation the entire scene is more interesting and appealing—it now has a punch to it. Knowing that colors and light have different associations to people, and that they can help create a more visually stimulating image, we can now use them to set the mood that we want for a specific image or for a game.

FIGURE 5.10   Saturated, dull, and boring realistic image.

FIGURE 5.11   Adjusted, alive, and stronger light, and colors.

In the *Battlefield 1942* expansion packs, the game takes place during World War II. We wanted the player to feel like he was playing the game in the 1940s, with the right weapons and vehicles for that time, not in the year 2000 with old rusted vehicles and weapons. Consequently, we could not create the game with comic or modern, strong, saturated colors. This would give the player the wrong message. We needed to make sure that the game felt old, but still new when played. To succeed in this task, we needed to know what color people associated with World War II. We know that photos from the 1940s were in grayscales, but oxygen makes photos on older photo paper become browner with age. Using sepia-toned images made the content appear older. Since we wanted to bring the player back to the 1940s, making the entire game in a sepia tone could definitely work—because the real world is in more saturated color, it would feel as if it happened in real life. Desaturated colors are also a sign of age. We created the game with a slightly desaturated color (see Figures 5.12 and 5.13), together with the loading screens in a sepia color like older photos, to give the player the feeling of going back in time.

Battlefield Vietnam presented a similar problem. The game takes place during the 1970s, which makes us thinks of flowers; hippies; brown, yellow, round curly shapes; and bellbottom pants. Photographs from the

FIGURE 5.12   *Battlefield 1942*—WW2 MOD for *Battlefield Vietnam*. © Digital Illusions CE AB. 2004 Reprinted with permission.

FIGURE 5.13   *Battlefield* WW2 MOD—Color scheme.

1970s have a tint of pink and yellow. To convince the player that he was playing in this epoch, we made the colors more saturated than *Battlefield 1942* to assure everyone that the game is closer to the time in which we live today, as seen in Figure 5.14.

We also updated menus and heads up display (HUD) so they reflected a more 1970s style, as in Figure 5.15.

During loading time, a feeling for the 1970s was created in colors and images that reflected the war and how things appeared for civilians (see Figure 5.16).

FIGURE 5.14   *Battlefield Vietnam*, with more contrast than earlier games. © Digital Illusions CE AB. 2004 Reprinted with permission.

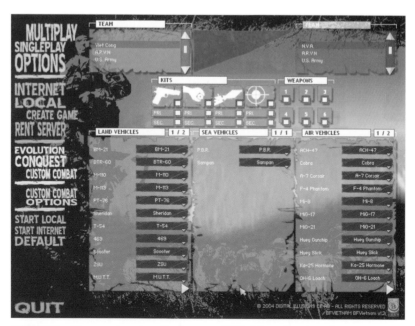

FIGURE 5.15   Menu system to reflect a more 1970s hippy, jungle style. © Digital Illusions CE AB. 2004 Reprinted with permission.

FIGURE 5.16   A loading screen with text and graphics, mentioning information on the war. © Digital Illusions CE AB. 2004 Reprinted with permission.

Dirt and Scratches

We live in a world where time affects all objects. All things in our environment look used in some way. The smallest screw has scratches, and an abandoned house will be dirty and overgrown with vegetation. Walls have bumps and scratches, floors are worn, and have dirt in every corner. This is what gives objects their character and history, and what makes them believable. Not all this dirt has to be visible. We do not see everyday dirt and scratches until we look for them, so in our art we should try to keep it subtle but make sure it is there all the time. It is a very important part of making something real and believable. Applying dirt and scratches to match with your story can be a challenge. It needs to be just the right amount to look believable. How does an object age? In what way will it look older and used? It is up to the creator to create a history for the object. It is important that it gets scratched and dirty at the proper place. Think of dirt and dust as layers added to the surface. It comes with rain and particles in the air. Even a regularly cleaned room has a layer of dust within days. Scratches appear when we drag or use an object in some way. A bolt becomes round when a wrench slips. Surfaces around the bolt are chipped with tightening. Surfaces, like doorknobs, get dirty from us touching them.

When you create your art and decide to have a history behind it, visualize a short history for everything. Keep it logical and realistic so people can visualize it. If you are modeling and texturing something, do not copy the reference material or photographs. The chance that someone else has seen it or even has copyright on the image does exist. You are an artist. Be creative and come up with your own ideas. Who and how has this object been used? A muscular mechanic on a warfront would use a monkey wrench very differently than a family man tightening a bolt on his new family car.

LESS IS MORE

This old cliché is amazing—and it will do wonders for your creations. Maybe it will make no sense at first, especially for people who love the technical part of adding detail in images. However, to reach your goal and higher quality, detail might not be what you need.

By creating less, we can let the viewer visualize the rest of the information. Do not overcomplicate things—keep it simple and understandable. If the player will not see the creation, do not spend time on it. Spend time on the art where it makes the most sense. By saying nothing, you can say a lot.

What message do you get when you look at Figure 5.17? Is the message shown with enough information? Explain it with simple emotional words—wet, fearless, strength.

FIGURE 5.17   A strong hero on a cold rainy night. © 2004 Tommie Lofqvist. Reprinted with permission.

Sure, Figure 5.17 shows a known hero, but is that where you get the information? Make sure that you really concentrate on the visual parts that carry the most impact for the viewer. In Figure 5.17, we get the message that it is raining—without drawing every drop. A few lines in the back are all that was needed—the rest we can visualize by ourselves.

In games where everything should be better graphics, more realism, more objects, sharper effects, and higher density polygons, how does a cliché like "less is more" fit in? Sometimes, we have to take a step back. In the inferno we call "game production," we need to concentrate on the special tasks that will give us the most, and know that we cannot get everything. It is important that the message gets through that we need to choose what to show the player.

Kill Your Darling

Knowing when to "kill your darling" will improve your artwork. When you have finished creating something that you are extremely proud of, you want to show your latest creation to everyone to get feedback. The feedback might not always be what you have expected from friends, the community, and other artists. It is better to know that you might have to "kill your darling" before you show it to anyone. For example, say you spent 20 hours on an animation, and just when you're done, you play it through and realize that the part you spent the most time on and consider the coolest does not match the scene and doesn't make the movie better. To achieve the best result, you would need to remove it from the entire movie. Would you do that, or would you rather sacrifice the quality of the complete movie? The less emotionally attached you are to your art, the easier it will be to accept necessary changes, and reach a higher quality, both for yourself and the production. If needed, take a break and look at it later with fresh eyes. Whatever you do, do not be afraid of ruining what you have created so far. Look at art and your creations as temporary tests.

Do not fall in love with the things you create; you will be blinded by your own creations, and therefore limit your abilities.

When judging your own art, judge hard. Do not settle with telling yourself that you did well if you know you could have done much better. Make sure you give 100% for every task. If you have a hard time taking criticism from other people, learn how to criticize yourself—you are the only one to blame if you fail. When assessing your own work's quality and what needs to be removed, ask yourself the question, "Does the viewer receive the message within the content before he becomes bored, and if so, does he stay interested?"

That is the golden rule for choosing your artwork for a demo reel; cutting your movie, drawing your concept, and making art and games. It is all about keeping the person interested in the content. What you think is a wonderful part of your creation might not be what the viewer finds interesting at all. Therefore, you might need to kill it. How does one know what is interesting? One question can be, "Is the content relevant to the viewer?" Learn from mass media, the best authors, and the best movies. What do people like, and how can you learn from what other people have done? If people hate solving the riddles that you love in a game, kill them. If you hate shooting barrels to see the large explosion, but the public loves it, keep it.

You should now have some new ideas with which to play. With these, you should consider setting up a goal to help you reach your own final quality. Think through the task before you start doing anything with it. Make a checklist that lists what the image/animation should show when it is finished. Does the image/animation communicate the right emotional feeling to you and to other people? Does it have the right light, colors, and composition? Ask yourself, "Is this the best I can do?" What could you have done differently? What can you improve on the next time? Always go over your creation a second time from scratch, even though you are 100% sure that it is finished. Then, do not look at it for one day. Look at other more experienced people's creations and then go back to your own image. Is there something you can change to make it better?

GAME VISUALS

A big problem with the development of games today is that we have conflicting ways of working with things. The procedures for creating art are always changing. There are always many "ifs" involved in the process . . . for this special case this should be done, but *if* that is done this way, we need to do it this way to get it right.

This makes the whole creation process confusing. Moreover, since it is hard to know everything in the development phase, it makes the process of creating game art stimulating and challenging.

To make things even more complicated, graphics change depending on the type of game you are creating, so there will always be new techniques to learn. For example, creating a huge, open-landscape multiplayer online game like *Battlefield Vietnam* compared to the advanced animated and detailed characters in *Soul Caliber II* requires different ways of thinking. Even if they share the same platform and the same engine, assets are built completely differently. Game design dictates the way we create art for the game.

Today, first-person shooters get the most attention. They are evolving fast with the best and newest technology. Even so, it is strange that we still have games that look like rigid worlds—stiff animation, empty worlds, and hard edges. Are games built with character, or are they merely a product for the mass market? Perhaps it is today's 3D programs with all their easy and perfect modeling tools that make everything look accurate—too accurate, in fact. The models are created with such perfect straightness and alignment that they don't represent the world in which we live—everything ends up looking mirrored and stiff.

To be convincing, we need to spend time making the objects and textures less symmetrical and "computer made" looking. Many games today do not try to make the objects look alive. They are more concerned with creating a good replica from the real world, but what we have as a reference might not always be what turns out to be the best for the game. In the game, we might need to exaggerate the pieces to make it more visible. If something is supposed to be a little bent, make sure that it shows up bent in the engine—it is more important how we experience the object in the game engine than how the object appears in the 3D program. Visualize yourself playing the game while you create the model, texture, effects, environments, or animations, and determine what will be needed to create your asset. Independent of the game we are creating textures for, we need to know where it is going to be viewed. CRT monitors, TFT monitors, and TV screens all show very different colors, and it is very hard to create a game that suits them all.

TEAM WORK PROCESSES (STYLE GUIDE)

Game art teams need to be highly efficient, accurate, and they should always follow the processes that have been established for them. For this to function throughout production, the project needs good documentation in the form of a Style Guide. This is where the artists can turn for questions regarding special rules and decisions. A Style Guide is especially useful if the person you need to speak with is not available. The Style Guide is a collection of Research & Development (R&D) for the game and the procedures for reaching the required quality for every asset in the game. It should include all the information needed for modeling; for example, measurements of buildings, vehicles, polygon count, texture sizes, heights of a character standing, crouching, lying down, and the size and height of doors and window openings. To make the Style Guide complete, it could also include:

- Tutorials that explain the different processes, such as collision creation, normal mapping, lighting, lightmaps, animations, and texture mapping
- The Art Director's visual goal for the game, in written and illustrated form, explaining what the Art Director wants to achieve

A Style Guide that is accessible by everyone saves a lot of time and frustration when a person is trying to solve a problem. One of the worst things that can happen to a project is that in the middle of production, the key person with all the information on a certain topic, for which nothing has been written down, abruptly decides to leave the studio for a new job—enter panic! The company would lose all of its information for this area, and someone would have to start from scratch and try to catch up very fast. It is very important to write down all processes and keep backups. A good suggestion for productivity is to collect and organize textures, references, and other related materials. Link these to the Style Guide so that all artists can achieve the same style and visual quality.

A Style Guide needs to be continuously updated when things such as game standards, AD visions, game goals, or other important processes change. This can become a big hurdle when you are on a project where the engine is being developed or upgraded at the same time you are creating your art assets. Researching to find new techniques and optimizing processes for continuity, you should remember that it is faster for 20 people to do the same task it takes a single person to do. Educating more people on a single task will gain long-term speed.

PERSONAL WORKFLOW AND SPEED

Everyone works at different speeds. What takes two days for you might take three days for another person. By working toward learning and understanding procedures, you can reduce the time you spend trying to achieve the best quality. Practicing each procedure will make it easier and faster with time. A good workflow can benefit you both in your personal creations and in your work for the game industry.

A proven workflow is the "rough to detailed" method. It applies to all art you would be creating—animation, concepts, effects, modeling, sketching, and texturing. Imagine yourself sketching a character. The first thing you need to establish is the pose and composition of the shot. When you are satisfied with how it looks, start adding more detail and shape, such as shoulders, torso, head, feet, and so forth. This process can be very important to learn and use. It will help you in several areas such as:

Too much detail at the wrong place: Concentrating on the wrong things and adding too much detail in the beginning creates a bad result.

Finish in time: Reduce the risk of working too long on one part, thereby losing time for the next section, and then not being able to finish the object in time.

Team process: Make sure everyone understands the mesh and can pick up where you left off.

All productions have a schedule, and it is very important to adhere to it. Using the "rough to detailed" process, time yourself and learn how long it takes to create a certain object a certain way at a normal pace. You are as responsible for your schedule and the time estimates as your manager is, when setting up the schedule together.

When you are checking over your creations for finalization, it is imperative that you go over them detail by detail. Go over the mesh one more time to find any technical errors that might exist. Make sure you work linearly when searching for errors, and restrain yourself from looking over the entire creation in one fell swoop. Focusing on each detail will help discover errors easier.

TECHNICAL LIMITATIONS

The technical requirements of creating game art present limitations to how creative you can be as an artist. Although you want to use all of your creative talents, the visual and technical aspects of the game will limit you. Games are products that have to appeal to consumers visually. Consumers want fast, quality graphics, so you need to understand frame rate, performance, memory, and graphic cards for each game. It's very important for you to get to know as much as possible about the system's technical aspects and what's involved in creating a game, so that you understand how to create art for each engine and console that you'll be working on: they all have specific hiccups that you need to know.

COPYRIGHTED MATERIAL

When creating objects for games, there will be occasions when you need to create objects that you need to find references for on the Internet. When creating these textures or objects, make sure you do not use the other people's material or ideas, just use them to generate your own ideas. Although finding images and objects on the Internet can be of great use and be great reference images if you add the material "as is" to a commercial product, you can cause the studio many legal and image problems. Copyright reasons aside, if you find an image on the Internet, you can be sure that others will too. If you create the exact model or texture as a replication of an image, people will notice. You are an artist, and there is little pride in replicating someone else's work. Come up with your own feel, look, and history for the texture of the object.

Use the references as a "guide" to create something interesting of your own. Make sure you have permission to duplicate the exact context of the object in the reference photos if you choose to do so.

Summary

1. You are an artist, not an assembly line. Use your imagination and vision!
2. For your personal evolution as an artist, question all decisions and make sure you test them yourself.
3. In your own development, stop creating what you find easy and fun. Struggle to learn what is hard and unknown. This will make you expand your art knowledge and let you evolve faster as an artist.
4. Buy a camera, use it often, and capture the world with interesting compositions.
5. When working with art, establish an emotional feeling for it before you add details.
6. To succeed in the games industry, you are no stronger than your entire team, so appreciate teamwork and share the burden to secure the game.
7. To gain personal speed, use the "rough to detailed" technique. Build an overview of the task before you delve too deeply into the details.
8. Learn to judge your own work; "kill your darlings" when necessary, and always remember, "less is more."

6

GAME MODELING

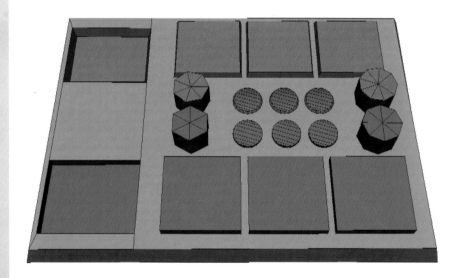

Every game artist needs to know how to model a low-polygon mesh with game production standard and quality. You might not be involved with creating assets for the game, but knowing its workflows will make you understand how a game is constructed, so it is necessary for each artist to know how to use a 3D program to be productive. With every new game released, we experience richer graphics and more detailed environments, characters, and objects. The complexity of the content consists of modeling the entire scene for the player to move around in. While this is made in real-time with limited resources, we need to know what we can afford and where we can place the information. Creating art for games with this process is different from creating art for movies, where each shot is planned for and the objects are modeled. If you work in the industry or study to do so, it is important that you have the basic understanding how low-polygon modeling works. In this chapter, we'll go over various techniques and examples that will help you understand, and practice different methods to get the best result when modeling meshes for different consoles.

MODEL AFTER REFERENCE

References in all productions are very important. We need blueprints, concept art, photographs, and clear images that can help us define the object construction and how things look up close. The more references you have, the easier it will be when you try to visualize the object's mechanical functionality and how to go about modeling it. You also need to know how the object is intended to work inside the game, based on the designer's thoughts about the object. Is it going to be used for something special gameplay wise? Answers to questions like this should be accessible and stated in a document such as the Style Guide for each object. If this information has not been collected and defined as you are assigned the task, make sure to get the correct guidelines before you start. If you can't find enough references and need to get more, verify that you have the right ones before you start to model and texture anything to protect yourself and make sure others know what you are about to create. Although blueprints can be visually boring, they are extremely helpful in defining the very basics of the shapes and for starting to create the rough model. Import them into your 3D program and use them as reference planes.

When modeling the objects that need to cover the entire inside of a game, we do not always have the time or data available to find accurate material. Sometimes, all you can find is a small blurry image, or just part of one. Visualize the object through these poor photos by drawing your own blueprints for the different angles Top, Side, Front, Back, and Bottom view, as shown in Figure 6.1. This can be very helpful with your creation process in the 3D program.

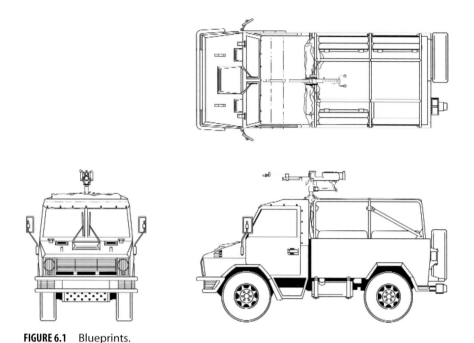

FIGURE 6.1 Blueprints.

Without the proper reference and research, you will most likely end up with revisions, so do not start to model anything until you have a clear idea of how the object really looks. Start with a rough model of the object by defining the correct aspects of length and measurements before you start going into detail. While modeling the mesh, go back to the real-life photos and verify what it really looks like. It is important to read the image correctly, and be aware of the photograph perspective. Although blueprints are easy to read and model from, there can be occasions when you might have difficulties reading the exact measurements and shapes. Look at and verify that specific details from the photos are what you want to replicate within the 3D world. When you go over your model and check its consistency in relation to your reference photos, make it a habit to see all pieces as shapes on your mesh instead of concentrating on their specific details. Start with the main object and verify its shape, and then continue the process with each shape in relation to each other. Go from the back to the front of the object. This way, you will not miss any areas of importance. You should be looking for how things relate to each other in the object by length, angle, and position. As an example, let's look at a gun. What is its main purpose? Aim, trigger, shoot. We tend to design objects with arcs and straight lines where parts line up with each other. Make sure you find these points, and then view each piece separately in relation to each other. As seen in Figure 6.2, the yellow color represents pieces of the same length; the height of the M16 at the magazine is as long as the lower meeting point of the stock and main piece. The green parts on the M16 represent more than a single length.

FIGURE 6.2   Each line with similar color represents an equal length.

Go over your entire object systematically. Are you giving the object's different parts the correct sizes in relation to each other? Then, continue with the angle of the different parts of the gun. Several parts will have the same angle, or meet up with other important points of the same object. If we study Figure 6.3, we see that the red line shows us that the angle from the stock lines up with the end of the top piece of the main part of the gun. It also shows us that all the yellow lines are parallel to each other, and we can clearly see the height difference between the barrel and the stocks upper part.

FIGURE 6.3   Each colored line represents the same angle.

When reading photographs, make sure you calculate the depth of view and its surrounding objects. Following this method will make you create objects that are more correct. Adding this to the workflow of starting with the rough mesh and defining the correct structure before you start with the details, you can easily secure your work.

Let's visualize how the object in Figure 6.4 is constructed. What can we tell from this single image? Visualize your reference images and draw your own idea of how you think the construction works, and how it would look from different angles, if this were the only image you had. How is an object like this constructed in real life and why? More often than not, fabricated objects that have a bend or curve have it for a reason, not just to look cool. Weapons, for example, are designed for usability and functionality, and have a logical reason for every shape. Remember that it is easier and cheaper for companies to make something boxy than to custom mold every piece. Take a gun as in Figure 6.4. Ask the question, "How would this handle feel during long periods of use?" If you modeled it too hard, it would probably even hurt the game character, if he had feelings.

FIGURE 6.4   How does this gun look from the other sides?

Remember that there is more to photos than reference details. They also give you the ability to read how light is interacting with the object. Study Figure 6.5 and you can see that the light shows how hard the edges are, together with the information of how smooth or round an object's surface is. By studying the light direction and shadows of the objects in a 2D image, you can determine the shape and depth between the different pieces and how they relate to each other. Think of the object as if you were putting a wireframe on it, drawing in the different depth with lines, as done in Figure 6.5, based on the light information on the gun. Learning how to read a 3D image for reference will benefit you in everyday work.

FIGURE 6.5 Simulated vertical wireframes, to visualize 3D within the 2D image.

POLYGONAL OBJECTS

When we create 3D objects, we connect points (vertices) to each other in the 3D world, creating surfaces (polygons). A single polygon is the smallest part of the surface in polygonal modeling, and is built from a surface of three connecting vertices, creating a triangle (Tri-gon). If the same polygon connects by four vertices, we refer to it as a face (Quad). If five or more vertices are connecting to the same single polygon, we refer to it as an N-gon surface (see Figure 6.6).

FIGURE 6.6   From the left: polygon (Tri-gon), face (Quad), and an N-gon.

All types of polygons are by default single-sided, but 3D programs can show polygons as double sided. Being single-sided, a polygon can only be seen from a single direction, controlled by the direction of its normal, often shown as a line pointing out from the center of the visible side on the polygon (see Figure 6.7).

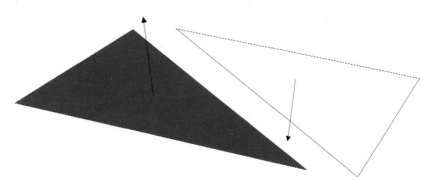

FIGURE 6.7   Directional normal shows the surface of a single-sided polygon.

POLYGON LIMITS

Hardware technology limits us to the number of polygons we can use on a single game object and in a complete scene. That amount depends on the system for which you are developing; therefore, there is no true definition for how low a low-polygon model is or needs to be. What we today call low-polygon modeling was once seen as high-polygon, depending on the technology at that time. Today, we create high-polygon models with millions of polygons, something that was impossible a few years ago. The numbers of polygons that we are able to use in the future will most likely contribute to changes in our workflow and the processes by which we create game art. Even today's hardware has limits, and we need to learn how to distribute the total amount of polygons the engine can render. Having huge amounts of polygons is a performance issue. If we can achieve the same visual quality with a low amount of polygons by placing them where they are most visible, it will help us achieve a higher frame rate. The way we determine the amount of polygons for each type of object can have a huge impact on how things are distributed within the game. You need to know how efficient the graphic engine and the console's graphic card are. If you can estimate how many polygons the engine can draw with the game's expected frame rate, it is easy to set up a guide for polygons that we can use. This process is vital for production and for artists to establish a quality standard for the art. When the numbers are tested and decided upon, it is important to document them so everyone in the project understands the target. This is where the Style Guide comes in handy, and will save production time because vital information is gathered for everyone to read.

More often than not, we are too optimistic with the polygons from the start. This mistake is usually made when the engine is developed alongside the game itself. While being optimistic with polygons, we should remember that it is easier to fill a game with polygons after the content is finished than to redo and remove polygons when the objects are already in use. If we add objects to a game that has a polygon buffer, it will give us breathing room later in the optimization process when everyone is trying to get the best performance out of the game. It is the responsibility of the artist to know where to place the polygons on an object. It is very important that the level designers know and understand what makes a level heavy for frame rate, and how they should place objects for the best and most stable performance.

With the many different game types created by various studios, it is important to know that the gameplay often dictates our visual experience.

We know that there are more than just the visual parts to a game. Physics, collision, AI, and networks—all require their piece of the processor power. Art limitations do exist, and we should be aware of them. We do not want to be in a position four weeks before Art Freeze where we get the order to cut all art assets by 40% to reach the performance needed. If this happens, be prepared for many long nights.

LOW-POLYGON MODELING

Knowing where to place vertices is the very key to low-polygon modeling, and will help improve your ability to create cleaner, more exact models. The process of creating a clean model requires both technical and artistic skills. Let's look at how to take your low-polygon modeling to new levels.

Polygon Placement

When producing content for games, there is an easy way to decide what is needed or not: polygons that will never be seen should not be modeled, or on special occasions, should be kept at a very low number. Why model and texture objects that the player will never see? Doing so only takes up production time, something we are short of in development.

We need to know what will be seen and when. Games are an open dynamic world, where we need to know how we are going to limit the player. Many single and multiplayer games take place in a closed environment where nothing is drawn outside established borders.

Many single and multiplayer games use objects as invisible walls to limit the way the player can move or see; this way, all things beyond this point can be removed. An outdoor environment works in a similar way. A closed house would be completely empty and act as a shell with no polygons inside it. Remember to distribute the polygons to locations where the player will see them the most.

Modeling priority can be broken into several levels of importance:

- Size
- Silhouette
- Camera distance
- Gameplay time
- Key area of interest

Size

The smaller the object is, the fewer polygons we need in relation to its shape. For example, a doorknob would require fewer polygons than a big oil cistern to make them both look equally round.

Silhouette

The object's shape is important when determining the number of polygons needed. If an object is round, you need to know how and where to place the vertices to get the best roundness for the object. Figure 6.8 Illustrates a theory with two balls, both with 11 sides. When both balls are facing us directly (furthest to the left), they look smooth in their centers, but the orange ball's silhouette is rougher than the green ball's. Turn the balls to see their sides, and we can see that the green ball has added polygons at the silhouette edge, which makes it look smoother from an angle.

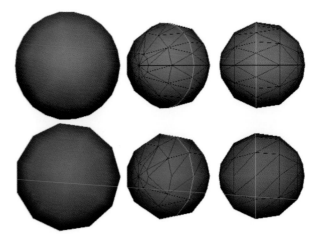

FIGURE 6.8   Silhouette is the key to a smooth-looking object.

The solution is not to add more polygons in the middle of an object, since it would not give the player more information. This is especially true when we use texture-mapping techniques like normal mapping (Chapter 19, "Normal Mapping") that simulate depth on the flat planes facing you but will not change the object's silhouette. With the object built in 3D and meant for the player to see from various angles, how can we know where the object's silhouette is? Well, if we know where the player's "camera" will be during gameplay, we can understand where the object's silhouette is, as seen in Figure 6.9.

Camera Distance

Not all objects need to be right in your face while you are playing the game. Many times, we will experience objects at unreachable distances.

FIGURE 6.9   Adding information in the silhouette makes the object more interesting.

These objects will not require the same amount of detail as those close to the player.

Gameplay Time

Time of appearance in gameplay is important when deciding what should be detailed. Let's say that you are playing a single-player game. You enter a room where there is a table lamp in one of the corners. If you see this lamp 1 minute out of a total of 10 hours of gameplay, spend as little time and polygons on this one as possible; you want it look good, but it doesn't have to be a masterpiece.

Key Area of Interest

While playing the game, human eyes will focus on what is important in the game, things that will affect the player such as characters, vehicles, or special objects. For example, a wall would be an object that the player would run past without noticing any specific detail in it. Some things naturally command more attention than others do. A character's head compared to his feet, a tank's turret compared to its tracks; all these objects are related to gameplay so we need to distribute the polygons accordingly.

Modeling Theory

Low-polygon modeling is challenging. There are no actual "rules" that dictate how to attain the expected end quality, but some processes and workflows are faster than others and give you more control. When low-polygon modeling, the fastest way to start is to use the box modeling technique, which is very similar to the "rough to detailed" method mentioned earlier in the book. The mesh starts with a simple box to which we add details and more polygons until finished. When working with polygons, it is important that you always have control of the polygon count; knowing where and how you add polygons to the mesh becomes extremely important. Start with a simple box, move, scale, and adjust the box polygons, edges, and vertices so it represents your reference images.

When adding detail, limit your tools to extrude, bevel, split, and cut (see Figure 6.10). Restrain from using Boolean, SubD, and smooth (subdivision smooth), which create more polygons than you need for low-polygon objects and cause unpredictable results that are hard to control. Try to get into the habit of planning your modeling before you start, so you always have control over polygon placement. In Figure 6.11, you see a green object modeled with the low-poly box method, and an orange object modeled with smooth and bevel. The green object has 51 polygons, and the orange has 10 times as many. If you are going to reach required quality in production time, sorting and optimizing a high-polygon model down to the required level is not where you want to spend your time.

FIGURE 6.10   Extrude, bevel, and cut.

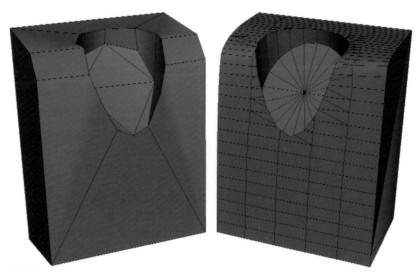

FIGURE 6.11   A low-polygon object versus a smooth and beveled object.

Modeling Using Polygons or Faces

Should we model with triangles or quadrants? The latest 3D programs support what we call *quad modeling*, where each object is maintained in its quad shape, operating on face select, split, bevel, and extrude. This works perfectly with the box modeling process, and gives the modeler fast and effective tools to use. Game engines read and use all the objects as triangles, so there are many things you need to verify to make sure your object looks like it will inside the engine. By converting the quads to triangles, you can secure visual quality in the mesh.

Arc Flow Edge Technique

Our goal is to make the object appear as smooth as possible with the polygons that we have available. To do so, think of your mesh as if it were clay; keep rotating the camera around your object to see it from all angles. This way, you will find areas that you need to tweak to achieve the roundness and smoothness needed for the best result.

If you look at Figure 6.12, there is a disrupted flow of the arc with a lower vertex in the center. Going over our object, we are looking for similar occasions, clean lines where the edges follow an arc within the mesh. To achieve this, we need to align the vertices to the right place as shown in Figure 6.13.

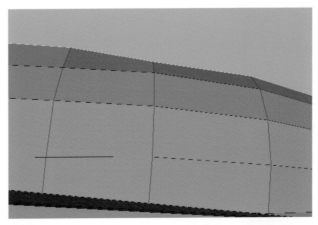

FIGURE 6.12   Misplaced vertex breaks the flow.

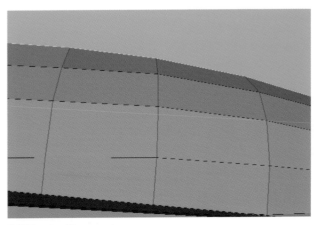

FIGURE 6.13   Corrected vertex.

If vertices do not follow the correct shape or add anything to the object's shape, they are not required. Let's study this example together with the flow in a more complex object. In the left image in Figure 6.14, you see the back piece of an airplane. There are several well-placed divisions in the mesh, but the yellow highlighted edges are not following the arc shape in the best way. The edge has such little alternation that it is unimportant for the object's shape. We can therefore delete it as shown in the right image in Figure 6.14.

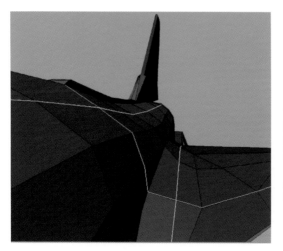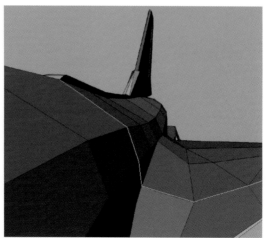

FIGURE 6.14   Left: Bad arc flow. Right: Deleted edges, leaves the same shape.

If the purpose of the object surface is to be smooth at these places, the edges would have needed to be tweaked to follow an arc instead of deleted as in Figure 6.15. To achieve a smooth object and arc with the edges, they have a good flow in all directions, even when crossing each other.

Rotate around the object to find breaks in the arc flow.

When you are creating and optimizing your objects, it's good to know how small the smallest visible polygon should be within the game to make a difference in the model. A good idea is for the team to have a standard set that depicts how small polygons in the game should be. Many times, small details will be lost in gameplay, thereby taking up memory and performance. Very small details that are not directly in the object silhouette risk disappearing in the object's smoothing groups. Pay attention to the structure of the model and try to find a continuous "flow" of the model lines, as how things are in real life.

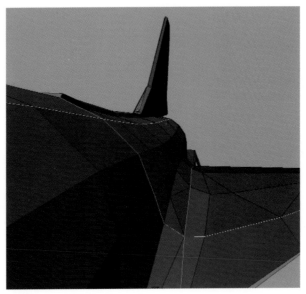

FIGURE 6.15   Object where the arcs are flowing correctly.

SUBDIVIDED TECHNIQUE

Structuring your model into sections is good for various reasons when creating meshes for games. Light reacts to how the vertices are placed in the object, and with good structured sections, you will be able to use UV coordinates in an efficient way.

Model for Lighting

Modeling for game engines that rely on per-vertex lighting requires you to understand how vertices react and work together with the light before you start modeling (see the section, *Per-Vertex Lighting* in Chapter 15, "Game Lighting"). Modeling for this lighting technique, we can decide where, what, and how the object should be lit by placing the vertices at certain points. For an even light intensity over the object, the mesh should be built with a grid system. The more vertices we can add to an object, the more detailed lighting we will be able to get. Keeping the same shape and size of the polygons over the entire object makes them react correctly to the light. See Figure 6.16, where the vehicle has been subdivided.

If we direct a light source onto the plane, you can see that the plane gets an even, smooth-looking surface (see Figure 6.17).

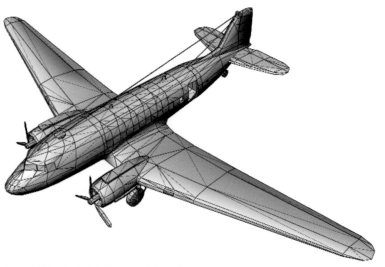

FIGURE 6.16   Subdividing modeling distributes the vertices evenly on the object.

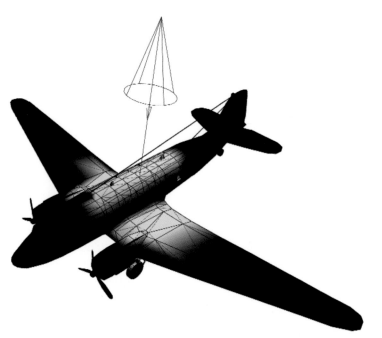

FIGURE 6.17   Evenly placed vertices on a model with a subdividing technique creates a correctly lit object.

If we had built the same plane with uneven shaped polygons, unstructured vertex placement, and turned edges, it could have looked like the plane in Figure 6.18.

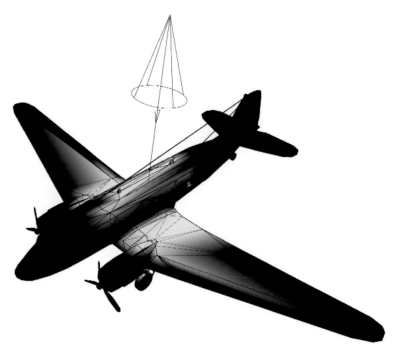

FIGURE 6.18   Uneven placed vertices and edges result in unwanted light calculations.

Modeling in this way spends polygons in areas where they might not be needed other than for the lighting to work within the game. Therefore, it is important that you know where and when you need to use this technique.

Modeling for UV Reuse

We can also use a grid modeling technique to split UVs to reuse or change UV coordinates over certain areas. This is very common in situations where we want to build something for tiling surfaces (see Figure 6.19). The orange color shows the horizontal tiling of the texture. The green color on the buildings represents a tile break with a new texture to add dirt and wet stucco under the windows. If you use the grid in a similar way, you can create extra polygons around doors, windows, and the corners of buildings to break the uniformity of the tile by applying different texture variations.

FIGURE 6.19   Object subdivided for tiling.

CHARACTERISTIC TECHNIQUE

Computers have a way of making things *too* perfect. To achieve a more natural and interesting visual quality, we have to address how we build the objects. We can do this is by:

- Shape
- Quantity of objects

Shape

One of the more difficult aspects with modeling is that we end up with too much symmetry. Objects are round in real life, but nothing in life is truly computer mirrored. The human eye distinguishes symmetry and repeated surfaces very easily. By taping faces, moving vertices, and tilting edges on the objects we are creating, we can break the uniformity and give each object a characteristic touch, which will make it look more true to life.

When creating a round object such as a cylinder, you can help the eye to *not* see the uniformity by using an uneven number of sides so no vertices are lining up with each other (see Figure 6.20). The large orange cylinder has an even number of sides compared to the green cylinder that appears rounder with the uneven number of sides.

As we can see in Figure 6.20, the green object has a taper and change added to it, while the orange one does not. This helps the uniformity, and shows more of the faces available on the object, making the player experience more angles in the game and get a richer experience.

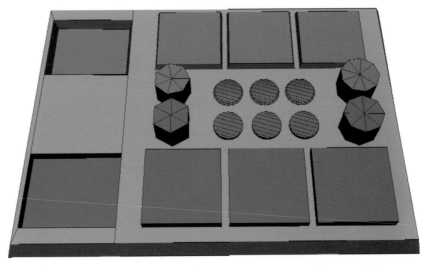

FIGURE 6.20   Object with taper lets you see more of the object. (Make use of all polygons and break uniformity with the correct shape in the object.)

Quantity of Objects

Together with the object's shape, games are normally very stiff and empty. Making a world look more alive requires us to fill it with various objects. Adding more objects and shapes can be done both in meshes and in the scene. For example, if we make an object such as a tank, it would be better to have many boxes with fewer vertices than to have fewer very detailed boxes. Even if they are just a couple of polygons, adding things like antennas, handlebars, windshield wipers, mirrors, and other small details on vehicles gives an impression of life.

When we fill the world with objects, we should rotate, tilt, and place them so they break the structured computer feeling of emptiness and exactness from which games often suffer.

OPTIMIZING OBJECTS

In the last phase of your modeling process, it is good to go over your objects to make sure you have built the objects to use the lowest polygon/vertex amount possible. If you need to reduce polygons, you have to decide what is most important on the object at this point. This could include:

- Size
- Silhouette
- Camera distance
- Gameplay time
- Key area of interest

The Art Director will be able to help you here, because he will know where the other objects in the game have their details.

Start removing your vertices and see if you can reach the same shape with the necessary amount of polygons.

Open-Edge Objects

A visual mesh does not have to be one closed mesh. A game model mesh can consist of several small pieces stuck into each other. This allows us to build objects that are more interesting and add many more details to large objects. If you look at Figure 6.21, you can see a gray base object with a mesh attached by welded vertices, and two white models stuck into it. This adds the same amount of vertices but gives more freedom to what we can create with the limited amount of polygons we have.

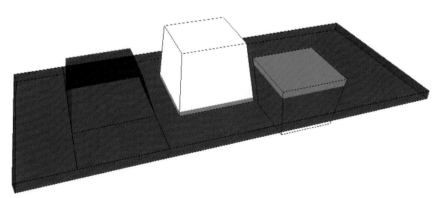

FIGURE 6.21   Several objects comprise one large one.

When we stick pieces into each other this way, there are faces that we can remove, because the player will not be able to see them as shown in Figure 6.22.

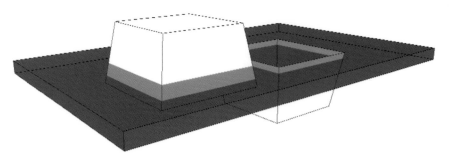

FIGURE 6.22   Deleted unseen faces inside main mesh.

This modeling technique is not without its flaws. It is not supported by tri-stripping and will in many cases become a larger cost than if the object were welded into one solid mesh. You can read more about the expense of vertices and polygons in Chapter 13, "Game Art Optimizations."

EDGE ROTATION

Game engines treat all created objects as if they were made of triangles. Therefore, it is important to look out for bad edges that could make the surface look corrupted or "bumped." This will occur when the triangles are turned the wrong way between two vertices. They will be clearly visible if you convert your mesh to triangles and view it in a flat shaded mode. In Figure 6.23 are three cubes. The orange is the original face mode cube with one if its vertices moved, and the two green cubes are duplicated and triangulated with different rotations of their edges. There are many possible combinations even for a small object like a cube. Therefore, it's important that you know how the object should look when you build it, and that you go over your final object, making sure the edges occur as you want them. If exported with the wrong turned edge, it will corrupt the visual experience of the object and show incorrect lighting.

FIGURE 6.23   Edge turning can have various results.

As you can see in the orange cube in Figure 6.23, it is very important to recognize this problem when you work in 3D/face mode. The orange cube does not show any edges, and you cannot tell even in face mode how the object will look within the game. If the exporter is converting the object, and you do not have manual control over the result, you'll have to go over and split or turn the edges that create problems before the conversion. Even if your exporter handles converting face polygons to triangles, it is best to always triangulate your objects and go over your mesh before exporting to the engine, or turn the specific edges that are creating the problems. Doing so will give you a better idea of what you will see in the game.

SMOOTHING GROUPS

Since we are restricted to defining shapes by the amount of polygons we have, a computer game relies heavily on a feature that gives us the possibility to give the polygons' edges a seamless look by manually controlling the edges as soft or hard. When using the 3D program to set an edge or a group to soft or hard, we change the vertex normal rotation angle and tell the engine what direction the vertex should have and how it should show the edge in the game. Vertex normal direction is handled by a common definition—smoothing groups, or hard/soft edges. Figure 6.24 shows two cylinders. The orange cylinder has all its edges set to smooth. Its edges are fading to dark as the engine tries to simulate that the object is rounded. Of course, to make this cylinder more normal, we need the edges to look hard. By changing its edges around the caps to hard edges or the cap faces to another smoothing group as the green cylinder in Figure 6.24, we get the hard caps yet keep the roundness around the cylinder's middle.

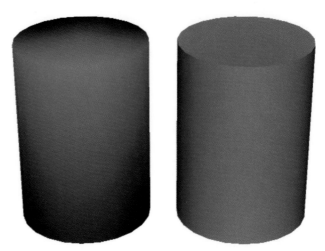

FIGURE 6.24   Smoothing the edges can drastically change the shape of the model.

For an area to work as smooth edges, it must have the vertices merged between its two polygons. The optimization option to stick meshes into other parts of the mesh will therefore not work. If your object requires a continuous smooth shape, you need its vertices welded.

 Through Mesh component display, Maya has the ability to filter out what types of edges should be visible, with hard or soft edges.

To learn more about the technical aspects of vertex normals and how you can control individual vertices and their control over light and smoothness, refer to Chapter 15.

CLEANUP AND EXPORTING

When you have finished the model, it is time for export. You should go over the mesh a final time, and once you have the mesh inside the engine/editor, you should go over your mesh again. Make sure it looks as it did in the 3D program. Perhaps some vertices need to be moved to make it look better, or you might see issues that you didn't notice until you placed the object in its correct placement in the game.

Clean Mesh

Adding details evenly over the entire object will help you decide where to distribute the polygons on the model. There should not be any extra polygons on the final object, so go over the object one last time to make sure all unnecessary polygons are removed before you export it. Make sure no intersections and vertices poke out unexpectedly. Clear and remove stacks or history and freeze/reset transformation.

Double-Sided Polygons

When you are handling polygons in 3D, you can see them from both sides. This feature is there to help you visualize the objects when they are modeled. In games, the engine has the capability to do the same thing; however, it will cost twice the performance and will create problems when used with per-pixel and per-vertex lighting. When modeling objects for games, you need to make sure that you have the polygons single sided; the polygon normals must face in the direction you want the polygons to be visual in the game. If you are going to model a window, a fence, or something that should be visible from both sides, your best solution would be to model two polygons close to each other with their normals facing away from each other.

Merging Vertices

As a final check, verify that the object does not contain any isolated or unwelded vertices. If your model has unwelded vertices, it's probably because the object's smoothing is not showing up correctly. Make sure your object does not include any isolated faces or vertices that might be unattached to the mesh.

Z Fighting

Z fighting occurs when you have overlapping faces drawn at the same position. This is something to avoid, since the polygon is "fighting" with another in the graphic card, trying to determine which of them should be drawn closest to the camera. This creates an unpleasant flickering. It will also be very expensive for the engine, because it draws things on top of each other and the fill rate is higher.

Animation Setup

The objects you create might be animated or moved within the game. You need to find out from the animators, the Art Director, or the designers how they planned to use these objects. Different setups and engines will require different ways to save the objects. Naming conventions, pivot location, rotations, and positions can all be dependent on the specific object you are creating.

IN PRODUCTION

Throughout the book, we will create objects within an "In Production" environment. This will help you verify what you learn in each chapter. In this chapter, we are going to create a low-polygon table using the box modeling technique. For this walk-through, we will be using Maya, but box modeling is a nonspecific modeling technique that is available in all 3D programs.

Box Modeling

We start with creating a simple box shape that represents a table, which will be our base object, so scale the box so it has the thickness of a tabletop. Box modeling bases its operations on faces, and uses the very basics of modeling operations—extrude and scale. We now have a tabletop and need to add four table legs. We want the legs to be correct in scale and position. We could create a single leg and duplicate it four times, but we are going to sculpt this table from a single object. Select a face of the table and extrude it in the X-axis, creating three divisions in the top face. (See Figures 6.25 and 6.26.)

1. Create a polygonal box.
2. Scale it down to represent a flat table.
3. Select the top face.
4. Extrude to make it smaller in the X-axis.

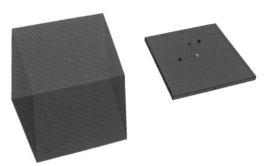

FIGURE 6.25   Create and scale the box.

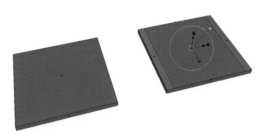

FIGURE 6.26   Extrude the face to become smaller in the X- axis.

The faces now represent the bottom of the table, and the two smaller divisions will be the leg thickness. To create the legs, select the narrow faces and extrude them in scale by altering the size of the Z-axis. By scaling an extrusion in one axis, the mesh will leave invisible faces in the mesh for the nonscaled axis. Merging or deleting the vertices will remove these. Select them and delete. See Figures 6.27 and 6.28.

1. Select the two narrow faces created.
2. Extrude them to become smaller in the Z-axis.
3. Select the leftover faces (marked as red dots in Figure 6.27).
4. Delete them.

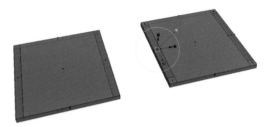

FIGURE 6.27   Select the narrow faces, and extrude them to become smaller in the Z-axis.

FIGURE 6.28   Delete the obsolete faces.

We now have one small square face in each corner of the table. By selecting and extruding these, we create the table legs and finish the modeling of the table, as shown in Figures 6.29 and 6.30.

1. Select the small square faces.
2. Extrude to create the table legs.
3. We now have modeled a table!

FIGURE 6.29   Select and extrude the square faces.

FIGURE 6.30   A low-polygon table.

Optimizing

We just modeled a low-polygon table very quickly. To make this table optimized for a game environment, we can optimize the mesh and delete faces that we will not see. Let's presume that the table will never be seen from underneath and the model will never be positioned upside down, making it possible for us to optimize certain areas that never will be visible. The legs will always touch the floor so the end polygons can be deleted (see Figure 6.31). In addition, the bottom plane of the table can be deleted as seen in Figure 6.32.

1. Select the bottom four faces on the table leg.
2. Select the three faces from the bottom of the table.
3. Delete them.
4. Triangulate the object.

FIGURE 6.31   Bottom polygons deleted.   **FIGURE 6.32**   Table polygons deleted.

Now the table is ready and converted to triangles. To finalize your object, turn on single-sided polygons, and confirm with face normals that your polygons are all facing the correct direction.

With the optimizing, we managed to remove 20 polygons, or 28% on the table. Using a similar process to model a larger object can save you many polygons.

FIGURE 6.33   Triangulated and ready to export to engine.

SUMMARY

1. Make sure you know all the object's features and have enough reference material before you start to avoid remodeling it later.
2. Keep modeling "rough to detailed." The less you add in the beginning, the easier it will be to add detail and change things that might go wrong.
3. Stop focusing on the details in the photos. Read the object's shape, length, and angles. Learn how to read the light and how it shows the shape of the objects, even within a 2D image.
4. Place your polygons where the player will see them the most in regard to gameplay and visual feedback. Remember, we do not need polygons that the player will not see.
5. Respect polygon limitations; they are there to maintain the game's performance.
6. Make sure the flow of edges is correct and that the vertices in the mesh are placed where they contribute to the shape of the surface.
7. Rotate around your object, and move and tweak the vertices from all directions until you find the right position that does not break the flow of the object.

UV LAYOUT

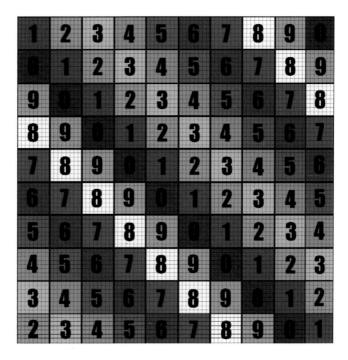

Vs are the 2D representation of a 3D object's mapped area. They are a representation of the texture space where each vertex on the 3D object represents a UV point. Today's games require a great deal of textures, and they represent a major part of the memory allocated for the art content in a game. Organizing the object's UV layouts and knowing how to use textures optimally can be crucial for performance. UV mapping from a production standpoint is time consuming. Setting up an efficient UV set for a complex 3D model can take several days, and that time will continue to increase with the more complex objects of tomorrow's games.

UV SETUP

Think of creating a good UV map as laying out a puzzle (see Figure 7.1). First, you sort and put aside all the pieces with the right matching structures and then make them all match up together. Our final puzzle should be placed within the 0 and 1 coordinates of the UV editor. This area represents the texture available for the object. If UVs extend beyond this range, the texture will appear tiled and repetitious. The more you can cover of the UV's layout, the less total texture you will use for the game, which results in higher performance and less memory used.

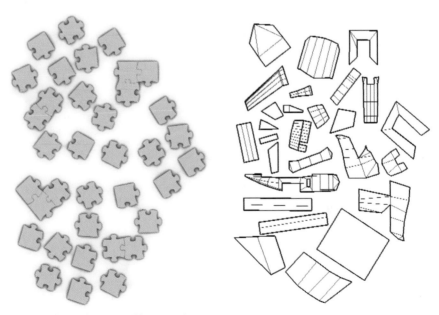

FIGURE 7.1   A UV layout is like a puzzle.

UV Resolution

We create textures for games by using square and rectangular shapes, with their lengths and height multiples of 2, 4, 8, 16, 32, 64, and so on as shown in Figure 7.2. A normal texture size for a PC game today can be a 2096 × 2096, while a 64 × 64 would be an optimal size for something that we use for a PlayStation® 2 console. It is important that you create the texture with the correct aspect ratio and for the texture's intended purpose.

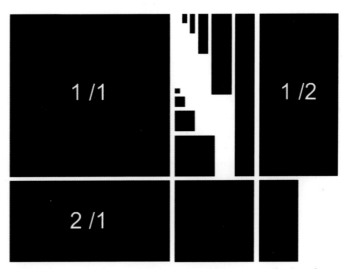

FIGURE 7.2 Texture sizes within game production—multiples of 2.

We can separate a texture object resolution into two parts: the game's objects related to other objects, and the single object's UVs layout.

Object versus Object

We will always have limited resources for textures, and deciding what size a certain texture should be for each object within the game is a complicated process. The computer game theory is that if an object is more visible or closer to the camera, it should have a higher resolution pixel ratio than objects in the distance or those that will never be seen up close.

This can be hard to control in some games where you have an open game area in which you can get close to all objects. Visualize a close-ranged single-player game, where you are standing on a cliff overlooking a landscape. You can see a building in the distance that you cannot travel to. This object's resolution would be very low in comparison to a barrel that you would have next to you on the cliff. Placing high-resolution textured objects near the camera will help give the illusion that the game has high-resolution, sharp graphics. Imagine playing a car game where you drive the car through city streets at an extreme speed. You will be concentrating on driving the car so much that you won't have time to study the quality of the textured buildings that flash by you on each side. Of course, when you are standing still, they need to look good, but in this case, it would be okay to map these walls with a lower resolution to make them have fewer details. The car, however, is the game's main object and the closest one to the camera. It needs to have the highest resolution and look the best. Arranging objects into groups and by importance will help us define the pixel resolution and the object's texture sizes. To keep the game visually balanced, a good idea is to keep all these groups mapped with the same resolution so you avoid visual mismatches, like when a barrel with four times as much detailed texture is next to some less-detailed, blurry, crates (see Figure 7.3).

FIGURE 7.3   Different resolutions on different objects break the unity of the objects.
© Digital Illusions CE AB. 2004 Reprinted with permission.

Let's say that all environment objects such as buildings, doors, barrels, crates, boxes, tables, cabinets, and chairs should have a texture ratio of 2 pixels per centimeter. Mapping a wall that is 2.5 meters high should take up 500 pixels in the texture height, while a barrel that is 1.3 meters high should have 260 pixels in texture height. It is important to have a concrete system planned out and written down in the Style Guide for the whole team to follow. This will greatly benefit the production process, because texture space for games is too expensive to waste in the wrong places.

UV Pixel Ratio

When you create UVs for an object in a game, you need to decide what parts of the object are the most important and will be seen the most. It is likely that you will not need to have the same pixel ratio covering the entire model. For example, when playing a game, the player will concentrate more on a character's face than the character's shoes. When you are laying out a UV map for this character, you would adjust the UVs to have a higher density of pixels on the character's head than you would on its shoes. The relation between the UVs for head and shoes for a character is shown in Figure 7.4.

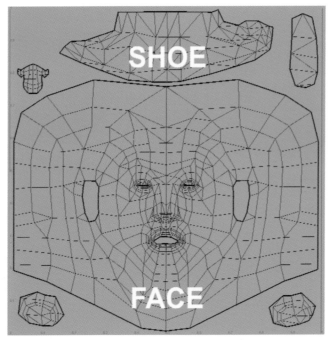

FIGURE 7.4   Face and shoe in UV map. © Digital Illusions CE AB. 2004 Reprinted with permission.

Even though in theory it is possible to scale down the shoes to save texture memory, it is a good idea to keep the differences to a minimum. Huge differences between the parts can break the overall presentation of the game.

When working with UVs, it is extremely important to avoid stretching at all costs so that you maintain the visual experience within the game. The barrel in Figure 7.5 has its side stretched. You can see that this is quite noticeable in a game environment, and it dispels the illusion of an object being realistic.

FIGURE 7.5   Stretched texture on a barrel. © Digital Illusions CE AB. 2004 Reprinted with permission.

The stretching on the barrel could be the result of a UV layout done with a planar projection without correcting the spacing between the UV afterwards. The smallest stretched UV can make the most beautiful object look awkward and break the realism of the game, so make sure you maintain the correct pixel ratio. You can apply a test texture as in Figure 7.6 to ensure correctness.

When applied to the object, this texture will help you notice stretching and other errors within the mapping. Make sure that the numbers and squares of the colored boxes are equal in size and shape. This helps you see if the object has any specific parts that are stretched and not square. Having the pixels square in a UV and in the texture is extremely important for making the object appear believable within your game.

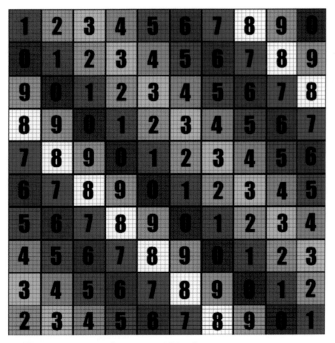

FIGURE 7.6 Test map for correct UV ratio.

Further technical information about processes to calculate the resolution needed, the sizes optimal for different consoles, and ideas on how to organize and optimize the textures in the game are discussed in Part III of this book, "Technical Knowledge."

PROJECTING UV

To get a good size with which to work, you need to project UVs so that you can work with them as a unit, and there are several ways to project polygons in a UV layout. Next, we'll talk about two processes that are commonly used within game production—both have their advantages and disadvantages.

Planar Projection

The most basic type of projection, planar projection gives you the most control of all the projection types, but is also considered the slowest process with which to work. Planar projection requires you to only use selected parts of a mesh at a single projection and angle your projecting plane according to the polygons. The biggest advantage with planar projection is that you have the option to specify the exact texture resolution for the projection, and that the projection will work with nonsquare textures. In Maya, this is done through the projection Height and Width options. 3ds max uses the planar projection options Length and Width as shown in Figure 7.7.

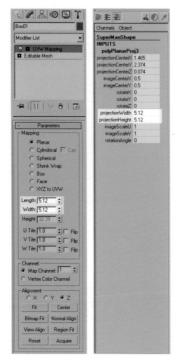

FIGURE 7.7   Planar mapping for correct size values in a scene, 3ds max on the left, Maya on the right.

These values represent the texture resolution depending on the world size and the object size. If you set Maya's Linear Working Unit (in preferences) to Meter, the value 5.12 in Height and Width specifies a 512 texture (5.12 meters where 1 pixel equals one centimeter). With the possibility for resolution size input, you will get the right size and pixel ratio throughout your entire mesh. For this process to work, however, it is important that you rotate the projection plane to be planar with the projected polygons, or it will result in skewed and stretched polygons. You would then need to correct the polygons within the UV editor with the help of the test texture, a process that takes a long time.

When using planar mapping, it is important that you do it on a per-selected polygon basis and not the entire object at one time. Doing so would create overlapping and stretched UVs.

Automatic Unwrap

The method that has become a standard for its speed and workflow is the automatic UV projection that comes with most 3D programs today. By using automatic UV projection, you can lay out the entire object's polygons at once without worry about overlapping polygons. Automatic projection options differ between 3D programs, but will most likely give you the option to choose projection angles. We want to use the box projection process, which uses six planar projections at a time. Automatic UV projection will not give you the option to input the correct texture pixel ratio for each projection. If your program supports the option to keep the polygons to the size seen in the 3D model by not scaling them to the UV 0 to 1 range, make sure this option is enabled. This is especially useful if you project an object in several selection steps. If not enabled, you will get each projected set of polygons covering the entire UV space. If you do not map everything at once, you will end up with several different resolutions on your polygons.

After you have projected all the polygons on the object, you need to match the pixel ratio with the size of the object in the world by scaling the UVs. Use the test image as a guide to determine the pixel ratio, and calculate with the grid how big your pixel resolution on the object should be.

Learn how to use automatic UV projection correctly and it becomes a very fast and useful tool. It will however, project and spread out several unconnected pieces that you will have to Stitch, Move, and Sew for your UV layout. A good workflow to build a correct UV layout is to project your final mesh with automatic mapping once, and arrange it in the UV editor. For more control, exact pixel ratio, to map something small, or to correct polygons within the same mesh, planar projection works well and can give you the very basic functionalities of mapping.

Maya does its Automatic Mapping in world axis. Make sure the object has correct rotation (planar to the ground grid) to get the cleanest UVs possible.

PLANNING UV LAYOUT

To get the most of your UV space, you need to organize and structure the layout to make sure that you stay away from using only 50% to 70% of the texture area. The tighter you can set the UV edges to each other at the given texture resolution, the more you can get out of the memory. Remember, we go over the UV planning process and arrange a good UV layout to:

- Reduce the seams in the texture map for a better visual appearance.
- Arrange the layout to fit more and use less texture overall.
- Overlay UVs to reuse texture.
- Tile textures.

When planning the UV layout it is important to keep as much of the object's edges connected to each other as possible so the player does not experience seams in the object's texture map. By arranging the UV layout, you can easily get more structure and get the most out of your texture area.

UV Editor

Working with game objects, you need to use the UV editor to arrange the pieces created by automatic UV projection. Move, Sew, or Stitch should be used to get all the piece edges together, and get rid of seams in the visual area. When using texture maps while sewing the UV together, you need to keep a close eye on the 3D model to see where the UVs are located. Make sure you sew the right pieces together. While arranging the UV pieces in the 2D UV editor, verify that your shapes match up with the right aspect and size in your 3D model. If your objects were projected with several pieces with bend, circles, and tubes, they will benefit from being straightened and aligned, before you Move and Sew them together. Figure 7.8 shows a transparent box extruded with sections, auto mapped, and then stitched together.

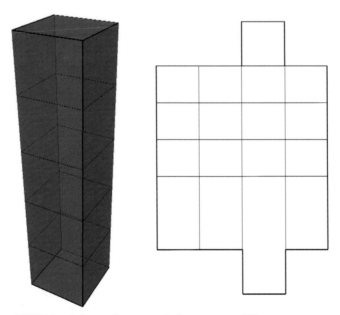

FIGURE 7.8   Cube sections extruded, easy-to-use UV.

We can see that the UVs line up perfectly with the size of the faces. If we tilt some of the faces, apply automatic mapping, and sew again (see Figure 7.9) the UVs' layout is corrupt due to the projection and the 2D representation.

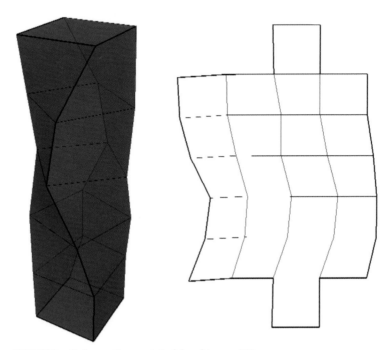

FIGURE 7.9   Cube sections rotated, hard-to-use UV

If we straighten the UVs before we sew the pieces together, we can get arranged UVs that work together with the tilted faces as seen in Figure 7.10. Always check your faces' size and shape on your 3D model compared to the UV editor.

Working toward keeping the lines as straight as possible for the UVs' edges will make it easier to draw clear lines in Photoshop, avoid blocky antialiasing, and free up space in the UV set. Maintain an edge padding when arranging the UVs by keeping the unfolded pieces' edges one to three pixels apart from each other. This will help the objects from getting color bleeding between the different pieces when mipmapping is used and the image is resampled to a lower resolution. This also secures the use of the extra space needed for methods such as normal mapping and other advanced texture techniques you might use in your game creation. Stay away from placing the pieces' UV edges at the very edge of the UV

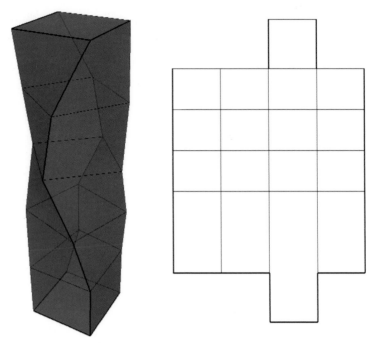

FIGURE 7.10   Cube sections rotated, easy-to-use UV.

Layouts 0–1 range coordinates. Using mipmaps that resample the texture will make the UV overlap the edge and read the texture on the opposite side. The UV has started to act like a tiling texture, and if the texture color has high contrast colors on its borders, it can create unwanted banding on the objects in the game.

If you lay out the UVs badly, you will end up with a lot of unused space, and you cannot use as high a resolution on the parts that you would have. Try to organize the similar unfolded pieces of the object to the same area on the UV layout. This will make it easier for the artist to find specific pieces within the texture, and you will have an easier time if you need to change it later. To get structure when arranging your UVs, begin placing all the flat rectangular UV object shells close to the edge of the UV Range coordinates. This frees up space in the middle of the layout for more unstructured, bigger pieces. Place these next. Keep the pieces organized and with their lines straight. Do not rotate them so they create problems for the texturer. Having two similar pieces where one is flipped horizontal will make it more difficult to create a texture. When the big pieces have been arranged and their size adapted to the pixel ratio, start to place the smaller pieces in an organized order. Fill the areas so the pieces cover the whole layout (see Figure 7.11).

FIGURE 7.11   A well-used and laid-out UV.

Within the games industry, many times we use a nonsquare texture (e.g., 512 × 256) to maximize the content and the layout. Working with these aspect ratios where the UV space is rectangular, you will experience a stretched appearance when rotating UVs in the editor. When rotating and arranging your UVs to match the UV space, you manually need to compensate for the image aspect ratio. Match them up with the test grid texture to confirm their proper square aspects. Planar projection lets you specify the projection rotation and therefore maintain the proper aspects. If you are forced to work this way with the automatic projection technique, it's best to use them both.

Tiling UVs

Tiling is a key part of texturing for games. We use it heavily in games to create a pattern that continuously loops over a long part of the surface. By using tiling as a technique, you are able to use smaller textures to create the same visual impact. The UVs extending outside of the 0 to 1 range in the UV editor will be treated as tiling information. When mapping a wall with a tiling texture, we would make the UVs continue outside the 0 to 1 range as shown in Figure 7.12.

It is possible to use both tiling UVs and nontiling UVs within the same texture. The tiling is set up as follows. When we create textures specifically for tiling, we need to decide what way the texture needs to tile. For example, if you are texture mapping a house, and a wall is 3.5 meters high and 20 meters long, if you let 256 pixels of the texture represent 2.5 meters, it needs to be tiled eight times. If you have a texture size of

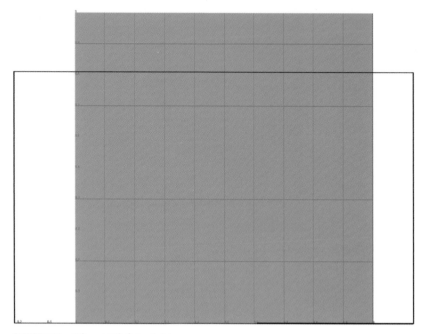

FIGURE 7.12   Tiling UV left to right.

512 × 512 for the entire house, you would need to change the aspect of the texture to 256 × 1024 to get it to work with the tiling you want. When using square pixel ratios, the height of the wall should take up 350 pixels in height of the texture and 256 pixels in width. This will give you 674 pixels of the texture's height to use for the rest of the house.

Mirror/Overlay UVs

In our attempts to save texture memory within a game, we reuse the same texture area for several objects by overlapping the UVs in the UV layout. Say you have 200 screws or 20 windows on one building that would take up a lot of texture if placed next to each other. By placing the UVs at the exact same position on the texture, we get them all to look the same.

Reusing texturing sounds great and can save you a lot of memory and time on painting textures, but several techniques such as Normal Mapping and rendered lightmaps conflict with overlapping and mirrored UVs and should be done with caution and understanding.

SUMMARY

1. Everyone can lay out a puzzle, and a UV is the same idea. Make sure you use the space as efficiently as possible; the fewer textures we use, the more memory we will save.
2. Games use textures that use multiplies of two in size.
3. Set up whole UVs before you arrange them outside the UV coordinates.
4. Arrange objects in the world in groups that have similar texture resolution.
5. Prioritize your pieces within the UV layout based on the importance of the object and what will be most visible within the game, keeping the differences small.
6. Sew together your pieces so there are no seams visible for the player.
7. Arrange lines parallel and straighten out pieces to make use of the UV space.
8. Start by laying out the biggest pieces along the borders, and then make the small pieces fit into the empty spaces in between, or what is left in the UV.

8 IN PRODUCTION: MODEL/UV

L et's test what you learned from the previous chapters by creating some art close to an actual development process. Let's say the studio you are working in is making a first-person shooter (fps) game on a PC and you are assigned a series of different objects. Throughout these tutorials, you should have a basic understanding of the 3D program with which you have decided to work; if not, please refer to the help guide for the task or command. For the tutorials, we will be using Maya 6, but the workflow and process will work in any other 3D programs with similar functionalities.

Low-Polygon Modeling

Before you jump in and start modeling our first project, you need some important information about the task. The following technical questions will help you understand what you are creating:

- Where is the screen placement of the gun in the game?
- What are its polygon and texture budgets?
- What texture-mapping techniques are used?
- How will the gun be animated, and what are its movements?

Let's see what games in general do and answer the preceding questions accordingly. In the game, we will place the gun on the right side of the screen so its left side will be facing the camera as the main interest and focus. This mesh will only be visible in the first-person view; for the-third person view, we will use a different mesh. We have a polygon limit of 2500 and can use a maximum texture size of 1024 × 512. The engine supports normal mapping, so we will be modeling with this in mind. We will not be using any vertex colors/shaders on this gun, so you do not have to be strict with the grid pattern when modeling. The safety mechanism is located on the right side on the AK47, so the animators will tilt the gun to the right side during the reload animation so we can see it during gameplay. Therefore, the right side of the gun needs to have a decent amount of detail. For moveable pieces, the animators need the magazine, the bullet chamber lid, the safety mechanism, and the trigger as separate objects.

This should give you a clear understanding of how the gun should look and act in the game. The next step is to know the exact version of the gun that the game designer wants in the game. For this task, you are modeling an AK-47 Kalashnikov in its original state.

Start by finding as much information about the AK-47 as you can. Research the specific gun on the Internet and find reference images to use as information about the model. You will find some images to get you started on the companion CD-ROM in the Chapter8\Blueprints_refImages\ folder (see Figure 8.1).

ON THE CD

FIGURE 8.1   Reference shots of an AK-47.

The more you know about the technical parts of the model, the easier it will be to understand how it works and why it was built the way it was. When you are finished with your research, import the blueprints to your 3D program and set them up as a reference image plane from which to model.

MODELING

Start by creating a box for the gun's housing and build the structure according to your backdrop blueprint. Make sure you verify the size of the gun to its real-life measurements and the size it needs to be in the game. Since you will have a limited amount of time to model this gun in production, you need to make sure that you get it right the first time—you cannot afford any mistakes in the workflow. Use the box-modeling technique to build a rough model so you can concentrate on its basic shape and structure before you start on the smaller details. Doing so will secure your workflow and make you reach your goal on time.

As a compliment to box modeling, you can subdivide the silhouette. Maya supports this with its Create Polygon tool. Draw your outline silhouette of the shape you need, then Triangulate the object, and then Quadrangulate the same object instantly. You can then extrude the faces to the right depth.

While starting to build the structure, do not add too many intersections; it is smarter to start with a rough shape. Barrels and round objects can be placeholder cylinders.

While creating your model, get into the habit of regularly checking your photographs and references over the entire object to make sure it is modeled correctly from all angles, and not only from the blueprint. (Revisit the section *Model after Reference* in Chapter 6, "Game Modeling," as a small reminder.) When you are done with the rough shape, it should look similar to Figure 8.2.

FIGURE 8.2   Rough and fast box-modeling mesh, iron out the shape.

The rough looks like a good start, so it's time to add a bit more detail. Go over all the reference photos, and look at zoomed-in photographs of various directions of the gun (see Figure 8.3). Every little groove is important. Make sure you add them at the correct place on the gun. Always check position in the real images while you are modeling; blueprints do not always provide you with the necessary 3D shape and depth of all the smaller details you need. Use the Extrude, Cut, Split, and Bevel tools to add details on to the mesh. If you want to make an extrusion in the middle of a face, or cut new edges through the polygon to build a face, Extrude works better than using Boolean tool.

Having a limited amount of polygons, it is important that you distribute them where they have the biggest visual impact. To get a better view of how the gun will be positioned within the game, set up a camera with

FIGURE 8.3   Details from all angles; look at several images to get information.

the gun positioned at the same angle as if it were in game. If possible, use the same field of view settings as shown in Figure 8.4.

FIGURE 8.4   Position the gun as it appears in the game.

The game will only be using this model in this first-person view and in any other angle created by the animator. You will never see the end of the barrel or polygons that face the same way you look. When adding smaller details like screws and round objects, the smaller/further away the piece is from the camera, the fewer polygons it requires. This gives you 2500 polygons to place where you need them the most, in the face of the player, closest to the camera, and in the silhouette of the gun. Prioritize the details based on what the player will see closest to the view as in Figure 8.5.

FIGURE 8.5   Importance factors of the gun details. White indicates more detail needed.

Right Side

Let's start with the right side of the gun where the bullet chamber and safety are the main visible parts when the player tilts and reloads in the game. Figure 8.6 shows what you need to focus on.

- Bullet chamber
- Hatch over bullet chamber, with pulling hammer
- Safety mechanism

FIGURE 8.6   Right side of the AK-47, up close.

When you add these things, keep in mind that you are still modeling the rough shape of the object. Do not go into any specific details yet, keep things simple, and work fast. Disregard any extra edges or mismatching

ON THE CD

shapes at this point. The companion CD-ROM contains the Rough mesh Ak47_AddDetail under Chapter8/3dsMax7_OBJ/ or Chapter8/Maya6/.

When cutting a hole for the bullet chamber, use the blueprint to get the correct size. Use the Split polygon tool to draw the shape of the chamber, and remove the edges that go inside the outline that you just drew. When you are done, you only have one big face. Extrude it inward.

We can use two methods to model the chamber lid. Using the chamber's edge, select the end edges and extrude them toward the backside of the AK-47. Detach them to a new object and move the new object inside the chamber slightly. Alternatively, we can start from scratch and create faces that follow the shape of the gun. Leave the piece detached so it only cuts through the lid, and continue to model the pin by adding a box and extruding the shape as shown in Figure 8.7.

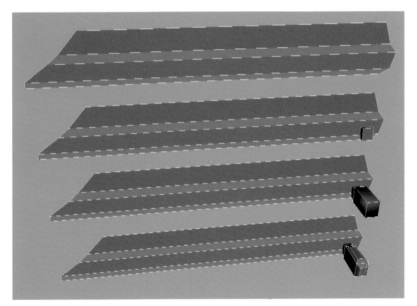

FIGURE 8.7   Chamber lid, modeled in steps.

The player will rarely see the right side, so we should keep the details low and concentrate on the largest and most noticeable things. Next, we add more detail to the safety (see Figure 8.8). To make it more interesting and look detailed we will add the small extrusion of its lower part. Splitting up the model to create a face to extrude and shape, we can leave this part attached to the model. It is going to be close to the camera when the gun flips for animation or when idle.

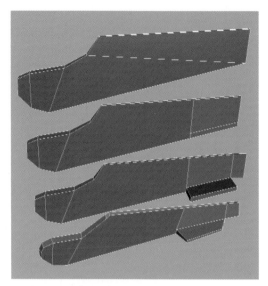

FIGURE 8.8 Safety piece, modeled in steps.

Left Side

The left side will be the part the player will see most of the time, so we want to make it as interesting as possible. Unfortunately, for the player's interest, the AK-47 is flat on this side (see Figure 8.9). We will add following:

- Smoother and correct shape on housing
- Ring
- Screws

Make sure that what is there looks as good as possible. Starting with the back of the housing, we need to make this shape more correct and smoother. Start with splitting up the mesh to get the intersections needed for the smoother shape. Then, manipulate the vertices until you find the shape you are looking for as in Figure 8.10. Look carefully at the reference images to guide you (see Figure 8.3). Because of the close proximity to the player, adding the screws and a ring adds a lot of interesting information.

Moving on to the front handle, we need to make the rough model smoother and add holes as the reference images. Start by splitting up the mesh so you have more intersections with which to work. Make the bottom rounder. When cutting out the holes, add single vertices on the edge and pull the newly created edges apart from each other as shown in Figure 8.11.

FIGURE 8.9   Left side of the AK-47.

Magazine and Normal Mapping

If you study Figure 8.1, you can see that the magazine has added details as smooth dents on its flat surface. Adding all this detail in the model would add a considerable amount of polygons that would take up most of our polygon budget. Luckily, this part of the magazine can never be seen in the silhouette and the game engine supports normal mapping, so we will save these details to be added in the texture (see Chapter 19, "Normal Mapping"). That way, we will be able to keep the mesh polygons low and the bumps will show up in the mapping. Looking at the housing (see Figure 8.5), this is the same case. It has indents on each side, information that will never become visible in the silhouette, so let's save this for the normal mapping as well.

Finishing the Model

Continue to work over the entire gun, adding polygons where you need them until you start to get close to your polygon limit. Remember to

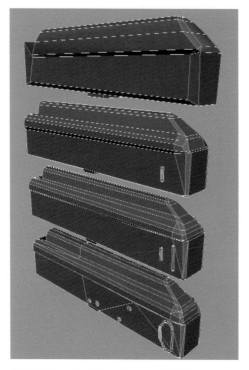

FIGURE 8.10   Main housing, modeled in steps.

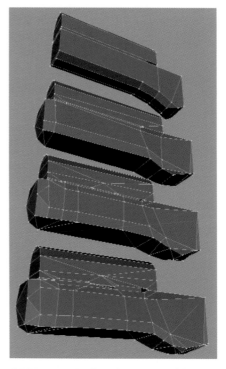

FIGURE 8.11   The front handle, modeled in steps.

switch to the "in-game position" camera to see where the information will be most visible and so everything looks good after you added it. Make sure the flow and shape of the object looks accurate from all angles.

Overlook Quality

When you are finished modeling, you need to go over the object to verify that it is ready for export. Smoothing groups, Turned edges, History, Pivot points, and Freeze Transformation need to be checked. (For an update on these tasks, revisit Chapter 6.) Shapes that appear as round should have smooth edges, and hard surfaces should have hard edges. Figure 8.12 shows the final AK-47 mesh with only the hard edges visible.

We have now finished the entire gun. Let your Art Director review it and confirm that it is up to par with the other guns in the game, and the detail is in the right places for the 2500 polygons you had at your disposal. The final mesh, Ak47_Mesh_Final, is located in Chapter8\Maya6 or Chapter8\3dsMax7_OBJ on the companion CD-ROM.

ON THE CD

FIGURE 8.12   Adding details until the AK-47 is ready for step two.

Setting Up the UVs

ON THE CD

It is time to set up the UVs for this gun. For this, you can use the Ak47_ Mesh_Final mesh on the companion CD-ROM. We will use a 1024×512 texture. Working on a nonsquare texture in a 3D program creates problems when scaling and rotating the UVs. To make our workflow faster, we will use a square texture until the final phase where we adopt the UVs. After loading the mesh, apply a test texture with square measurements (1024×1024) onto the mesh, available in Extras\Textures\ TestMap.jpg.

Apply an Automatic mapping with the option to not scale the UV coordinates within the 0 to 1 range. This will lay them out, ready for you to create your UV layout.

Stitch, Move, and Sew

When sewing together pieces, a good idea is to start with the biggest shapes and work with the edges in the UV editor. Select an edge and move and sew (stitch) them together. Make sure you look at the 3D mesh while you are doing your UV layout so you can see where the different parts are located. Try to keep as much as possible sewn (stitched) together. If you need to have a seam, make sure you place it so it does not appear in the player's view after the information seen in Figure 8.4. When sewing the different parts, try to create as little distortion as possible, and always check against the test grid bitmap to see if any problems occur due to size and stretching. While sewing and stitching, pieces can move around very easily, so make sure no areas overlap each other.

Straighten the UVs

To use as much of the available UV space as possible, we will straighten out the pieces that were projected incorrectly. Select the end points on the object and rotate them until they line up with the main piece of UV points as done with the magazine of the AK-47 in Figure 8.13.

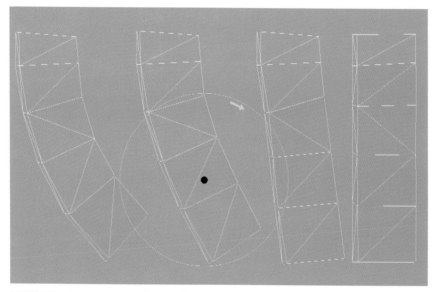

FIGURE 8.13   Straighten out the UVs for easier texturing and better UV space.

It is important that you verify stretching with the test map after you have straightened the UVs.

Straightening it out will give you a UV that is much easier to work with. Even after you have sewn the projected pieces together, you need to go over the mesh and look for pieces that have uneven edges and lines (as seen with the AK-47 stock in Figure 8.14). Compare each face shape and size in the UV compared to the mesh in the 3D view.

Arranging the UV Layout

When you are finished sewing the different pieces together, arrange all groups referring to their placement on the gun (e.g., aiming, handle, main

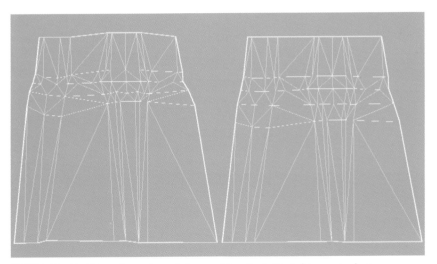

FIGURE 8.14   Verifying the scale and shape of the stock. Straighten out edges.

part, stock, magazine, and barrel) outside the 0 to 1 coordinate range (as shown in Figure 8.15).

FIGURE 8.15   Lay out the pieces together as different groups.

Now it is time to decide how large the different pieces should be, and the pixel density of the gun. We will start to scale all pieces to an average good pixel resolution. To do this, you need to calculate how big the object is compared to the pixel resolution it should use. This AK-47 will have an overall pixel resolution of 10 pixels per centimeter. Using the grid in the UV editor, the full height (10 grids) represents our total texture (1024 pixels), making every grid 102.4 pixels high. The AK-47's stock measurements are 27 cm long in real life. The 3D model should then have 270 pixels, or one-fourth of the UV editor grid length. Since all the UVs are the same ratio at this point, select everything and scale it so the stock has the correct size.

Using shell selection to select and move the UVs will save you a lot of time.

While you arrange and lay out your UV, you want to keep you work-space square. Doing so makes it easy for you when you need to rotate and scale the pieces, and you do not have to compensate for any stretching or mismatching. Your final texture size will be half the height of the work area. We can simulate that you have the same aspects by limiting the view on which you place the pieces. To do so, either load a 1024 × 1024 texture with the bottom 1024 × 512 colored black, or if your program supports it, limit your texture visibility within the UV editor so it only shows the 0 to 0.5 coordinates in height. Figure 8.16 shows you the dark area where you need to squeeze in all your UV pieces. Remember that we also want to add higher resolution to the pieces closest to the camera if possible, thereby making the UV space of these pieces even bigger. It may look like there is not enough room, but it will be an easy task.

Always start with the largest parts first when moving the pieces into the UV range, and then work down to the smaller pieces. By placing the large pieces first, you can quickly and easily see how much of the space they will take up. Arranging the large pieces also creates small holes in between them where you can place the smaller pieces later. Do not place the pieces too close to the texture border or too close to each other. Keep a 1- to 3-pixel safety zone for the edge padding.

When arranging the UVs into the coordinates, try to retain the grouping of the different pieces (stock, aiming, handle, safety, and barrel) if possible. By keeping them organized in groups, you give the texture map a clearer structure if someone needs to go in and find something specific, or to make changes.

Start with the gun's stock, housing, magazine, aiming, and the front handle. You will quickly see how much space you will have left, as shown in Figure 8.17. This allows you to scale up the pieces closest to the camera for sharper graphics; something we should do gradually, because we do not want a visual separation between the various pieces. Let's start with the gun's main piece (colored green in Figure 8.17) and scale it up 20%.

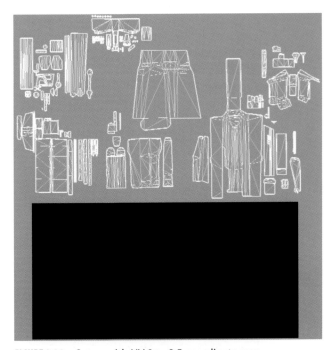

FIGURE 8.16   Setup with UV 0 to 0.5 coordinate area.

FIGURE 8.17   Start with the biggest shapes first, with straight edges along the sides of the texture.

When you start arranging pieces inside the coordinate space, you might need to rethink the way you folded some pieces together. Some pieces might need to be cut and detached to make them fit better. Notice the orange part on the AK-47 stock in the top-right corner of Figure 8.18. The stock piece fits well but we need to separate the end piece and place it somewhere else. Do the changes we have gone over, and add more of the large pieces into the coordinates. You will need to rearrange several of the pieces due to our resizing of the gun's main piece.

FIGURE 8.18   Scale up the selective left-side parts of the gun.

We have now placed all the large pieces into the texture, and as you can see, we still have quite a bit of space left. There is always more space than appears to be, if one lays out the puzzle correctly. Before we start to move in the smallest pieces, let us scale up some more of the parts on the left side (colored green in Figure 8.18) to make better use of the texture. When selecting pieces to size up, consider what is important for the player to see on the left side—the magazine, handle, left side buttons and ring, and the wooden front handle.

To gain even more space, we can see that the aiming construction UVs (colored orange in Figure 8.18) are unfolded in an inconvenient way for what we need, and its shape takes up unnecessary space. Separating this piece into two pieces will let you have better control over the space.

Now that we are finished with the large pieces, let's place the small pieces in the areas where they fit. Remember that some of the smaller pieces are not facing the camera and we will not see them much, like the end of the muzzle, for example. We can scale these down 20% or more depending how little we will see them. Some other ways to save UV space as mentioned are to overlay UVs and reuse the texture space for several pieces. A perfect situation for this would be the screws on this model, or to mirror the stock to look the same on both sides. However, we have the space for this model, so we will keep this as clean as possible if we ever want to make some of them unique. As you see in the final UV in Figure 8.19, we have rotated the gun's main piece, scaled it up together with the rest of the left parts, unfolded, and sewed together the left side of the front handle and brought in the smaller pieces.

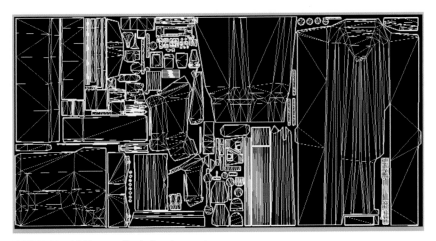

FIGURE 8.19   UV layout, final visual aspect.

We are almost finished with the layout mapping, but we are still using the lower part of a 1024 × 1024 texture. Create and apply a new shader with the correct texture, or reset the visibility of the UV coordinates. Set the UV editor to show the texture aspect ratio; this will squash all your UVs to look like Figure 8.20. Select all UVs and scale it up to the top of the UV area to regain the correct UV ratio as in Figure 8.19.

FIGURE 8.20   Squashed UV set.

ON THE CD

You are now finished with your AK-47 model, with full production quality. As a final touch, go over the object and verify that nothing has been changed (smoothing groups, edge directions, pivots, and then delete history, and freeze transformation). You can find the final mesh Ak47_UV_Final in the Chapter8\Maya6 or Chapter8\3dsMax7_OBJ folders on the companion CD-ROM.

SUMMARY

You now know how to model a first-person gun from scratch using the box-modeling technique together with applying the low-polygon techniques to determine where to visually gain the most out of the mesh. You also learned how to set up and arrange a correct UV layout quickly and efficiently. Some things to consider:

1. Do not start modeling your creation before you research it thoroughly. Knowing its technical and mechanical functionality can help you understand its shape better, making it easier for you to replicate it in 3D.
2. Always start modeling by the "rough to detailed" method and the box-modeling technique. Block out the shapes and work fast to get the correct structure on the object before you start adding details.
3. Box modeling will give you control and structure and keep you on schedule. Your management will be also able to see very easily at what stage the model is and how much more detail you will need to add in the mesh.

4. Add detail where it will be seen, model a clean mesh, and put in sections where they are needed, in curves, not where the surface is straight and the vertices don't add anything to the shape.

5. Keep the more important parts visibly detailed, and the secondary parts interesting.

6. To achieve more control and to work with the same scale on all projected polygons with Automatic projection, project them without the options scale or uniform 0 to 1.

7. Straighten out UV pieces for a more organized UV map, and always check the stretching with the Test map.

8. Project all pieces, move and sew them, arrange them, and then lay out all your pieces in your UV space; working with a structure will keep things arranged and keep you on schedule.

CHAPTER

9

TEXTURE CRE/

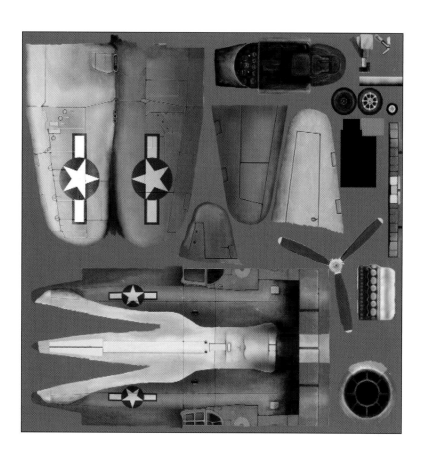

Texture mapping greatly adds to the visual experiences of any game. Being a part of the team that creates the textures gives you the chance to add important input to the content of the game. In the early stages of games, objects were mapped with a simple painted texture, a process that has evolved to a very technical one for artists. Today, the 3D engine combines several layers of textures with different capabilities together with advanced shader systems, something that takes more time and is more complicated. There is still a need for an artist to be able to create an interesting texture with highlights, shadows, scratches, dirt, and character; however, the new techniques have separated the process.

Textures for games can consist of two parts—the color channel and the alpha channel. The color channel holds the RGB (Red, Green, Blue) values, and the alpha channel contains gray values. When saving textures for games, we use various color depths and formats depending on the usage in the game, something the book covers in-depth in Chapter 14, "Texture Technologies." This chapter teaches you about the information a texture can contain, and how we can use textures in games.

For creating textures in games, Photoshop is the most commonly used program and is what is used in all tutorials and examples given in this book. However, any program with similar functionalities should work.

COLOR CHANNELS (RGB)

The color channels contain the main texture and the visual information of the objects. To be fully experienced, every mesh visible within a game requires a color texture. We can create the texture for the color channel in several ways, depending on the visual style of the game and the technology used. There are two main variations: diffuse map and color map.

Diffuse Map

The diffuse map contains the colors, shadows, and light all in one texture. This process of only using one texture is being used less frequently, and is therefore used in the former generation graphics engines that may not support the new shader or light capabilities. In this process, you draw the diffuse texture exactly the way it is seen in the game, and it is mainly up to the creator to make it as aesthetically pleasing as possible, without relying on any graphical programmers' features. By creating a diffuse texture, you can include things like shadows, highlights, and metallic reflections, and simulate fill lights by painting in the sun direction by drawing the texture whiter on the topside of an object. In addition, you can draw small brightness variations for each polygon so its angles are clearer. Figure 9.1 shows a diffuse map, which has everything included.

FIGURE 9.1   A diffuse map. © Digital Illusions CE AB. 2004 Reprinted with permission.

By having a texture that always looks the same, we are able to make it look good in all environments—good but rigid, since it does not interact with what the player is experiencing in the game world (e.g., darkness and sunlight). Texture mapping using a real photograph that contains both strong shadows and lights would be a way of defining a diffuse texture. Shadows and highlights, which you would have difficulty removing, create a lot of contrast and makes the texture realistic.

When adding light to the diffuse map, you can also add objects in the texture to simulate a more detailed modeled object, a painting on a wall, cables, wires, and other smaller things. It is, however, important that you do not add them in places where they will break the visual illusion in the game. Adding lights and small details will add illusion of depth to a flat surface, and can look good when looked at straight on, but if you view the object from the side or from a closer range, it can look skewed and fake.

In Figure 9.2, we see a brick wall with an air vent and a pipe. All details are in the same diffuse map. The pipe has a painted highlight, and casts an illusion of a shadow and depth from the wall. If we align the texture to a perspective, we notice that there is something wrong (see Figure 9.3).

FIGURE 9.2   A diffuse map, with large painted-in objects.

FIGURE 9.3   The diffuse map contains wrong information, and seen from the side makes the pipe look wrong.

The silhouette clearly shows that the object is still flat. The pipes are neither convincing nor good looking. Painting large objects within a texture can break its illusion. You can add light and shadows in diffuse maps, although it should be done with care and understanding. In this case, it would have been better if we had modeled the pipe to give the object depth and get the proper silhouette. If we are limited by our polygons on the environment objects but still want to make them interesting, make sure you test the object from all angles and keep the shadows subtle and the depth to a minimum. Painting the texture in a way that includes everything as this diffuse map does can look great. However, if used together with a normal map and specular map, the painted shadows and highlights will make the textures respond badly and limit the object's visual impact.

Color Map

Color maps only contain the simplest color values. Shadows and highlights are not colors, but an absence of light, and should not be included within the color texture. The color map is not a representation of the complete texture, but rather a representation of the colors the object has. We use them together with shaders in today's graphics systems, where games start to use more real-life lighting techniques. This allows the materials to react better to light and the environment. We combine the color map with other mapping techniques such as normal maps, detail maps, bump maps, and specular maps to get a final texture. Creating each map separately makes the process more complicated and can take longer to visualize when created. Although, when combined within the shader, surfaces will look more true-to-life when interacted with, since light and shadows do not exist within the texture. Figure 9.4 is a good example of a color map.

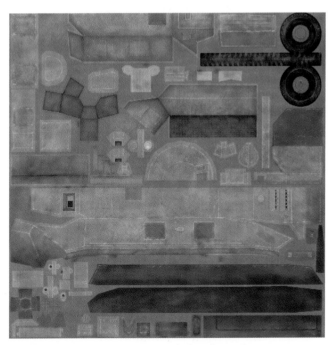

FIGURE 9.4   Color map contains no light information. © Digital Illusions CE AB. 2004 Reprinted with permission.

It is a good idea to start the creation of the color map in conjunction with the creation of textures. This will help you define where you have different types of materials and objects when you decide how the specular, transparency, and bump maps should look.

Alpha Channel

As important as the RGB channels are, giving the object a face in the game, the alpha channel helps us add extra richness to the texture, or decide what should be shown when and how. The alpha channel is built from grayscales, which work like a gradient ramp to give each pixel of the texture a value and a feature (e.g., transparency, reflection, specularity, bump maps, displacement, refraction, illumination, glow, and many more) (see Figure 9.5).

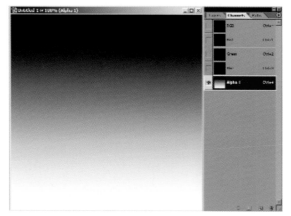

FIGURE 9.5   Alpha uses the grayscaled fourth channel in a texture.

The ramp will always go from white to black in the alpha channel, but different engines may invert the values. For ease of explanation, we will presume that white is maximum in future reference. In Photoshop, when working and saving in its own file system (PSD), you are able to create and have several alpha channels within the same image for different options.

Transparency Map

Using the alpha channel, you can determine, per pixel, how transparent or opaque a surface should appear in the game. We can also decide where an object should appear as completely transparent. Using the alpha channel, we can create objects in the game that would require too many polygons to model—wires, grids, fences, and trees are perfect examples. If you were to model an entire tree, with all its branches and leaves, you would need several hundred thousand polygons for each tree. By using the alpha channel to mask out the surrounding areas of a branch and for each leaf, you can create a tree with as few as 500 polygons as seen in Figure 9.6 and its texture in Figure 9.7.

FIGURE 9.6   Trees with alpha on a *Battlefield Vietnam* level. © Digital Illusions CE AB. 2004 Reprinted with permission.

Although transparency allows you to create many interesting structures without using any polygons, there are some drawbacks. First, just because you cannot see the information does not mean that it is free for the engine. Having large parts of the scene drawn with transparency hinders performance because they need to be sorted when they are drawn. Another problem with using transparency to determine the shape of a structure (e.g., wires and tree branches) is that the transparency masks out a single flat plane. If you look right at the edge of a branch, you will not see any depth, and the illusion of a 3D object disappears (see Figures 9.8 and 9.9). With more powerful graphics cards, there is more power to

FIGURE 9.7   The alpha texture for the palm leafs shown in Figure 9.6. © Digital Illusions CE AB. 2004 Reprinted with permission.

push polygons, so it has become less important to rely on transparency texture objects. In any case, you should rely on transparencies as little as possible. They are best suited when there is no other solution and where players would have limited access to see the plane from the edge.

FIGURE 9.8   Alpha with thin objects; alpha masked texture contains no depth. © Digital Illusions CE AB. 2004 Reprinted with permission.

FIGURE 9.9   Texture with alpha for scene shown in Figure 9.8. © Digital Illusions CE AB. 2004 Reprinted with permission.

Transparency is used with specifics like refraction and fraction to make an object look like glass (in cockpits and windows) where they need a reflection map to achieve a smooth, glasslike surface. With the exception of vegetation and objects, the largest area we use transparency textures for is effects.

Gloss/Specular Map

Specular maps work with the in-game lighting. When the object is in line with the sun, its lighting will depend on the information it gets from the specular map. By using the alpha channel, we can determine, per pixel, where the object should be lit, and with what intensity. We can define the characteristics of the object and how hard or soft the specular is. Normally, the specular map's maximum value is white (255) and its minimum value is black (0). The value 128 represents an average specular value. Metallic surfaces that are hard and shiny would be painted with a whiter specular value to achieve a stronger highlight than wood, for example, whose surface features are more subtle with a wider and lower visible highlight, and therefore painted darker.

When creating the specular map, we base the colors on the material as we have painted the color map.

The Specular map decides the amount of light the material should absorb, something we can control by painting the areas with various shades of gray as we can see in Figure 9.10. If the texture is converted (straight) from a diffuse, it will get structures and high contrasts within the specular map values and create an incorrect representing of the materials. If a texture representing a dark poster with white text were converted into a specular map, the text would have a higher specular value than the rest of the poster.

FIGURE 9.10   Specular map, and gray values for the specular values for each material. No shapes added.

These are the basic features and guidelines for specular mapping. There are several tricks where we can use the specular map in ways it was never meant to be used. Doing so will give you extra quality and help you achieve a higher visual experience in the game.

If the engine does not support self-shadowed objects, we can use the specular map to specify areas that will always be in shadow with a dark specular value. This means that if an object's surface is facing the sun direction, but part of it is shaded by its own polygons, it would look strange if the object received very glossy specular. Painting these shadowed parts close to black in the specular material can make it look like they are not being lit by the sun. This will help make the object look more true to life and self shadowed (see Figure 9.11).

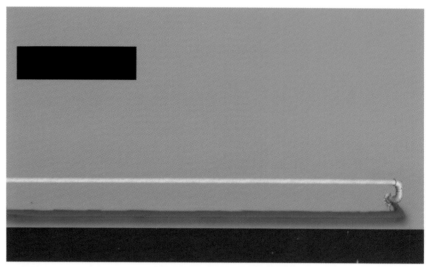

FIGURE 9.11   Specular map, added brighter pipe, and darker area for simulated shadows.

Another possibility for the specular map is to let it help show the shape of the objects inside the engine. If we have an airplane in a game, we can determine where the high light should appear, instead of having the same material characteristics over the entire airplane. The specular map can be used to depict its shape so that at specific bends, there would be more intensity than where the object is flat. The same idea can be used to depict bricks more clearly. If we paint the specular map for a texture with bricks and masonry to have the same specular strength, they are lit with the exact same value, washing out structure and shape. By painting the masonry in between the bricks with a brighter/darker value, the shape of the bricks will remain.

By adding a small noise level to the specular map, we can let the object become a bit noisy as flicker or dust on top of the object, thereby appearing rougher and less flat and shiny, All these techniques make the world less computer clean—the more dirt we have, the more realistic it looks (see Figure 9.12).

FIGURE 9.12   Full specular, each object reacts differently to the light. Even the sprayed color and dirt on the wall will get another specular feeling from the light. This method creates a very dynamic world and variations in the light.

SKY AND ENVIRONMENT MAP

In games, we create a sky by projecting a texture onto a cube or a sphere that covers the world like a lid and is parented to the camera. This makes it impossible for you to get closer if you tried, making it act like a real sky. When creating a sky map or an environment map for outdoor environments with the cube method, we use five textures that are planar mapped on each side on the box, where each represents a side of the world—top, bottom, north, south, west, and east as shown in Figure 9.13. We can also use the same technique to create reflections inside a game by creating an invisible cube that casts reflection onto the tagged objects. For an outdoor environment, it would be ideal to use a smaller version of the texture that represents the sky of the level.

If the game needs an indoor environment map, we can use the same system, although the texture needs to represent an indoor average room of some kind to simulate all the rooms in the game. A good idea when creating reflection maps is to keep them sharp and detailed so they can represent the whole world. It is also a good idea to have a contrast in the reflection map, which will make the player see the difference in light and reflection easier, and make it interesting and make the objects look shiny.

FIGURE 9.13   Sky/environment map/reflection map. © Digital Illusions CE AB. 2004 Reprinted with permission.

TILING TEXTURES

As mentioned in the section, *Object versus Object* in Chapter 7, "UV Layout," a tiling texture overlaps outside the 0 to 1 range of the UV coordinates. When a texture is created to be used for tiling, it would best if we make it narrow in one direction so we can tile that length several times as shown in Figure 9.14.

This gives us the possibility to repeatedly reuse large parts of the texture but still have a very small texture for the entire mesh, especially when we split up the model for use tiling grids as mentioned in the section, *Subdivided Technique* in Chapter 6, "Game Modeling." When you create textures for tiling purposes, it is very important that you remove unusual strong details within the pattern—these break the illusion of realism. When working with tiling and small textures, restrain from having high contrast at the texture's edges. When the texture is using mipmapping, it resamples itself in the distance, and you risk ending up with lines and streaks near the tiling borders.

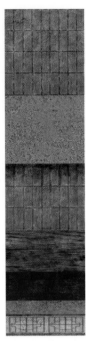

FIGURE 9.14   Tiling texture from left to right. © Digital Illusions CE AB. 2004 Reprinted with permission.

DETAIL MAP

A detail map is a small tiling texture that we add on top of the color map to give it more structure and details when we view objects at a close range (see Figure 9.15). The detail map is only visible at close range; moving away from the object fades it out.

Buildings, ground, and characters all benefit from having a detail map because it makes the objects appear to have a higher resolution texture. To create a more detailed outdoor ground, a detail map is multiplied on top on the main texture to add rocks and dirt. Moving away from the ground, the tiling detail texture will fade away to save performance and show the main texture, which we can keep small and without details.

You can learn more about multitexturing and advanced handling of textures with different files systems and compressions in Part IV of this book.

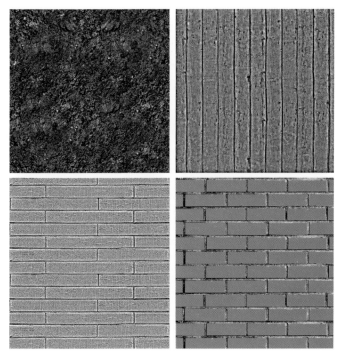

FIGURE 9.15   Four different types of detail map structures.

PRACTICAL PHOTOSHOP TRICKS

When we create textures for games, we need to spend some time making them believable. Compared to the movie industry, we have a very small amount of texture space at our disposal for each object, so it is important that we maximize its quality. The examples later in this chapter concentrate on the high-resolution textures that we expect the new game consoles to use in the future, since they have more memory and will remove some of the limitations that exist on today's consoles.

Layers

Although Photoshop is famous for its filters, very few are useful in everyday game production. Where Photoshop really shines is its capability to use layers. Using layers is like working with composition (see Figure 9.16). It is a great way to build up an image, and test your way to the best result. It is also a good way to add details. Learning how to use layers to their full potential will give you great flexibility and more possibilities. The various layer blending modes give you millions of different combinations.

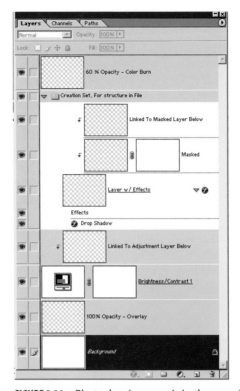

FIGURE 9.16 Photoshop's power is in the use of layers.

Let's say you need to darken a part of your texture, but you do not know how strong a brush you need to get the right darkness. If you create a new layer over the photo and paint the area with 100% darkness, you can change the opacity for the painted layer and set the amount of darkness. Later, if you need to darken other areas in the same texture, you can continue to paint with 100% in the same layer to get the correct values you need. Then, when you are finished, you can change it all or remove some if you do not like what you see. Layers work not only as composition tools but are also as an easy way to keep the quality of the texture, and as an UNDO function.

Photoshop comes with several layer-blending modes, and they are expanding with each new version of the program. Learn more about the different blending options in Photoshop's instruction manual, and experiment to gain the best possible result.

When working with colors within Photoshop, keep in mind that you are not able to change completely a gray color's hue. However, painting your layers with a tint of color will enable you to correct and tweak colors more easily later, and if you want it just gray in the future, you can desaturate it.

To maintain the quality of the image, never manipulate, filter, or flatten your working layers with any type of noise, scratches, or dirt. Keep them separated in layers and blend them with Overlay, soft light, or opacity levels. This will save you many hours if you need to update or tweak the original image. If you flatten the image with noise, it becomes impossible to remove it, and you'll need to redo the entire image.

If you need to add noise to a texture, create a new layer and fill it with a 128, 128, 128 gray colors, and then apply a monochromic noise to it. Change the layer's blending mode to overlay, and you have a fully controllable noise layer with opacity level that you can remove.

Get into the habit of structuring your layers and naming them according to what they are used for within your texture. Doing so will help both you and your teammates find layers more easily when doing advanced textures that might require over 100 layers. We are all working on a team, and a simple process like this will help others read and understand the texture you have done. For further tweaks on the texture, you might not be the person who does the final touchups and color tweaks. Therefore, it's a good idea to arrange them after the main parts of the texture, and for each piece of the texture. For example:

- Color
- Dirt and Noise
- Rust
- Scratches
- Shadows
- Highlights

Having a structure for your textures as shown in Figure 9.17 makes it easy for everyone to understand it. Using this technique to create the layers will require you to adapt your workflow. You need to place all the highlights in the same layer, and you cannot start adding a white highlight in the dirt layer since it will make it difficult to tweak them as separate layers. Mapping a texture with layers used as composition, you can decide how much of each layer should be visible. You can decide the amount of dirt, shadows, or highlights just by changing the layer's opacity level. Creating the texture might slow things down if you are not used to it, but when you have adapted to the workflow, it will help both and the entire team to gain speed.

Dirt and Scratches

As mentioned previously, nothing in the world is untouched by dirt, and it is the object's history that makes it interesting. It is very important to know where this dirt appears on an object, and how to make an object believable.

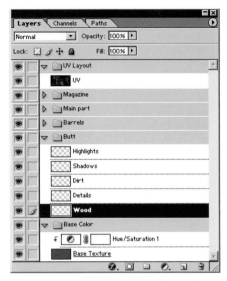

FIGURE 9.17 Structure the use of your layers, for both you and your team.

When you use photos as a base layer to make the texture look like metal or to add dirt or scratches, it is important to know the aspects of that photo. Beware of the pixel resolution of the details in the dirt. We do not want to use a texture map that, in equal size of our object, represents scratches many times larger in our texture. Try to use textures that are the appropriate scale in terms of details.

Due to the limited texture usage within game development, if everyone uses the same scratch maps, you risk creating a uniformed look for all textures in the game. By blending several different scratch and dirt maps, thereby making up your own history for your object, you will be able to break this behavior (see Figure 9.18).

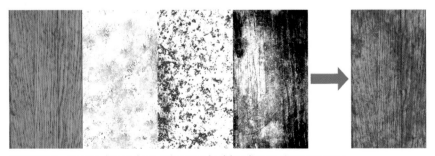

FIGURE 9.18 Create dirt and scratch maps by blending various textures.

We can also easily create new and interesting scratch maps using different variations of the advanced blending tool in Photoshop. Let's go over this process:

1. Start with an image that has an interesting structure.
2. To make this easier to visualize, create a layer filled with a gray color under the layer with your image that you want to become the new scratch map.
3. Select the layer with the texture.
4. Enter its blending option, either by double-clicking on it or selecting Layer/Layer Style/Blending.
5. Change the general blending mode to overlay.
6. Next, change the advanced blending at the bottom (see Figure 9.19).
7. Adjust the This Layer option's white arrow until it's at the middle. We are masking colors within the image. The more you pull this arrow, the more you will remove the scratches. Now you will be able to see the gray layer that you created earlier.
8. Close this window by clicking OK.

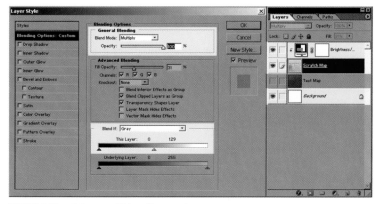

FIGURE 9.19   Advanced blending options.

9. Next, create a new contrast and brightness adjustment layer above this scratch layer, and group them together with Layer/Group with Previous.
10. Open the options for Brightness/Contrast and change the levels until you can see the entire image again. Accept your changes by clicking OK.

There, now everything is set up. You have now created a very powerful and adjustable scratch map. By controlling the opacity of the adjustment layer, you can adjust the amount and structure of your scratches. With the scratch map's layers, you control how much of the texture should fade into the underlying textures. With the adjustment layers mask you can paint out areas that you do not want to be affected (see Figure 9.20).

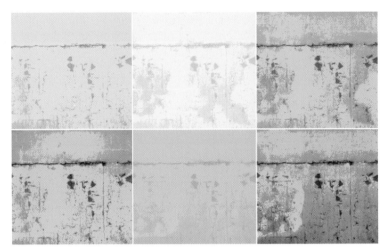

FIGURE 9.20   Different possibilities with the scratch map technique.

Even though it is perfectly okay to create these within your texture, to create various scratches you can instead save them out or just flatten the image. There, now you can create endless amounts of interesting scratch maps. For each new image, there will be new unique scratches. This is a fast and easy way of creating new and interesting scratches for your texture. The final process is included as a PSD on the companion CD-ROM for you to explore its possibilities (Chapter9\ScratchMap\Texture_ScratchMap.psd).

ON THE CD

Cleaning Up Textures' Highlights

With contrast in textures, we can add interesting variations. If we paint with light inside the textures to get what we are looking for, we can improve the flattest objects in the crudest 3D engine. Light is not always good, though; if we use tiling textures, a highlight at the wrong place can create a repeated look to the tiled surface. When we use photos as reference to our textures, we need to make sure we even out any highlights. This is especially true when we use our own textures for a texture library. To take good photos for use as textures, it is important that you use a tripod, a long exposure (shutter) time on the camera, no flash, and little environment light. The longer the exposure time, the more evenly lit the object will become. Most of the cheaper digital cameras do not support a variable shutter speed, so you should know how to clean up highlights in a photo. The main problem with cleaning up a photo taken with a flash at very close range is that it can have large areas of completely white values that contain no digital information. Do not clean these up. It is better to choose another image for your mapping or try to retake the photo. To clean up a texture with a small highlight you can use this technique:

1. Duplicate the texture with the strong highlight and change its blending mode to color.
2. Desaturate your original image. The layer with the color-blending mode should now be on top.
3. Add a layer in between these two layers with the blending mode set to multiply, and paint it with a 100% black smooth-edge brush to cover the areas where the highlight is. See Figure 9.21 for the result of this technique.

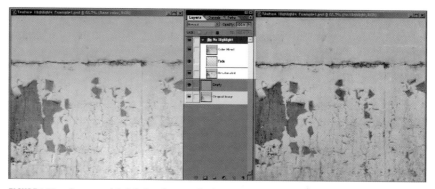

FIGURE 9.21   Remove highlights from a flash.

If you have a texture that is badly damaged and contains high contrasts from a camera flash, and you want to unify the light values within the texture, you can apply a Filter/High Pass. The High Pass filter helps us average out the contrast and light values within the image, which can be used with good results for tileable textures

Texture Quality

When creating textures for games, it is important that we use the pixels as efficiently as possible. Textures in today's games take up more memory than the models do. This means that we need to try to get the most from the pixels we have and keep the amount down, both by using an efficient UV map (Chapter 7) and the size of the pixels. Making a high-resolution texture blurry with large lines and unclear content will give you the same result as if you were using a smaller texture. The sharper you make the details with smaller pixels, the more information you will be able to get into the texture and the game.

As shown in Figure 9.22, we want the pixels as small as possible. If you create each line with two pixels on the texture, it will be twice as blurry as one that is one-pixel wide, and if you create the whole texture with two-pixel thickness, you can scale down the whole texture resolution to half its size. It is important to use the pixels in a way such that they represent their actual size on the object and that you never blur the information, which should appear sharp and clear. Never scale up any textures that you want to use in production (this also blurs them); always work with larger textures than your mapping area, not the other way around.

FIGURE 9.22   Blurred (left) versus sharp texture (right).

It is difficult to sharpen a texture that has been created too blurry. The easiest way is to scale it down 50% or repaint it. One could use Photoshop's sharpness filter, but it creates highlights and white rims around the contrasted areas. This is not what we want, since the white rims and highlight add incorrect information to the textures in the game.

Color Matching, Histogram

When creating textures for a game, or any art production, make sure to double-check your monitor and Photoshop settings for color calibration. This will assure you that others correctly experience the texture you create. If you work in a studio, consider purchasing a monitor calibrator. This allows all of the artists in a team to achieve the same color and light values when creating textures, something that will reduce the time spent on adjustment and color tweaking of the art at the end of a project.

Instead of using a calibrator, each artist can learn how to use the histogram. It amazes us that every digital camera bought today shows you a histogram, and many artists working professionally in the industry do not know how to read or use it to their advantage. The histogram becomes very important when you need to verify the luminosity (light value) of the entire image or per each channel of the image to match it with other textures in the game.

A histogram illustrates the amount of pixels (vertically) and their light intensity (horizontal) of the selected texture area (see Figure 9.23).

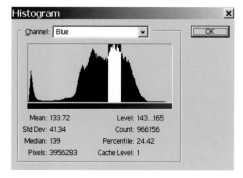

FIGURE 9.23   Histogram with Blue channel analyzed.

Photoshop's histogram presents the result with the options for each RGB channel, and independent of the color setting on your monitor, you can verify if the colors in the texture are too red, too blue, or too green, together with too much light or dark. Each vertical line represents the number of pixels for light intensity. With this tool, you can see if there is a gap between colors or if there are any peaks.

If your team can't calibrate the monitors, the histogram will give you valuable information since it is independent of the monitor settings.

If you have the option, it is very important that the team calibrate all monitors to the same values so all the art is produced with the same quality and with the right light intensity. Teaching yourself and everyone in your team how to use histograms will assure you get final art at consistent color levels. Expect the artists to set their monitor a bit brighter than normal settings or with a tint of blue, depending on the environment they are located in and their ability to see colors.

In Production

Before you begin to create your texture, it is very important that you finish your UV layout. Starting the texture while you still are arranging your UV pieces will leave you with a lot of unused space. If you start to texture something and discover that you need to rearrange the UV layout, you'll lose valuable production time when you try to match the texture with the updated UV layout.

Let's texture the AK-47 that we created and finalized the UV for in Chapter 8, "In Production: Model/UV." For this tutorial, we will use Photoshop, but any 2D program with similar functionalities should work.

ON THE CD

To see the progress of the texture, load the scene Ak47_UV_Final on the companion CD-ROM in the folders Chapter9\3dsMax7_OBJ or Chapter9\Maya6, depending on your software.

The assignment is to create a realistic-looking texture for the AK-47. The texture size is 1024 × 512, and should have all light burned into the diffuse texture. This gives you the chance to add light, shadows, and all kinds of things in the same texture. While you do the task, remember what you learned in Chapter 5, "Growing as an Artist," about colors, light, darkness, scratches, and dirt. The way you create the texture will heavily influence the game's visual quality.

References

To map the AK-47 realistically, we could take photos from a real gun and apply them to our model. Although this would make the texture look real, it is hard to find photos for all objects within a game with the same style and quality. It is also difficult to match real photos with our own created UV layouts. The photo will give you a real-looking gun if you are able to apply it correctly, but you will not have any options to tweak the different layers within the texture to match the rest of the content in the game. Mapping something that has a similar look to photographs is easy when you can use the same photos to see the location of the dirt and scratches. These can also give you ideas for your own object and techniques to get the best realistic feeling. To create the textures with the right feeling, you can choose to work from real photos of different material, metal, rust, dirt, and scratches. Having a library with good textures that represent different types of scratches, dirt, metals, and wood will become very valuable in your texture creation.

developer.NVIDIA.com provides the community with a set of photos that you can freely use in your game production.

Import the Object UV

Let's start by bringing in the UVs from the AK-47 into Photoshop. Snapshot the UVs of the AK-47 in your 3D program as a black-and-white color texture and load it into Photoshop.

You will have the UVs as the base layer. You need this as the top layer, so you need to unlock the base layer. Double-click on the layer in the Layers window, or select menu Layers/New/Layer Set. This opens the Option window; confirm it be clicking OK. This is now treated as a normal layer, which you can move around. To follow the steps with the PSD, it is located on the companion CD-ROM in the folder Chapter9\PSD\ Ak47_UV.psd.

ON THE CD

Work Layers

To draw a texture, think of it as making a set composition with layers, where you have all the options to blend between. The more layers you create, the more control there is to tweak the texture in the end—and the more difficult it will become to keep track of all the different layers. We are going to create a diffuse texture, but paint it with the different properties that give us more control. So, set up the layers by fill light, highlights, shadows, dirt, rust, and edges. This will keep the texture adaptable and allow us to convert it into a color map later by simply turning off highlights and shadows. We are going to create a separate set for each part of the UVs. Start by creating sets (folders) named after the parts of the gun. Then, create layers for specific content—highlights, shadows, dirt, scratches, and edges—inside these sets as shown in Figure 9.17. Depending on what you are adding to the texture, you can add several other layers. The more you split up the layers, the more control you will have in the end. Finally, create a set for just the UV. Drag it to the top position and change the UV layer's blending mode to Screen. Lower the opacity to about 10%, which will make the black disappear and the white lines in the UV map appear as a guide on top of the lower layers. From now on, make sure you always work in the correct layer in the hierarchy.

When you are looking at your mesh in the 3D program, make sure you use a shader (like Lambert) that does not produce specular highlights. By making the mesh show the texture without influence from the scene's light, you can see exactly how the texture looks.

Let's start by deciding what type of materials and images we need for our gun. The AK-47 is a metallic gun with a brown wooden stock and handles. This makes us need images representing different types of wood. For the structure of metal, we need different dirt, mud, and scratch maps so we can achieve the correct visual feeling.

Main Color

Let's decide what the main color should look like in the base layer. Remember to work with a bit of hue inside the texture so you can adjust it later. Let's make the base have a brown tint. Then, we need to create the metallic noise on the entire gun, which will make the texture look less flat and give it more real-life characteristics. Create a new set above the Base Color named Base Dirt. Pick some photos that represent dirt, scratch maps, and apply them to the whole texture with a low opacity level. This will give us a good base-metal look. The other main part of this gun is wood, and we should establish the feeling of this next. Pick a wood texture that you feel would work for the task, and cut and paste it to the place it needs to be. Remember that the veins in the wood need to follow the flow of the object and represent the same size as they would be on the handle. For continuity, always color tweak and handle all the wood at the same time to make the wood look and behave the same on the gun and make it more natural. So far, so good, as you can see in Figure 9.24.

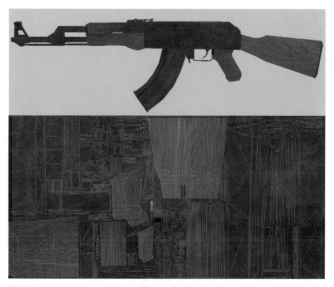

FIGURE 9.24   Base gray metallic and wood colors.

Fill Lights, Shadows, and Highlights

With the two main colors established in the texture, we have created a rough color map. What we need, however, is a diffuse map that shows more of the object's shape in the texture by using shadows and light. We will now start to paint with light and darkness to build the shape of the object. This means that in the first pass, we are not adding highlights or shadows, but rather a vague fill light within the texture to give the object a more 3D feeling. When painting light values, they should affect the areas that should appear in front of the base color. These places would be on the topside of the main part, the back of the main part, and top of the wood. Select a smooth brush 100% White and paint in the Fill Light layer over the surface with broad strokes. (Remember to change the layer for each part of the gun, and add a Fill Light layer if the part needs it.) You can also add soft indents where the shape appears to be sunken compared to the light values you painted in before. Painting with 100% Black, adding darkness, we will again try to give the feeling of a surface that goes in slightly compared to the original color. This will help the object have a clearer shape. When finished, make the painted layers have a low opacity value so they act like fill lights and added darkness (see Figure 9.25).

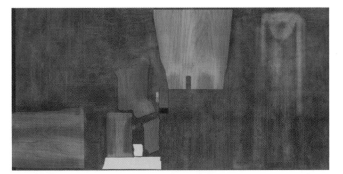

FIGURE 9.25   Fill Light areas added for added shape.

Next, it is time to add the hard highlight and shadows to the object. They are more visible, and we need two more layers, one for each part of the object. We are going to paint with the same technique but with a smaller brush, and in the end leave the opacity at a higher value. Paint the gun at its top and at places that you would see a strong highlight on the materials (see Figure 9.26).

Scratches, Edges, and Dirt

We now have a gun that starts to take shape within the texture and the 3D program. However, it looks very clean and new, so it needs some scratches, dirt, and marked-out edges. Let's start with the edges. New layer is needed; name it Edges. Painting edges takes the longest time in

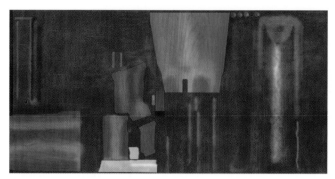

FIGURE 9.26   Highlight added.

creating a texture, but doing so separates the polygon angles and enhances the 3D feeling of the object. Paint noisy lines at the edges of the polygons to represent scratches and wear. To make it look real, you need to add lines to all edges on the gun and make sure they are thin with a low opacity, blended into the base texture. If the edge lines are too thick or too strong, the gun will look like a cartoon painted gun (see Figure 9.27).

FIGURE 9.27   Edge definition added.

Create new layers for each new effect needed. To create dirt, scratches, and oil stains, use the same technique as shown earlier to create a scratch map; multiply or overlay them together with the base texture with a very low opacity level. Using several different scratch maps will make it look more natural, and break it up. Remember to make the scratches sharp and clear. All scratches, dirt, and edges will show even though they are very subtle; in fact, if you just show them slightly they will appear more realistic. A common problem is to paint all the highlights, edges, and dirt to thick and strong in the texture, which breaks the realism and can make the texture look cartoonish. Figure 9.28 shows where we added the dirt and scratches to give the gun its history. This amount of scratches will become very clear in the game and will make the object more realistic.

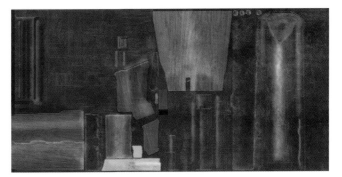

FIGURE 9.28   Dirt and variations added.

These are the basics of how to build a texture from scratch. For more details, keep on adding noise, structure, and shapes to what you want to have in there. Working with very low opacity levels gives you more control. When working, if there is something that you want to test, just create a new layer, and if you are satisfied with the test, merge that layer. We can continue to work on this texture and add more scratches, edges, and details. However, let us wrap it up by adding a GI render (shadows) on to the gun for more depth. See the result so far in Figure 9.29.

FIGURE 9.29   Final texture for the AK-47.

You can find the final PSD on the companion CD-ROM under Chapter9\PSD\Ak47_UV.psd.

Summary

In this chapter, you learned what different types of texture maps a game uses, how they relate to each other, and how to create them in a team-oriented workflow. You also learned the importance of detail within the texture, together with several useful tips on how to produce dirt and textures within Photoshop. Some things in particular to consider include:

1. Always finish your UV map before you start texturing.
2. Structure your workflow and the files so others can understand and continue your work if needed.
3. A color map does not include any light information.
4. The texture alpha contains the specular, transparency, and the added information to a texture.
5. A specular map can help simulate shadows and create dark areas on objects with darker parts of the texture.
6. Remember that just because you cannot see transparency does not mean it is free.
7. The Diffuse texture contains all information within the same textures. Yet, you should paint them separately so you can easily tweak the result.
8. Work with layers like composition. The more layers, the more control you will have.
9. Paint in a subtle fill light and a darkness value to help the object maintain its 3D feeling and difference between facing polygons.
10. Place the dirt and scratches where they reflect the use of the object; it is what creates the object's history and makes the object believable.

10

SPECIAL EFFECTS

The special effects that players experience during gameplay are what make the games so satisfying. It is invigorating to see your enemy blown up in a cascade of debris and smoke when hit by a tank. It is equally exciting to see dirt, mud, and smoke spray across the road when driving a rally car.

While effects are exciting to experience when playing a game, they are one of the most challenging and fun tasks you can work with in production. Most of the art creation within production is very structured, and effects are often given time to be tested to achieve the best "wow" result. This extra time can grant you more freedom. Creating effects is, however, a very technical process that may pose inventive problem solving and keep you on your toes at all times. Since functionality depends heavily on each studio's in-house particle system, this chapter will explain things that we have worked with and have seen in different programs.

EMITTERS

Getting an effect visible within the game requires an *emitter*. An emitter is an invisible object placed or attached to objects in the world, from where the particles emit. In addition, it has variables to control the particles, such as the amount of particles, time to emit, direction, spread, and gravity, among others. By attaching emitters to other objects that uses physics in the game, we can create effects like trails of smoke after a car.

PARTICLES

A *particle* is the emitted visible object in games. A particle structure can have different shapes, as point, mesh, and polygon particles built of three and four vertices. Each has specific features and capabilities in the game.

Sprites

The most commonly used particles in games are the four vertex particles, which are built up by two polygons building a face—we call this type of particle a *sprite*. The sprite is a flat camera-aligned face that aligns itself to the camera angles at all times. Each face has a planar mapped UV layout where the coordinates 0 to 1 are equal to the sprite size. Some systems will allow you to make adjustments and tweak the placement of the vertices on the sprite. The UV points connect to the sprite vertices, so by moving them you might end up with stretched sprites. Instead of moving its vertices, a particle system should support the scaling of the sprite in length and height so you can scale the sprite to simulate smoke similar to fog. By emitting sprites, you can create smoke, fire, and most of the game's effects. Sprites have specific variables such as size, lifespan, gravity, rotation, color, and blending modes. Many of these are controllable over time so you can start with a small-sized smoke that grows over time. Several systems will also support per-vertex lit particles, making the sprite inherit the directional light in the scene, creating volume and depth to the sprite.

By mixing different sprites with different colors, we can build various combinations of structure and colors as shown in Figure 10.1.

FIGURE 10.1   Mixing smoke and fire. © Digital Illusions CE AB. 2004 Reprinted with permission.

You can also use sprites when creating snow, rain, and vegetation. Depending on how you scale the sprites and show them in the world, the only restriction is that they will always aim toward the camera.

Mesh

If the system supports meshes as particles, it gives another layer of functionality and you are able to create many exciting things with them. When emitting meshes as particles, you have the advantage to use any shape with any amount of vertices. In theory, it should be possible for the system to use any mesh within the world. You create meshes for a particle system just as you create a normal object. One of the big advantages of a mesh particle versus sprites is that a mesh is not camera-oriented. With full control over angle and placement in the world, you can create wreck pieces flying out of exploding cars, shockwaves, shells, water, and simulate thickness in your effects (see Figure 10.2). You can also connect these meshes to the game collision and physics engine for bouncing wrecks and artifacts. Using meshes as a particle affords you endless possibilities.

FIGURE 10.2   Huge explosions with mesh pieces flying away. © Digital Illusions CE AB. 2004 Reprinted with permission.

TEXTURES

Since the mesh particle handles like a normal object, the UV points are connected to the sprite's four vertices, making the texture cover the entire sprite. To define various shapes on a sprite we use the alpha channel from a texture to mask out the shape, as transparency works in Chapter 9, "Texture Creation." Because the sprite uses a lot of transparency, it gets rather expensive. By keeping the texture small, we can retain performance. In Figure 10.3, we see a muzzle flash where the alpha masks out the shape.

FIGURE 10.3   Muzzle flash effect with texture and alpha. © Digital Illusions CE AB. 2004 Reprinted with permission.

Since sprites are camera-oriented and the UVs lock to the face vertices, we need to mask sprites with a round shape. This will allow a uniform appearance no matter what position or angle your camera is located. If you create textures that have specific shapes, you should make sure they cannot be seen from any angle other than that for which they were created. We can decide the sprite's texture sizes depending on the level of detail and the distance of the effect. Creating a smoke effect shown 100 meters away would not require a large texture. An explosion or fire with flames would, however, look better with a larger texture to achieve a convincing effect with added detail.

Animated Textures

Some engines support the use of 3D textures (also called *volumetric textures*) or animated sheets of textures. This useful feature will let you add extra quality and life to your effects.

An animated sheet texture is a large texture subdivided into sections. Figure 10.4 shows several 512 × 512 textures with 16 frames each. When the engine reads these, you can specify the start frame, and it scrolls through the sections like a cycle, as a looping sequence. Using animated textures within games will allow you to create very true-to-life fire and water effects.

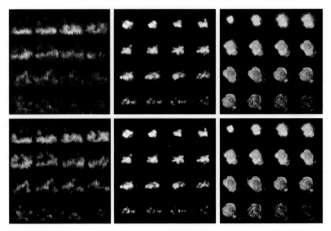

FIGURE 10.4   Animated sheets of effects. © Digital Illusions CE AB. 2004
Reprinted with permission.

Animated UVs

Animated UVs are another very useful feature. They let you, with a mesh or sprite, move the texture along its UV coordinates. With this feature, you can easily create running water, smoking pillars, and other things that must appear to move seamlessly at long distances.

BLENDING MODES

Blending modes decide how the sprite blends with the scene behind it, and there are several different types:

Additive blending: One of the less costly blend modes, since it does not sort any of the sprites and adds the layer of sprites together to what it is behind it, without blending. It ends up saturating the texture, making very hard and strong colors, which can be used for fires and strong internal light simulations. Additive blending works well alone, but becomes hard to control when several sprites with different colors are added.

Alpha blending: Although more expensive, alpha blending gives full control to the artist. With each alpha blending, you can decide the structure and shape of the texture. Because alpha blends the different textures in use, it can become expensive, but it blends smoke and fire seamlessly.

These are just two of the many options available. By blending your particles differently and trying different textures, you will be able to make things look like they are burning, smoking, or have other strange visual combinations.

Performance

The graphics processor calculates everything seen on the screen. All sprites that the emitter emits face the camera and overlay each other in depth, creating layers of transparency and blending modes. Each blending mode has different properties and costs. Mixing different blending modes and textures will require the graphics card to switch modes, which causes a slow down in performance. Further, large sprites that cover the screen become even more expensive to draw, due to the addressed fill rate of the polygon sizes that the graphical card needs to calculate. When creating particles such as smoke and other lifelike particles, you would most likely want to use around 100 to 200 sprites to give it volume and height. However, using fewer sprites and playing with colors to achieve the same depth would be the best solution. In a good environment, you might not be able to use more than perhaps 40 to 100 sprites to get the performance needed. One way to work with optimizing the look of textures is to work with the size and the texture's alpha channel to make the particles blend into each other. When the engine renders sprites with its transparency, it needs to filter the objects behind them. The more of the screen a sprite covers, the more expensive it gets; creating a single sprite that is hardly visible for its transparency and covers the entire screen will slow performance.

The three-vertex sprite is the most render-efficient sprite, but it has the disadvantage that it's hard to texture and use with the camera angle. The mesh particle is the most useful, but when we use it with collision, it is by far the most expensive to use. When creating effects, you need to be aware of when to use the right technique, how to keep them as performance friendly as possible by using fewer textures, the correct blend modes, and to use a decent amount.

DECALS

Bullet holes and dark splashes, colors on the objects and ground left after impact from a grenade or projectile—these are all decals. A decal is a face that shows on the terrain or structure to which it is attached. When a projectile hits a surface, it leaves behind a small texture that shows the impact. We can trigger a decal in several ways to make it show up the game objects. One method is to tag a texture or shader with a value saying what decal it belongs to, so when triggered, on impact the correct decal shows. We can also make use of the collision mesh system to decide what the type of decal should show when the polygons of the collision object register an impact.

WATER

Water is for the most part a programmer-driven feature within games, but the artist should have control over the tweak values that affect the visual context, transparency, color, speed, direction, reflectivity, waves, and, if used, fresnel. By applying a bump (normal) map to the water surface, the water gets a feeling of depth and 3D movement. Water often appears as reflective, something that we can simulate by connecting an environment map to the surface, and decide how much of its value should show. Water has become a large factor of realism in many games. The newest engines support shaders, which gives them the possibility to create real-looking reflections and height displacement waves of the water.

SUMMARY

1. An emitter is the source from where the particles emit inside the world.
2. A sprite is a camera-aligned face that has a planar-mapped texture to its vertices.
3. Creating effects is very satisfying, and good effects make a great impact on the game visuals. People will cheer when you have done something impressive.
4. Using the right blend mode for sprites can be performance effective, and help you create interesting variations.
5. By using meshes as particles, you can lock them in the world, as they are not camera aligned.
6. Particles with the use of transparency demand a lot of performance, so it is important to know what and how to optimize the effects, depending on their size and amount.
7. Animated textures and UVs can create animations that are more realistic within your sprites, by looping images.

11

CHARACTER ANIMATION IN GAMES

Jumping, running, leaping and shooting? We have come quite far from the first games created with character animations, where the character showed emotion by moving sprites. A few years back, animators worked with very limited tools and restrictive parameters. Low bone counts, linear f-curves, and keyframe optimizations made producing good-looking animation very difficult or just impossible. Today, we have physics, and motion capture, and have implemented much more technical functionality within the development process. However, we still have ground to cover before the process is perfect. Animation for game creation is very similar to the movie industry. It has some specific technical differences that the player needs to know to be able to interact with the animations at all times. There are hundreds of special cases, and variations to how an animation system works in games. And with all the different systems and engines out there, this chapter is at best generic.

ANIMATION: GAMES VERSUS MOVIES

Disney® defined the western animation standard by establishing the "principles of animation," something we still use and hold true. Squash and stretch, follow through and overlap, slow in and out, anticipation, and secondary action are all applied to characters in film animation. So is the principle of character animation where timing, weight, balance, and strong poses are all important features of game animation.

Adopting animation to games requires certain changes to the very basics of these principles. Games are highly interactive, so when players press a button, they need instantaneous feedback on the screen. If they do not get it, the result is a broken illusion of player control and a sluggish game. So we need to adapt the animations for games so that they become intuitive with the game speed and controls.

To set up animations correctly for real-time use, we need to eliminate the use of "anticipation time" for actions. A punch animation, for example, when done for television or film would contain anticipation movements and a moving hold, before the actual punching action. In game animation, the punch comes instantly with almost no anticipation. The punch animation must be at the full range of its motion, but should work seamlessly if the player presses the punch button repeatedly, thereby making follow-through harder to implement. Therefore, the animation needs to be quick enough so the visual feedback is fast and accurate.

Animations in films are most often linear, where the shots are planned and the action is predetermined. Once everything is ready, the animation is created, finalized, and eventually rendered and composited.

In videogames, the character animations are nonlinear, so each game animation needs to be built as short segments that the player can trigger at different occasions within the game. Movements are created like a library, where a jump animation would consist of at least three parts—the initial leap, the moving through the air, and the landing. When in mid air, the player can then trigger another animation segment, making the animation blend to several other options and variations instead of the landing animation.

These different segments control the main movements within the game. There are, however, things that are not animated—for example, a character jump in length and height. Several games support different heights in jumps or double jumps, which are gameplay and player dependant, and code needs to specify the behavior, to be altered and tweaked easily. Animating characters for video games also requires animators to sometimes move away from subtlety in their work and secondary motion. Often, characters in games will be very small on the screen, and to read the particular motion, the animator needs to focus on strong poses and exaggerated movements.

CONTROLLING THE MESH

Characters in games are getting more complex as the hardware develops. At its early stages, inverse kinematics (IK) chains were unsupported by game engines, and bone limitations were very low. Character animation was restricted to the very basic body motions and polygon counts were limited. Hands and fingers were sometimes just not technically feasible, or were managed with a single bone.

These days, the number of bones used in a character skeleton is much higher, and the detail of the animations much finer. To control the mesh, game engines have an exact representation of the 3D software bone setup within the engine, and the animator is able to use 3D program-specific manipulators such as morph targets, expressions IK/FK toggle, IK splines, nonlinear animation, and other features that will create more realistic-looking animations.

Each type of game will have special features and requirements for character setup. In general, the skeletons within games are split into different parts within the engine—upper body and lower body—to keep things interactive with the different animation set created. For example, if the player runs forward and shoots, the legs will use a set for forward run, and the upper body will use a set that shoots the gun. This way, sets change in between the skeleton to be able to blend and work with the interactivity needed.

There are different interactions between the engine and the 3D program, with various methods to control the skeleton movements. The most common process is using bones. Each bone in the 3D engine represents a bone on the character within the game. Game engines commonly support both rigid and smooth binding. When the amount of vertices weighting in smooth binding is limited to the hardware's performance, two or four bones per vertex are most commonly used.

Each keyframe in the animation is stored as separate data that takes up memory. The keyframes can, however, be compressed, and as a result are uniformly spaced, which can result in unpredictable animations—something interpolation compensates for between adjacent keyframes.

BLENDING AND CYCLES

With games today, where the game characters have a lot more freedom, we need to create many more segmented animations to support each action. With so many different actions starting and stopping in succession, you could wind up with some very jerky movement if they are not set up and blended correctly. A blending system is something the engine uses to smoothly transition between animations. It takes the end position of one animation and morphs the bone positions to the start of the next required animation. For example, a player who has just jumped over an exploding barrel and wants to keep running will see the animation of the character jumping two times, and then blend into the run animation once the character lands. The blending process will usually begin in an animation within the last three frames of the first, and end by the first three frames of the next. The animator's job is to make these blending animations as seamless as possible.

There are a few ways to do this, including using a character animation viewer tool to tweak the motion, but most important, animations need to cycle. This is especially noticeable on commonly used animations, such as walks or runs. If you have a run cycle that is around 20 frames long, the last frame of the animation must have the same pose as the first frame, so that it loops seamlessly. Cycles like this are common in pre-rendered productions such as film or TV. However, in a nonlinear production environment, it is common to find cycling animation in many types of motions. Attack movements, jumps, and idles will often be cycling animations.

MOTION CAPTURE

As with pre-rendered animation made for film and television, real-time animation also uses motion capture to produce quick and realistic character animation.

In motion capture animation, the human or animal performs the game movements in front of special cameras or in a bodysuit with sensors so their movements are captured and then every keyframe gets stored. Several games today rely heavily on the character's exact movements; for example, sports games where the result with motion capture is very noticeable and correct. A signature basketball dunk, for example, looks even more authentic in the game, if the recorded motion is from the actual athlete. The motion capture process is somewhat messy, and the recorded motion data can be full of anomalies and artifacts that need to be cleaned up to work with a game engine.

PHYSICS

When applying physics to an object, that object will react with the world around it in a realistic manner, with weight and friction properties representative of its real-life counterpart. For example, take a box that is assigned with a particular weight and friction value, and is designated a "hard body," meaning it is rigid. (The opposite, a "soft body," would be designated to a flexible material such as cloth.) Now this box can react to forces within the game in a believable way, much like effects due to gravity. Depending on the engine's forces, this can be done without the need to set a single keyframe. If the box is dropped, it will bounce depending on the height and speed at which it fell. Real-time physics engines increase the immersion of the game world and add many gameplay opportunities, which make the game feel more alive and real.

Physics applied to characters is referred to as a "ragdoll" system. This system acts like a replacement for keyframed or "canned" death animations. Ragdoll has attachment points where the mesh is weighted. When the game enables ragdoll physics, it lets it take control over the selected pieces and it reacts to the game physics instead of using the animation keyframes. If enabled on an entire character, it would fall or crumble with physics, without any keyframes needed. If a ragdolled character dies on a staircase, it will topple down the stairs, and land in a crumpled pile at the bottom. If a character is blown up in an exploding car, its body will be tossed limp into the air, limbs knocking off other environment objects as the character falls to the ground. This type of detail and realism would be impossible to keyframe for all the different possible combinations, which makes rag doll physics a very popular choice.

SUMMARY

1. Timing, weight, and anticipation are all important functionalities that are still used in game development.
2. The animator animates segments of the character's body and movements.
3. Game animation differs from movie animation. A game triggers the animated segments, which blend together depending on the player's input and actions.
4. Bones and character setups represent the same setup in the 3D engine as in the game.
5. Motion capture is the most accurate way to create animation data, where characters' movements often need to be "cleaned up" before use within the engine.
6. Physics and the ragdoll system have become standards for game animation and provide the player with fast feedback of dynamic movements in a character, without any content creation.

CHAPTER

12

COLLISION

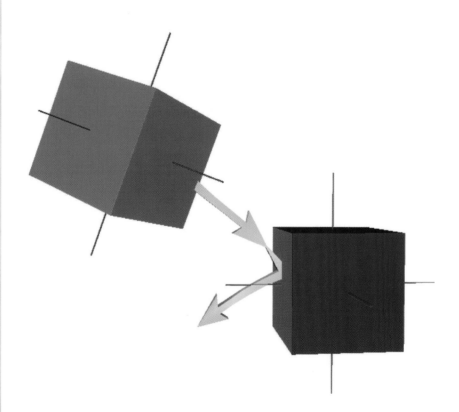

S o far, we've looked at some of the visual possibilities within game production. With gameplay, we need to be able to control the player to do what we want. The game does not use the visual mesh to interact with the player, so we need a collision object—an object that is invisible to the player but is capable of limiting the player from going through the visual meshes. Different collision systems work in different ways, and they all differ in construction and performance, depending on what they are created for. An intense Beat 'Em Up game would use a different collision system with more detail and accuracy than a massive multiplayer online game that needs the bandwidth for other things.

PROGRAMMER-CONTROLLED COLLISIONS

There are several types of collisions, some of which an artist will very rarely be involved. Character collision setup and how projectiles work are two examples. For characters, the collision structure could be made of bounding boxes, collision points, cylinders, or boxes that follow the bones or the mesh itself. All these depend on what features and details the character needs to have within the game, and what your engine supports. The projectile reacts and triggers a collision depending on the action; for example, it specifies the impact of a bullet within a game.

OBJECT COLLISION

Object collision is the main type of collision in games, and the system that the artist creates. These objects are generally handled by a mesh system, meaning there is a second mesh located at the exact same position as the visual mesh, acting as the colliding part for the same object.

Mesh Collision Setup

The theory behind the collision mesh is that the engine checks and collides with it depending on the direction of the polygon's normal. This means that you need to have the polygon normal facing the way you want the object, character, projectile, or vehicle to collide on both the colliding objects as shown in Figure 12.1 where the orange cube is falling, hitting the green cube, with facing normals. If we flip the normals so they face the opposite direction, the collision will be inverted and the orange cube will go right through the green cube.

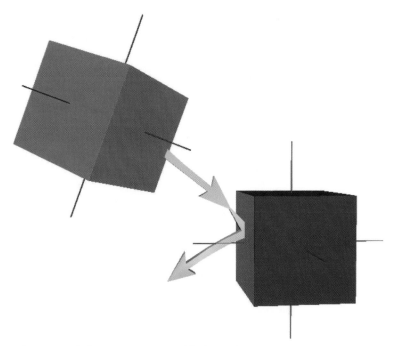

FIGURE 12.1   Collision occurs toward facing polygons.

A collision object differs in construction compared to the visual mesh. UVs and texture do not matter, but the collision object can contain information about material specifics; for example, if the surface is wood, rubber, or concrete. By connecting these values to the game physics, we can control how different objects interact and collide with each other. Although it is not necessary for all engines, it is always preferable to try to create the collision mesh closed, with all vertices welded and no open edges.

It's important to know how accurate the collision system is in the game engine you are working with, and what is required for the game. It will help you understand how detailed the collision needs to be on the objects. Very simple shapes (e.g., boxes) are the most performance efficient for game engines, and as long as they provide enough detail for the gameplay, there are no specific rules on how to create collision meshes. A general rule can be to keep them as low on vertices as possible, and as close as possible to the visible object as shown in Figure 12.2.

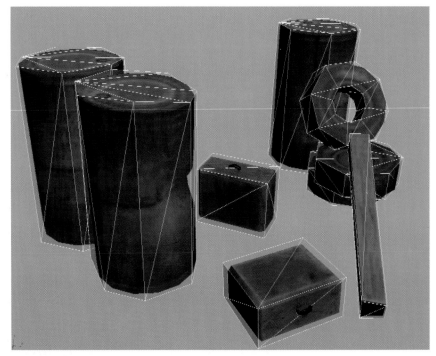

FIGURE 12.2   Collision mesh, a bit larger than the visual mesh. © Digital Illusions CE AB. 2004 Reprinted with permission.

PERFORMANCE

Mesh collision is expensive for the CPU to calculate, and the more physics and collisions the game engine has to calculate, the more impact this will have on its frame rate. You need to keep the polygons and vertices in the collision as low as possible—merely boxes in some cases. Make sure vertices are merged together and no extra polygons are used where they are not needed by following the principles of low-polygon modeling in Chapter 6, "Game Modeling."

Using the correct amount of polygons in a collision mesh is important; if too few are used, the characters will float, and projectiles will limit the gameplay. Too much detail in the collision mesh results in bad prediction, and can cause other objects to start to interact strangely—characters fall through, intersecting, and getting stuck. It is very important that after you create a collision mesh, you test it thoroughly, making sure it functions as intended. Collision meshes are commonly one of the biggest problems in the bug-testing phase.

We're sure that you have played a game where you got frustrated because you hit mid air instead of what you were aiming at. You have seen places where you float above the object, or a hole in an object into which your character clearly would fit. This can be the result of insufficient collision meshes being used or restricted collision for performance. Figures 12.3 and 12.4 show examples of an environment in *Battlefield Vietnam* where we use a lower polygon mesh to interact with vehicles. This way, we save performance. If this collision were to be used for characters and projectiles, they would have been standing and shooting in mid air.

FIGURE 12.3   *Battlefield Vietnam* with some placed objects, visual mesh.
© Digital Illusions CE AB. 2004 Reprinted with permission.

FIGURE 12.4   *Battlefield Vietnam* with some placed objects, collision mesh.
© Digital Illusions CE AB. 2004 Reprinted with permission.

In games that we can control where to place the objects (e.g., a car game or a scripted single-player game), we can choose more precisely what needs to have collision. In a car game, for example, we know that the cars will never leave the ground or the track, so we can easily make the collisions mesh end above the car height on buildings and only provide collision on objects along the track. Objects at a distance that the player will never reach, such as trees and houses, would work without having any collision.

SUMMARY

1. The programmers normally handle character collision, without artist involvement.
2. Collision is an invisible mesh, an extra modeled mesh.
3. All visible objects that the player will interact with need a collision mesh.
4. The modeling principles for low-polygon meshes are applicable for collision meshes. By keeping the collision mesh closed without open edges, you will restrain from misbehaviors and bugs.
5. Collision mesh polygons should be kept as close as possible to the visual mesh, so they do not limit the player's actions in the game.
6. Collision is expensive. To retain performance, you might need to cover up holes and keep objects less detailed than the visual mesh. Start with the positions that are not as important, places that the player will not reach.

III

TECHNICAL KNOWLEDGE

You are an artist, and you wish to remain so, but to become a full-featured game artist you need to understand why the art is done the way it is. You can be the best artist on the planet and create beautiful art, but to be able to use your artistic knowledge for games, you need to know the technical limitations for the gaming platform with which you are working.

Each platform has its own limitations, where techniques are adapted and constructed around the graphics cards and machines that we have to our disposal. Learning how to use the power of the machines to their maximum will help you understand why processes and workflows are the way they are.

When finished with Part III, you will have in-depth technical knowledge about the most relevant processes and techniques, and know how to solve problems and think when creating art for games—something that will make you very valuable as an artist in production.

13 GAME ART OPTIMIZATIONS

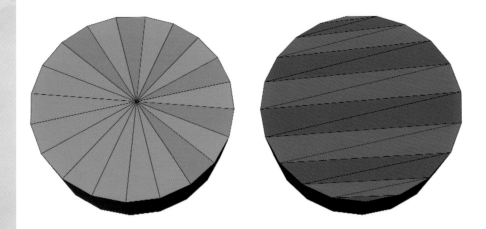

MEMORY VERSUS PERFORMANCE

When adding artistic features to a game, we divide them into two categories: memory-intensive content, and processor-intensive content. If we cannot afford the processor power, there may be a solution by creating art that takes up memory instead. If we had unlimited resources, we would use code to create all the special features in real-time and model the most detailed models with unlimited polygons. Yet, there are limitations to the amount of content that we can add to a game, and technology usually forces us to sacrifice one feature for adding something else. We can prioritize content by assessing what gives us the most "bang for the buck." Artistic features such as shadows, colors, lights, collisions, and textures can be implemented by code, but games need the processor power to do other things as well, so we end up using art for many of these solutions. Some solutions that will require memory to create the similar effect include the use of light maps, various colored textures, and lower poly collision meshes.

RENDERING PERFORMANCE

In Part I, you learned how to build and optimize objects after art creation and what makes assets look good in games. We will now take the modeling process a step further and look at the very basic features of a game engine to analyze how we need to build objects and scenes technically, so that the level designers and artists can reach the required frame rate.

As we know, an object is built with vertices and polygons. If we look at a level where the game engine calculates every polygon and vertex visible on the screen, the more depth we have to the scene, the more expensive it gets. So which is more expensive: a vertex or a polygon?

Polygons versus Vertices

Vertices are the very structure of our meshes. Without vertices in an object, there would be no polygons. For each vertex that exists on an object, the engine keeps track of its transformation, position, and angle, which requires a lot of processor power.

Thereafter, the engine creates triangles in between the mesh vertices by connecting each triangle to three vertices. When drawn on screen, they create what we call *fill rate*, which specifies the amount of "filling" each polygon uses of the graphical processor on the 2D screen—that is, the visual polygons within the field of view. Objects that have extremely large polygons covering the full field of view require more process power than if the same large polygons were divided into smaller polygons. While a polygon's cost changes depending on the size drawn on the 2D screen, the vertices cost is constant. When polygons get smaller in the distance, they require less area to fill between the vertices and become less expensive, while the number of vertices stays the same in all positions and distances, and requires the same processing power regardless of the situation.

CULLING/CLIPPING PLANE

A huge world where all art assets render everywhere requires a lot of processing power. Therefore, we need to limit the visible objects at any given time. Having a huge, open-range gameplay area as in a *Battlefield* game requires a different approach compared to a linear corridor, single-player game. They do have something in common, however: they need to reach the highest performance possible to give the player an immersive experience. To do this, we need to remove everything that is not visible to the player and only show what is in front of him, because those objects will require additional processing power (see Figure 13.1).

FIGURE 13.1   Having a huge world with a far view distance means that the graphics card will need to calculate a great amount of information and objects. © Digital Illusions CE AB. 2004 Reprinted with permission.

As you know, the engine does not draw all the objects at the same time. A system commonly used is to have a far and a near plane connected to the field of view. These planes define the outer areas where the objects surrounding you clip away, depending on the angle of view of the camera. This is unnoticeable to you, of course, since they are attached to the camera, following you in every movement. With the far clipping plane, we can decide the distance of the scene and how far the objects should be visible. Using a view distance feature like this, we limit the polygons and vertices to only appear between the plane and the camera.

Object Culling

If an engine supports object culling, you will have control of when the objects disappear in the distance depending on the size of the object and the distance to the camera. An example would be separate objects attached to larger objects; for example, steering wheels, and separate interior objects in a vehicle or a house. When the level of detail (L.O.D) starts to show, they would not need to be visible anymore since their size on the screen becomes too small to justify the performance hit for the player.

LEVEL OF DETAIL

As discussed earlier in the book, we want the objects close to the camera to look as detailed as possible, but those viewed from a distance do not need to be as detailed. Polygons become less expensive at a distance, but the amount of them and the vertex costs stay the same. L.O.D works for objects in the way that mipmapping works for textures with several smaller mesh changes, depending on the distance to the camera.

With the limited pixel resolution that exists on a TV or computer screen, the information within a detailed mesh becomes obsolete and less visible when the object is viewed at a far distance. By removing the details that are not visible into a second mesh that replaces the high-resolution one at a certain distance, we can achieve higher performance. The L.O.D objects need to match up as closely as possible to the original mesh so the player does not experience a "POP" when the engine switches between them. The distance to the camera usually defines the switch.

When building the L.O.D, the amount of polygons is irrelevant, as long as the L.O.D represents the silhouette of the original object well. To maximize performance with the L.O.D objects, you need to concentrate on reducing the vertices. As discussed earlier, the polygons fill rate becomes less when drawn in a distance, but the vertices cost stays the same. Therefore, the lower vertex amount we have on the L.O.D objects, the better performance we will receive in the game (see Figure 13.2).

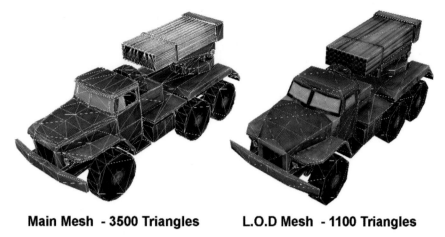

Main Mesh - 3500 Triangles   **L.O.D Mesh - 1100 Triangles**

FIGURE 13.2   L.O.D objects. © Digital Illusions CE AB. 2004 Reprinted with permission.

L.O.D objects will help performance, but each extra object we place in the world will take up more memory. This is something to keep in mind when each object in a game needs about three L.O.D objects each. An optimal L.O.D system would only use the amount of L.O.Ds needed for a specific object's complexity. If the original model were boxy, we would probably get away with one L.O.D, while a very complex model might need three L.O.Ds to make the transition down to a good amount of polygons as smooth as possible.

To obtain the low vertex count needed for the L.O.D objects, we need to keep just what is important on the mesh, the very silhouette of the object. Create an L.O.D by reducing polygons from your high-resolution mesh. You will save time by specifying what needs to be visible in its silhouette and then work to remove the larger shapes before the smaller ones. Remove smaller structures such as edges, bolts, and handles that are located on flat areas, and show them with textures instead. If your object has a very complex silhouette, you can replace it with boxes or other simpler structures that cover the same area. Another performance solution would be if the L.O.D used a lower mipmap texture level than the original object. This way, the graphics card would not need to reload textures, which reduces draw calls (see Figure 13.3).

Creating several L.O.Ds manually for each object in the scene requires a lot of work for the artists, but there are other solutions done with code. Game engines can support the use of progressive meshes, a system where the mesh bakes in its own L.O.Ds. The engine will merge vertices together automatically based on the least-needed edge within the mesh. Progressively reducing the mesh's total vertices and polygons saves draw

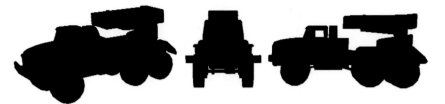

FIGURE 13.3 Keep and concentrate on the object silhouette. © Digital Illusions CE AB. 2004 Reprinted with permission.

calls compared to switching each separate mesh with a unique object. However, more mesh data needs to be prestored within the object, increasing the overall memory usage.

Tri-Stripping/Tri-Listing

Part II of this book discussed the very basics of polygon modeling, where we mentioned many artistic ways of how to save on vertexes and polygons. Yet, consoles and PC hardware may require a stricter and exact way of constructing the objects. To understand how to model even more efficiently for the engine, we need to know how the graphics cards treat polygons. There are two commonly used processes when handling triangles: *tri-stripping* and *tri-listing*. Tri-listing is a technique in which each triangle is treated and saved individually into an index, which keeps track of the different placements of the triangles. Tri-listing is quite forgiving to how the artists build the object, and we can be more creative without concentrating too much on performance. In Figure 13.4, we see a model using tri-listing. This technique saves each colored triangle in an index so it can have any shape and position possible.

FIGURE 13.4 Tri-listing saves each triangle to an index.

Tri-stripping, which has been around for quite some time, has some unique requirements when it comes to modeling for the highest performance. Tri-stripping builds up the polygons by creating continuous strips over the object. The longer the strip of bundled polygons an object can have, the faster the drawing of the scene (see Figure 13.5).

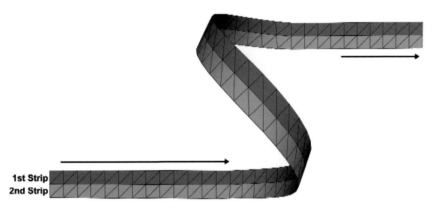

FIGURE 13.5   The optimal structure for tri-stripping.

Today, most exporters will handle and arrange the content within the meshes created, making the modeling process less of an issue. With future consoles and new powerful graphics cards, the specific modeling techniques for tri-stripping will cease to exist, and open the door for more artistic modeling methods. Modeling and texturing objects for tri-stripping requires practice and work, but the very basics are to keep the flow of the strips together by modeling polygons as squares. This can occasionally be broken when you create T-junctions.

T-Junctions

By splitting an edge in two, the continuous loop will break the strip. It is important that you do not place edges or vertices within the continuous strip, as doing so will stop the flow (see Figure 13.6).

Fan Polygons

When we model things like vehicle wheels, barrels, and bolts, it is common to use cylindrical caps where several faces attach to a single point, creating so-called *fan polygons*. These react badly with the tri-stripping method, as do other things like vertex lighting and bad edge flipping.

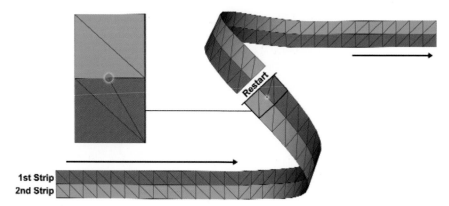

FIGURE 13.6   T-junctions—an extra placed vertex within the polygons breaks the continuous strip, and it restarts with new strips.

Keeping the polygons square and equal in size will solve this problem (see Figure 13.7).

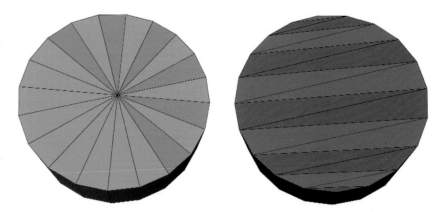

FIGURE 13.7   Fan polygon—the orange wheel is more expensive than the green wheel.

Noncontinuous or Intersecting Meshes

As mentioned in Chapter 6, "Game Modeling," when modeling pieces so they "stick" into each other, you can add many details yet keep the mesh optimized. You cannot use this feature with the tri-stripping method; an object that uses tri-stripping needs to be modeled as a single block, with no intersections. For example, a character with a head stuck into a body would break the continuity of the strips. When we create objects where we need to use tri-stripping, each intersected mesh on a tri-stripped model will make it restart a new strip as shown in Figure 13.8.

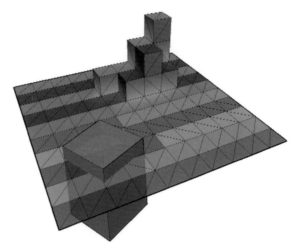

FIGURE 13.8   Noncontinuous or intersecting meshes.

Modeling for tri-stripping with these things in mind will help the engine achieve speed, and benefit per-vertex lighting. There is, however, more to tri-stripping than modeling. Other processes can stop the continuous flow of strips depending on the engine system.

UV and Material Borders

When you are UV mapping a tri-stripped object, the UVs need to be as unfolded and attached as possible to maintain the flow of the strips. By breaking up the UVs, materials, and the use of different textures within the mesh, we create breaks and start a new tri-strip.

Vertex Splitting by Surface Smoothing and Prelighting Vertices

The vertex normal has great meaning in the process of game creation. By changing the smoothing groups to hard, you will also break the strips. You can read more about how this works technically in Chapter 15, "Game Lighting."

To achieve the best performance within a tri-stripped model, it needs to be one uniformed mesh with no intersecting parts or smoothing. There should be one texture, one UV set, and no breaking vertices or polygons within the mesh.

DRAW CALLS

Every time the graphics card needs to access new information for the game, it needs to go through the application programming interface (API). This can be for loading a new object or new materials that were previously not cached. Requesting each of these tasks creates what we call a *draw call*. Graphics cards are sensitive to draw calls due to the bandwidth it requires when transferring information through its pipeline. If the amount of draw calls exceeds the graphics card bandwidth, it will choke the rendering process and the game will become slow. As artists, we can keep the draw calls lower in several ways.

Clustering of Objects

For each unique object drawn within the world, the graphics card needs a new draw call. If we create larger clusters of the objects within groups, we can reduce the amount of draw calls that the CPU has to do. A fence made up of 20 pieces in a level requires a call for each part. We can reduce the draw calls by clustering them as one piece. Having one piece of geometry is, however, not always preferable, and it's important to know where and how the parts merge. Say that you merged the fence into one large piece as a fence surrounding you. While standing in the center, you will have information drawn behind you even though you cannot see it. Large merged objects also make it harder to cull the L.O.D away, since the bounding box (area) of the object defines from the center of the object. Draw calls have become a serious performance issue on some graphic hardware, more so than the amount of drawn polygons. To solve this problem, a new technique has been created: geometry instancing, which reduces the API penalty for the mesh information that the engine needs to redraw for each instanced object.

Reusing UVs and Textures

To improve the performance of draw calls, we can reduce the overall trashing of textures. We can get the graphics card to reuse the same texture on as many objects as possible instead of having millions of small ones. The graphics card swaps and calls less through the API, and we reduce the draw calls considerably.

Structure your objects into groups. Make buildings, characters, and other objects reuse the same textures as much as possible within the same field of view. By storing a single large texture within the graphics card, the card can access it quickly for all its objects. Take buildings, for example. When we construct a city, if we can make 10 buildings use one texture map, we reduce the total draw calls within the scene to a bare minimum.

Atlas Textures

There are other techniques to optimize performance besides reusing UVs on objects. One is to bundle all small textures used within a scene into a larger texture. NVIDIA has released a texture tool that gives us the ability to create Atlas textures. It combines selected smaller textures into a large texture map. An index keeps track of the position and the different sizes of the various textures. By linking the various textures inside the Atlas to the objects within the scene, the graphics card can get fewer draw calls from this single large texture (see Figure 13.9).

FIGURE 13.9   Combined Atlas texture. © Digital Illusions CE AB. 2004 Reprinted with permission.

Creating bundled objects, reusing textures, and building Atlas textures are great ways to keep draw calls to a minimum. However, optimal performance of draw calls requires that the level artists/designers know how to distribute and build the level with the objects' placement in mind. By arranging and placing the objects within the field of view, the level designer can minimize draw calls even in the worst-case scenario of gameplay. That is, when the game is at its critical point of what it can handle performance wise, with all its features gathered to a single place on the screen.

Alpha Blend/Alpha Ref/Sorting

In Chapter 9, "Texture Creation," you learned what you can do with Alpha textures. We also mentioned briefly about their expense—objects are not free just because we cannot see them. When you create transparency, there are ways to define how it reacts with what is behind the transparency. We will go over two different methods here. The first is *Alpha blending* (see Figure 13.10). Alpha blending is when each object filters and blends behind the transparency texture. This makes the texture fade out the background according to the alpha information, where it uses the black and the grayscales to blend them with the world behind it. To get other transparent objects behind this to appear correctly, you need to add a sorting system. This sorts the different transparency textures in depth and keeps track of which one is in front of the other. This becomes expensive very fast when several objects are overlaying each other.

FIGURE 13.10   Alpha blending. © Digital Illusions CE AB. 2004 Reprinted with permission.

Using Alpha blending with sorting creates the most artistically pleasing results. There is, however, a much faster and less expensive option available called *Alpha reference* (see Figure 13.11). Here, the transparency texture is a 2-bit image, where we use the power of an input value to mask out the black color in the texture. The higher the number is the closer to white, the more transparent the image appears. A very low number would keep the entire polygon the same color, and a very high number would remove the entire polygon from view. Alpha reference is much faster since the engine does not have to sort the geometry. However, Alpha reference makes it harder to control the visual quality, and creates flickers, artifacts, and hard aliased edges if masked out improperly.

FIGURE 13.11   Alpha references. © Digital Illusions CE AB. 2004 Reprinted with permission.

SPRITES AND BILLBOARDS

We can use sprites for much more than explosions and smoke effects. By attaching sprites to trees as leafs, we can make the leaves rotate toward the camera at all times, overlaying each other and making the tree look dense regardless of what direction you are facing them (see Figure 13.12).

Since the sprite will rotate even at close range to the camera, standing under a tree or over a bush will make the entire bush rotate under you. This can create an awkward visual experience. To solve trees in a distance, we can use billboards.

FIGURE 13.12   A tree, the leaves of which are built up by sprites. © Digital Illusions CE AB. 2004 Reprinted with permission.

A billboard is a polygonal object locked in its world-up axis, facing the camera position at all times. There is a similar functionality here to the rotation of sprites for effects. This way, we can create L.O.D for trees and other objects in a distance very cheaply.

To take the L.O.D even further, we can use billboards with an animated texture, which we connect to the rotational camera angle. By implementing a generation of rendered images to the animated texture, we can create L.O.D objects using billboards. A method like this would be good for trees and other static meshes in the distance. Then, when we move around the L.O.D, it shows the animated texture representing the main object from all directions.

Ambient Objects—Grass

To get a visually appealing outdoor environment, games should never have flat and boring ground planes. What we need is to do is populate the world with objects to achieve a more realistic, dense feeling. For this, we can use an ambient placement system, which places small objects such as rocks, leaves, sticks, and, of course, grass on the ground.

To start creating art for a system like this, we need to know how it works. Drawing objects representing grass over the entire world would be too expensive. By connecting the system to the player's camera, we are able to set a separate view distance for this process, making the grass appear around you while you move forward. We also need to blend toward the bottom color of the ground, to make the transition and fade as smooth as possible. The meshes for this grassy look are going to have a lot of transparency and overlaying in them. To keep the performance optimal, we need to be efficient when modeling the polygon planes, and keep the polygons single sided. Since they are single sided, we need to make them visible from all angles by crossing the polygons in a star formation or by creating cubes (see Figure 13.13).

FIGURE 13.13   Modeled single-sided polygons, visible from all sides. © Digital Illusions CE AB. 2004 Reprinted with permission.

The system then fills the surrounding world with transparent objects looking like grass. By letting the system use an independent culling distance, we can manually decide at what distance they should disappear/appear, and by making the system keep the amount of vertices constant means that the shorter the view distance, the higher the density of the grass.

Now the grass will look like it's just floating on the ground, if it doesn't inherit some of the base colors or get shadowed by trees, buildings, and so forth. This can be done in two ways: by vertex coloring or by per-pixel shading. With vertex coloring, we let the end of the polygons fade to the color of the underlying ground. Using pixel shading, we can sample the ground color, projecting the color up per pixel toward the polygons. Both methods will do the trick, but per-pixel shading will create sharper shadows and visuals that are more correct.

IN PRODUCTION: OBJECT INSTANCING

Grass and small objects on the ground give depth to the world, but we cannot afford to have them drawn forever. It would be great to have a system where the artist/game designer can place instances of objects that stay on screen even in the distance effectively and intuitively—a system that would allow for fast and random generated placements when creating forests, cities, and interior and exterior objects.

To create a decent forest that we can approach, enter, and move around in, requires a great deal of geometry to look good, but with all the trees placed, it will also require many draw calls. We can combine the various techniques mentioned earlier in this chapter to construct a system that works the way we would like it to:

- Independent distance clipping
- L.O.D objects in a distance, with few vertexes
- Auto-generated clusters from the engine
- Few draw calls
- Few textures
- Correct Alpha sorting

A system is at its best when it empowers the artists, so when using the system, we need to be able to have full control and a seamless workflow. Things to consider implementing to make it easy for the artists include:

- Separate view distances
- Manual and automatic placement of the objects
- Variables for size, angle, spread, distance, and amount of objects
- Color control

A system like this can, of course, be used to place debris, houses, and all kinds of objects randomly in the world. Here we will concentrate on creating an outdoor environment. Let's start by modeling a single tree, for which we need two models: one high-resolution (for the up-close detailed mesh), and one for the low-resolution (L.O.D) mesh.

The polygon amount of the high-resolution mesh (Figure 13.14) depends on the system's (game console's) performance. Modeling the trunk and branches, and using Alpha textures as leaves together with folded polygons we can create more depth on the tree.

 The numbers of trees mentioned for the clusters and groups are only examples, not actual or suggestions for the system.

FIGURE 13.14   High-polygon trees. © Digital Illusions CE AB. 2004
Reprinted with permission.

To keep the L.O.D mesh as low as possible yet resemble the silhouette of the main object, we can render images of the high-resolution tree and planar map it onto planes. This way, the low-resolution mesh (Figure 13.15) consists of merely a part of the total vertices of the high-resolution object, and is cheap to view in the distance.

We solved the main mesh and the visual L.O.D. Now, let's create a forest. If we built a forest with this tree, it would require over 1000, all visible at the same time to make it believable. That equates to one draw call per tree; therefore, thousands of draw calls—something of which performance would not approve. As you probably figured out, we need to

FIGURE 13.15   Low-polygon trees. © Digital Illusions CE AB.
2004 Reprinted with permission.

reduce the amount of draw calls by bundle and merging textures. By creating groups of our single tree, we can create variations of other trees and break up the visuals of the groups. The L.O.D then needs to be created to represent the new groups. To reduce the draw calls further, we can use a single texture for all the trees in the level, and another separate one for the L.O.D trees. Now the draw call cost is the same for an area with 1 tree as it is for a group containing 10 trees.

Looking at the world through the field of view, we see a few groups of high-resolution trees close to us. There are many L.O.D groups visible in the distance, and although low-polygon, they still create draw calls. We need to be able to get these L.O.D objects merged into even larger clusters.

This cannot be done in art. We need the programmers to specifically generate and bake the groups of several L.O.D trees into larger clusters. From having one tree for the L.O.D that stood alone when we started, we now have a cluster containing hundreds of various-sized trees with the same cost of draw calls.

As you can imagine, performance-wise this system is a near-perfect solution. However, nothing is useful until the artists have full control over the process. We need to implement several intuitive controls for the artists so they do not have to manually place every tree in the world before the engine bakes them into clusters. We also need the artists to spec-ify to the system what type, spread, size, rotation, and angle the trees should have depending on world position.

Having a material map covering the entire world, we can let the artist paint the areas with a specific color representing the type and size of the trees. Through this method, artists are able to paint where roads are lo-cated, where no trees should be.

If we link the system that automatically generates the placement of the trees to the material map, the artist can achieve fast results. Every-thing in games is about control, so we need to have a feature that if the automatic generation does not suit the artist or designer, it lets him go in, delete specific trees, and move the ones needed for gameplay to another location.

To be able to maintain maximum speed, the system needs to be able to integrate the manually placed trees into the larger baked sets of trees.

To stretch a system like this even further, we can add pixel shaders and vertex shaders to the objects, where we let the objects sample the ground texture's light intensity and colors under it. This would let the ob-jects go darker or lighter depending on whether they were standing in light or shadow (see Figure 13.16). Using vertex shaders, we can also make the leaves of the trees wave and move, making them more organic.

FIGURE 13.16   Light and dark areas, sample of the ground darkness, per-vertex, and per-pixel. © Digital Illusions CE AB. 2004 Reprinted with permission.

SUMMARY

1. The amount of memory or processing power decides the artistic quality.
2. Polygons are expensive up close due to fill rate; at a distance, vertices become more of an issue.
3. Using culling techniques will let you decide how far the objects in the scene should render and be visible.
4. When you create L.O.D, it is important to keep the silhouette as close to the high-resolution mesh as possible; only save the vertices that help to define the shape.
5. When Tri-stripping is used or required, you need to model the objects with performance in mind, adding polygons where needed. Adding a few more polygons to help maintain the stripe is cheaper than breaking it.
6. Modeling, layout, and change of materials, smoothing groups and intersection between objects all break a Tri-strip.
7. Draw calls are expensive for graphics cards; clustering the objects and using larger textures will help keep the number of draw calls low.
8. Atlas textures save draw calls and clean up the structures of the folders.
9. Trees can use geometry, sprites, and billboards. Depending on the system's requirements. Geometry has the highest quality, yet highest performance requirements.
10. Object instancing can be done through automatic placements, which later can merge into larger clusters of objects. This is to reduce unique draw calls for meshes and textures throughout the level.

TEXTURE TECHNOLOGIES

Textures are the most memory intensive assets in game production. Each console has its own way of handling textures, and supported file systems. With the resolution and the information needed in textures, it starts to become very important to be able to compress the textures. Compression methods are important, since compression distorts colors and content depending on the format and the color depth.

COLORS

Digital images have a limit on the amount of information that can be stored and viewed on a screen. Using textures, we store the information with RGB digital colors, which have a maximum range between R0, G0, B0, to R255, G255, B255, or the mathematic values 0–1 for each channel. We can divide colors into two categories, palette-indexed and non-palette-indexed.

Indexed textures have each pixel representing a value of an associated palette. The bit depth would represent the total amount of colors available in the texture palette. For example, an 8-bit texture using a palette would have 256 variations.

A nonindexed 8-bit texture represents the bit depth of each channel, where they together add up to 24 or 32 bits according to the amount of channels.

Color-Indexed

An indexed texture can have various bit depths up to 8 bits.

> 1-bit = 2 colors
> 2-bit = 4 colors
> 3-bit = 8 colors
> 4-bit = 16 colors
> 5-bit = 32 colors
> 6-bit = 64 colors
> 7-bit = 128 colors
> **8-bit = 256 colors**

This is the indexed texture bit value, where the entire texture shares a palette (see Figure 14.1).

Color Depth

Non-palette-indexed textures use the bit depth to describe the total amount of color variations that each pixel can have. Instead of using a palette, the textures use channels with a set amount of color depth. We can divide palette-indexed textures into two formats: software codec (ex: jpg) and

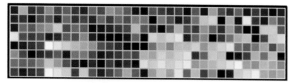

FIGURE 14.1   Indexed colors, each color has its own slot.

hardware codec (ex: dds). Software codec is most commonly used by artists when working inside 3D programs. Both systems behave differently in bit depth. Non-palette-indexed textures can make use of less bit depth and AU:combination depending on need. The most common formats for game texture codecs are shown here in bold:

What does combination mean here?

- **16-bits: 4-bits colors/channel (65,536 colors) + 4 bits alpha**
- 24-bits: 8-bits colors/channel (16,777,216 colors)
- **32-bits: 8-bits colors/RGB channel (16,777,216 colors) + 8 bits alpha**
- 64-bits: 16-bits colors/RGB channel + 16 bits alpha
- 128-bits: 32-bits colors/RGB channel + 32 bits alpha

The 16- and 32-bit formats are 4- and 8-bits per channel, with one extra channel storing a 4- or 8-bit alpha channel. 24-bit mode is merely the texture without any alpha, by storing only the 256 colors/per channel, it creates 16,777,216 colors together. The true 24-bit without any alpha is rarely used within the game developing because graphics cards do not support it. Depending on quality, the game, file format, and compression, we use different color depths for various situations in production. The smaller bit depth we can create the textures in, the smaller the textures become, which let's us add more of them in the game. The result of compression and fewer colors is that they create distortions and color bandings between the interpolations of colors. Figure 14.2 shows the principles of a per-depth texture.

1 Pixel / RGBA

FIGURE 14.2   Color depth, the texture use channels.

With current software technology, we are limited to 8 bits per channel, or 256 light values in each color of red, green, and blue. The human eye can visualize more than this color range, which makes it possible to experience banding even in 24-bit color. 16 bits is commonly used for games due to the speed gains, but creates even further bandings (something we artists need to be aware of) by creating fewer color variations in the textures and applying a small level of noise, or dithering to make them appear smoother.

RAW IMAGE

A *raw image* is a color-index texture format. As the name implies, the raw file format is the raw information of an image. The image is stored without any compression, information of color, depth, or size. It is stored exactly as the main processor would read the information, in binary form. In this uncompressed state, it can assemble the data quickly. To access a raw image file, we need to specify the color depth, size, and structure when it is loaded into the game or for edit in Photoshop. Raw images are good examples of informational images, where you need to specify a unique color to a value and a function within the game. Supported by the hardware, their main disadvantage is that they become very large.

Targa (TGA)

TGA is a software texture (format) that we can save as an 8-bit index texture, as well as 16-, 24-, and 32-bit depth. TGA supports compression methods but is rarely used in the PC environment because the format tends to become quite large and the graphics card decompresses it in the engine. Having larger TGA, as the PC environment requires, tends to be very memory expensive together with the higher bit color depth. For use in a game environment, the TGA texture needs to be small and use a low color depth, where the object mapping relies more on a tiling and vertex coloring for creating variations for texturing. TGA is still an interesting solution when quality needs to be exact, since nothing in the image distorts when saved.

Direct Draw Surface (DDS)

DDS is a DirectX file hardware format created by Microsoft. It has been adapted and streamlined to graphics cards and for use in games. DDS supports compression with a fixed ratio depending on color depth. The format supports fast decompression by the graphics cards.

 Developer.Nvidia.com has a file plug-in that allows you to be able to save this format from Photoshop.

DDS supports various color depths and compressions by default (see Figure 14.3).
Compressed formats:

- **DXT1 RGB: 16-bits with a compression ratio of 8 to 1**
- DXT1A RGB: 16-bits with 1-bit alpha, compression ratio of 8 to 1
- DXT3 RGB: 32-bits with 4-bit alpha, compression ratio of 4 to 1
- DXT5 RGB: 32-bits with 8-bit alpha, compression ratio of 4 to 1

Uncompressed formats:

- 16-bit (4444): 4 bits for alpha, red, green, and blue
- 16-bit (1555): 1 bit for alpha, 5 for red, green, and blue

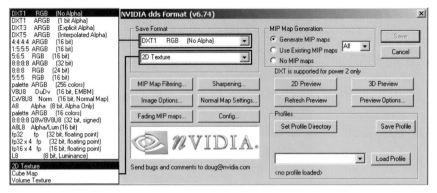

FIGURE 14.3   DDS Photoshop options.

- 16-bit (565): No alpha, 5 bits for red, 6 bits for green, 5 bits for blue
- 32-bit RGB: 8 bits for alpha, red, green, and blue
- 64-bit RBGA: 16 bits for alpha, red, green, and blue
- 128-bit RBGA: 32 bits for alpha, red, green, and blue

The DDS file format has many different compression methods and possibilities to save your textures so they match the quality and speed that you might require in your game.

DXT1 is a 16-bit compressed texture without an alpha. This format is the most commonly used in games, but also gives us the lowest quality. By having the highest compression ratio, it creates artifacts on textures that have a large range of gradient colors.

HIGH DYNAMIC RANGE IMAGE (HDRI)

HDRI changes the limitations we have with RGB images. An HDRI image uses floating-point numbers instead of 0 to 255, and contains a higher range of light values for each channel.

The most common problem with working with RGB images is that you run out of contrast values. It is hard to get contrast within an image without cutting areas to completely white.

VOLUME (3D) TEXTURES

We often visualize our textures as a single flat plane. Although we still work with them as 2D images, we do not have to save them as 2D planes. There is a system available where we can use all axes X, Y, Z where the Z-axis stores frames (see Figure 14.4). This way, we can integrate several

Loan Receipt
Liverpool John Moores University
Learning and Information Services

Borrower   Mohd Mohd Ariff Sabri
Borrower ID 194258
Date 06/04/2008   Loan Time 15:21

Game level design
Byrne, Ed
Barcode: 31111011273313   Loan Type 21 Day Loan
Due Date 28/04/2008   Due Time 23:59

Game art
Lee, Riccard
Barcode: 31111011344940   Loan Type 21 Day Loan
Due Date 28/04/2008   Due Time 23:59

images into one file, reducing the amount of swapping from various single textures if a sequence is used. As with other image formats, multiply by two limits the height, width, and frames of the 3D images.

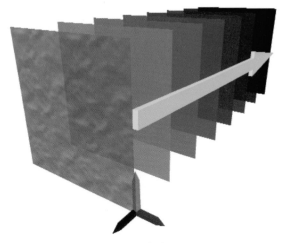

FIGURE 14.4   A 3D image reads the image in X Y Z.

A 3D texture in game production is good when we want to create and use animated textures in effects, or create image sequences for water. When the texture uses a sequence sheet for effects as shown in Chapter 10, "Special Effects," each frame represents a small part of a large sheet through which the engine scrolls.

3D images use layers of images, making it possible for the different images to interpolate between each other, and making the transition smoother when fewer frames are used.

By using a smaller sized texture with less alpha transparency, 3D textures help to gain speed when sorting is used, because the engine reads it as a single looping texture. We edit and use 3D textures in strips, as shown in Figure 14.5.

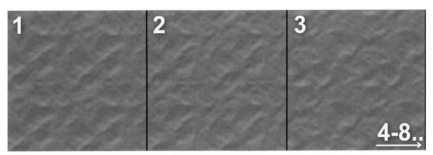

FIGURE 14.5   3D textures in Photoshop appear as 2D, frames from left to right.

TEXTURE RESOLUTION FOR GAMES

The resolution of computer games is increasing rapidly. Graphics cards today finally have support for textures that are not a power of 2, meaning that we will be able to specify the exact width and height of the texture areas when we create our art. However, it will take some time before it becomes a standard because of the amount of old hardware that does not support it. With the graphics cards today, we can also use larger textures, like 4096 × 4096 pixels.

In Chapter 7, "UV Layout," we talked about the right UV size for the right object in the game. With so many different types of games in production, most studios use different techniques. Should a chair have a 1024 × 1024, or is 64 × 64 enough? Who decides what resolution a certain object should have within a game? Can all objects have different resolutions within the game, or should we keep them the same?

Before we decide the final texture resolution for an object, we should understand the technical side behind the process. We need to know the intended resolution for the game. Games created for consoles are suited for TV screen resolution, either PAL or NTSC, or in certain cases HDTV. On a computer, the player has the option to change resolutions and color depth. You should try to optimize the texture to a resolution where each pixel of the texture shows up on the screen and takes advantage of that particular resolution. If you create a higher resolution texture than the screen needs to show, you will have antialiasing problems and flickering will occur. In Figure 14.6, you see a gun on screen. In this set resolution, it uses as much texture space as the texture has.

FIGURE 14.6   Maximum size needed for texture versus screen size. © Digital Illusions CE AB. 2004 Reprinted with permission.

TEXELS VERSUS PIXELS

To understand how pixels show up on the TV/monitor screen and at what resolution we will achieve the best quality within the texture, we need to know the basics of what texels are and how they relate to what we see on the screen.

When we create our textures, we visualize each pixel as a square area on the texture. However, the engine does not see the pixel as a square shape. In the middle of each pixel, we have a round circle. This circle is what we call a texel (see Figure 14.7). It holds the information for the co-ordinates for each pixel location.

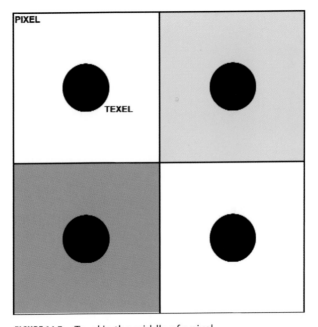

FIGURE 14.7   Texel in the middle of a pixel.

What we see on the screen is texels; the pixel in 3D view becomes a round dot in the middle of that square and interpolates with the surrounding texels. A texel is the pixel on the screen at a given resolution, which gives us the ability to calculate how many pixels are needed for each texel size. This is something we can decide with each mipmap level.

Each pixel on the screen is calculated compared to the texel that can be shown on the monitor/TV. When there are more pixels than the monitor can show, a single texel can contain more than one pixel. If you create textures with a higher resolution than there are texels to show them, you use more memory than needed and reduce the graphics card performance.

MIPMAPPING

Mipmapping is a way to simulate perspective for textures, or if we want, a method for L.O.D for textures. When we start to move away from a texture in the game, the engine will try to draw the actual pixels, which creates an irritating flickering noise.

A texture that uses mipmapping has a sequence of textures stored within the same image, where each sequenced image scales with the power of 2 to a smaller size in height and width, from the previous level. For instance, having a texture of 1024 × 512 would create mipmaps that are 512 × 256, 256 × 128, 128 × 64 continued to a single pixel, or depending on the mipmap sequences specified when saved (see Figure 14.8).

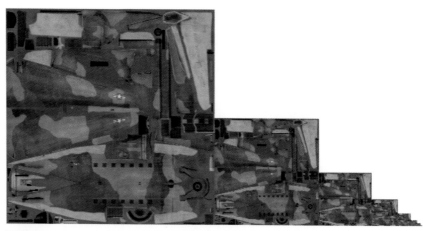

FIGURE 14.8 Mipmapping texture. © Digital Illusions CE AB. 2004 Reprinted with permission.

The closer we are to an object with mipmapping in a game, the larger the level of the texture the engine will draw of the mipmaps. Moving away from the object, the mipmaps will interpolate to a smaller texture. Having several levels of mipmaps stored in each texture consumes more memory.

To visualize mipmapping easier, you can color each mipmap in the texture with a different color.

Mipmaps increase the rendering speed due to the number of texture pixels becoming less in the distance when the engine draws a smaller level of the texture. Using a smaller image in the distance also reduces the flickering we notice when the engine tries to draw the actual pixels from the large original texture. In this case, what we win in performance and rendering quality, we lose in memory.

Even though you cannot create mipmaps when you save the texture, the option is to let code create them in the game.

The algorithms in today's graphical engines are able to calculate the amount of the pixels needed for the textures compared to distance. If you create and apply a 2048 × 2048 texture to an object that does not take up more than a few hundred pixels on the screen, the engine will choose to show a smaller mipmap closer to the screen resolution. This makes the largest mipmap of the texture unused and will only be stored within the graphics card and take up extra memory. If we see an airplane from 100 meters, the object will not require as large a texture as if we saw it up close, since it takes up fewer pixels on the 800 × 600 screen (see Figure 14.9).

FIGURE 14.9   Depending on the camera distance, the game uses different mipmaps.
© Digital Illusions CE AB. 2004 Reprinted with permission.

Graphics cards also decide how the texture quality is going to look. To gain speed, you can choose a lower graphic setting that would make the engine choose a lower mipmap closer to you. It draws fewer details and reduces the memory in the graphics card.

SUMMARY

1. A texture can be saved and used in both index and nonindex textures.
2. The most common bit depths in graphic production are 16 and 32 bits, where the alpha use the last 4 and 8 bits.
3. There are both software and hardware formats, where the hardware format does not have to be converted inside the graphics card. Software codecs are too slow for the graphics card to use them in real-time.
4. The DDS format supports several unique ways to store the texture. It supports compression for more memory, but compression can create banding within the textures.
5. A 3D texture adds another dimension where images can be stored as frames in depth.
6. To keep memory to a minimum, do not create textures in a higher resolution than that in which the game is intended to play. Developing for various screen resolution will decide your size.
7. Texels are the very definition for the pixels in the screen, and the way the engine knows where the pixels are in 3D.
8. Mipmapping reduces flickering and speeds up rendering by storing smaller images in the same texture, something that also requires more memory.

GAME LIGHTING

L ight is everything. Without it, the world would appear black. It is through light that we experience the world, and so it is in computer games as well. We are moving toward a new generation of game development, where the implementation of light makes the world more true to life. GI in real time, HDRI, Bloom, and others all work to achieve this goal. With dynamic lights, we can create muzzle flashes that interact with the environment, torches, and explosions that light up the surrounding area or a specific area of interest. Lighting will not just change the visual experience of the game, it can be used to determine the gameplay. Game lighting uses several different methods. For us to know how they work, we need to learn the very basics of how models are lit inside a game engine.

PER-VERTEX LIGHTING

All objects have vertices. A vertex is the smallest part of a mesh, yet it is so powerful. Each vertex on the mesh has its own normal vector, and just as the polygon's normal, it decides the direction of the vertex. However, the polygon normal only has two directions, while the vertex normal is a rotational value of all axes. Each vertex normal rotation angle can be controlled manually, controlling the edge smoothness of the polygons and its intensity. In games, where vertex lighting is used, it decides what part of the surface is light or dark. If we use a directional light to light up a vertex on an object, we get two values: one light vector, which is the bouncing vector from the vertex toward the directional light position, and the angle of the vertex normal. When we take these two values and measure the difference in angle, we get a value that specifies our intensity for the vertex (see Figure 15.1).

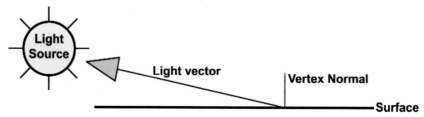

FIGURE 15.1   The calculation of the intensity of a vertex.

If the value is low, the vertex becomes bright, since the light vector is parallel with the normal directly facing the light. If the value is higher, the angle is larger between the light and the vertex normal, resulting in a darker vertex. See Figures 15.2 and 15.3, where the red color represents the angle and value.

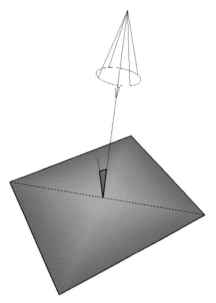

FIGURE 15.2   Small angle = light vertex.

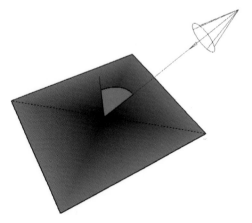

FIGURE 15.3   Large angle = dark vertex.

The engine samples each vertex and sets its intensity. Then, an interpolation takes place between the vertices (see Figure 15.4).

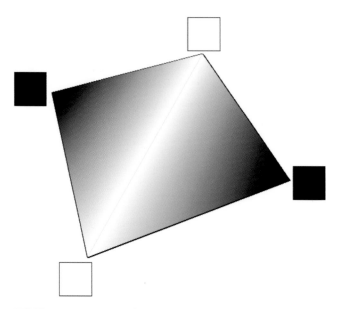

FIGURE 15.4 Two interpolating vertices' light intensities.

Polygons are always triangles, even when we model using Quads (faces), and they have hidden edges in between the triangles. Each triangle edge dictates how the interpolation occurs between the vertices. Turning the edge on the mesh will change the interpolation and the visual content on the mesh (see Figure 15.5).

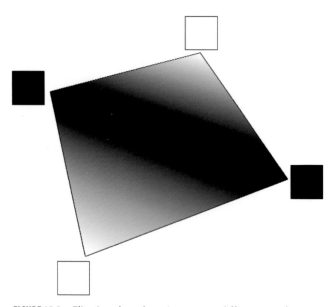

FIGURE 15.5 Flipping the edge gives a very different result.

Together with the edge direction, the amount and the spacing of vertices of the object have a direct effect on the lighting quality. To get the vertex to react to the light, it needs to be within its light cone.

For instance, if we direct a spotlight into the middle of a plane that has no vertices, there is nothing to affect, so the polygons will remain dark, even though the light lit them up (see Figure 15.6).

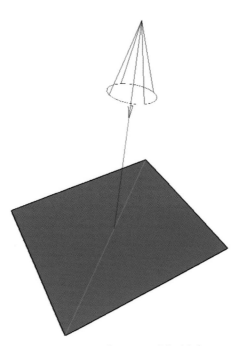

FIGURE 15.6   Low-polygon model with few placed vertices.

If we subdivide the same object evenly, the vertices will be able to see the light and receive an intensity value that they can use to interpolate. Figure 15.7 shows an evenly modeled plane with a projected light that has edges turned in the middle to make the light react better to the light source.

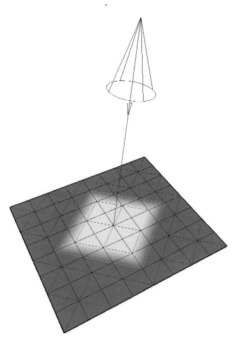

FIGURE 15.7   Low-polygon model with evenly
spaced vertices, together with tweaked edges.

VERTEX CONTROLLING

Vertices can be controlled in several ways, and give the artist freedom of
how the objects should look within a game development.

Vertex Color

Coloring vertices bases its technique on the very construction of game
lighting. In addition to light and darkness, vertex coloring gives us the
ability to give each vertex a color that interpolates the color value between the surrounding vertices, as seen in Figure 15.8.

Combining vertex coloring and lighting with textures on an object, the
vertex information multiplies its value together with the texture. This way,
we can make use of vertex painting in many ways, by adding colors to the
entire object and creating different variations within the scene, or by painting parts of the object darker, lighter, or a color value to create variation in
the objects and minimize tiling and uniformity (see Figure 15.9).

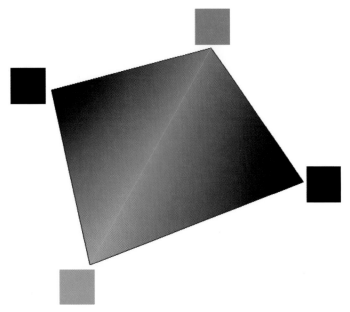

FIGURE 15.8   The interpolation between vertex colors.

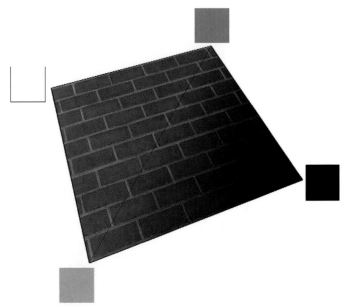

FIGURE 15.9   Various different colored objects with vertex coloring.

Vertex coloring is a commonly used feature within game production. Although it is hard to achieve visually satisfying results with a low-polygon mesh, it gives adequate results in comparison to the performance and the memory required, since vertex colors are stored within the saved mesh and are practically free for the engine.

A single colored vertex that connects to four polygons interpolates to all surrounding vertices.

Vertex Alpha

Vertices also have the capability to store a transparency value. When we apply information of alpha value to the vertex colors, we make that specific vertex on the object and the interpolation disappear, as shown in Figure 15.10. With this, we can create objects that simulate fog and other transparent objects without using any textures.

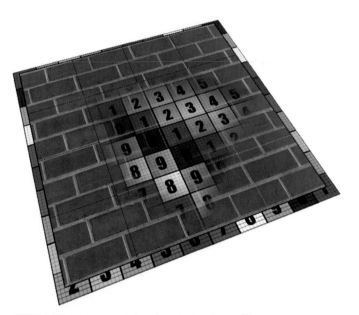

FIGURE 15.10   A vertex alpha plane in the form of fog.

Precalculated Vertex Lights

When we develop a game, performance can limit our use of light sources. To save performance, we can prelight (bake) the vertices' light values into the objects instead of calculating the light in real time. This means that the vertices will become self-lit within the game with a burned-in color value. With prelighting, we can also paint in shadows and other artifacts to give the objects a more interesting look. Prelighting is becoming less common in PC games due to the more complex hardware and the shader systems that can make real-time per-pixel calculations. However, consoles still use prelighting to a great extent.

 By turning off all lights within the 3D scene, we can see the exact prelit result better.

Today's 3D programs support the functionality to take a light source and bake the vertex intensity into the object.

VERTEX SOFT/HARD EDGES

Lighting determines how the object surface appears—in fact, the vertices do. The object's smoothing groups and edges determine if a polygon should appear hard or soft within the game engine. By rotating the vertices' normal, we can change the direction to where the light should hit it from, changing the amount of intensity the vertex will have. The vertex normal's most common direction is the face direction.

An object that uses hard edges has one separate vertex normal in each edge direction, as shown in Figure 15.11. What looks like one vertex becomes three vertices in the game engine, and therefore more expensive to draw.

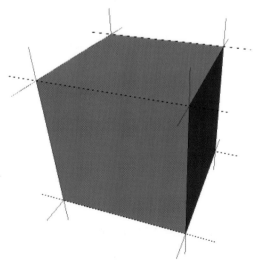

FIGURE 15.11   Hard edge (split) vertex normal angles

When you move the vertex normals toward each other so they share the same direction as seen in Figure 15.12, the edges connected to the vertex will appear smooth. Changing the vertex so it only has one normal makes it require less data for the engine to calculate.

Due to the higher cost, only use hard edges where your objects really need them.

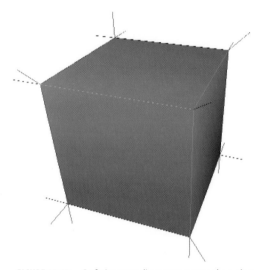

FIGURE 15.12   Soft (merged) vertex normal angles.

If a polygon appears completely black, check its vertex normal angle and align its direction toward the polygon.

PER-PIXEL LIGHTING

Vertices might be the smallest part of the mesh, but there are many more pixels within an object. Using per-pixel lighting, each pixel in the texture is calculated and given a light, which gives us extensive possibilities (see Figure 15.13).

The amount of pixels within an object gives us sharp shadows, realistic lighting, and other special features that can occur on each pixel on the polygons. The resolution of using per-pixel lighting is unlimited, compared

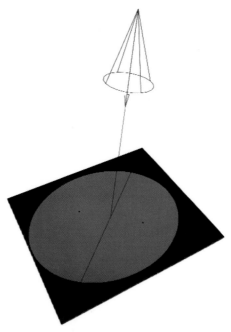

FIGURE 15.13   Per-pixel lighting creates an exact shape from the spotlight.

to having to model the same amount of vertices within a mesh. The accuracy and the functionality does come with a price, since it requires much more processing power to do per-pixel lighting than per-vertex lighting, so games are still implementing and mixing old and new methods.

 This is the base system for the new and more advanced texture techniques that we have today (specular maps, gloss maps, normal maps, etc.).

Bloom

One very true-to-life light effect that is becoming more common is to simulate light bloom, created when the surrounding area of an object is lit up due to an overexposed value facing the sun, often experienced when photographs are taken. As a feature within a game, it will give you a real light feeling when you look at a strong light source since it blurs and blends your image.

Bloom is a postprocessing technique that sets up what should glow. You can use an Alpha texture to determine what parts of the texture should affect the bloom.

GI Lighting

These are all versions of systems where the objects in a scene sample the textures on the sky to inherit an intensity value. Using HDRI in games is still uncommon, but there are other methods of calculating the intensity of the texture so it transfers its lightness to the objects, per pixel or per vertex. From having a single light source that the vertices got their intensity from, we are moving toward a sky acting as a light source and determining how bright objects will need to be. These techniques create a type of GI lighting depending on the sky's darkness/brightness.

DYNAMIC LIGHTING

Adding interactive light sources in the game influences the environment, making the light dynamic. With attached light sources to weapons, effects, and vehicles, we can create searchlights, torches, and exploding effects that emit light.

Dynamic lighting can be functional with both per-vertex and per-pixel lighting methods. It is still expensive to make per-pixel dynamic lighting in large scenes in combination with shadow calculations. It is also common that the engine mix the techniques, where objects use per-pixel lighting up close, but per-vertex further away since the accuracy is less important.

GAME SHADOWS

Having light in a scene does not make much sense if we do not have shadows, especially if we want to make things look realistic. Creating shadows for games is complex, where we are moving toward using more programming techniques. We will go over some techniques that are commonly used and where it is common that artists need to create specific art.

Because shadows are a processor- or memory-intense process, the system or the type of game determines what kind of shadows we should use. There are normally variations used to create shadows within a scene:

- Code
- Vertices
- Textures
- Meshes

Code Shadows

Several various techniques are available for programmers to create shadows, a workflow that does not involve much artistic input. The goal is to make them as true to life as possible and tweakable for the environment. Some commonly used technologies include:

- Stencil buffer shadowing
- Projected textures
- Shadow maps (depth map)

When we use code-based techniques within the games, it is dependent on what technique and what objects can afford them because it is a processor-intensive task. Developers normally use them for dynamic meshes (characters and vehicles) and static meshes (buildings, objects).

The main functionality of code shadows is that they read the silhouette of the object and cast rays, project a texture, or a shadow map. To reduce the costs, artists can create a low-resolution shadow mesh that simplifies the silhouette calculations for the engine (see Figure 15.14).

FIGURE 15.14   *Battlefield Vietnam* dynamic objects use projected texture shadows.
© Digital Illusions CE AB. 2004 Reprinted with permission.

Vertex Shadows

As discussed in per-vertex lighting, we can create shadows using the vertices' dark intensity values. It is very important to remember that the engine treats polygons as triangles within the engine, and that the direction of the edges will change the interpolation and the shadow's visual appearance. Although creating shadows using vertex shadows requires many more polygons on the objects, it does not require any additional textures or memory other than the added vertex cost (in memory size and rendering).

Texture Shadows

If the system allows us to use a lot of memory, we can use so-called lightmaps. The lightmap is a pre-rendered shadow from the position of the light source. Mulitplied over the main texture, each pixel on the lightmap represents a light intensity. Lightmaps are independent of color depth. Color lightmaps can simulate radiosity, while the grayscaled lightmap merely adds a layer of darkness (see Figure 15.15). Lightmaps are most suited and used for static meshes (buildings, objects).

FIGURE 15.15   A typical lightmap texture multiplied over the object texture.

Lightmaps make the objects more appealing and believable, as shown in Figures 15.16 and 15.17.

FIGURE 15.16   A *Battlefield Vietnam* building without lightmaps. © Digital Illusions CE AB. 2004 Reprinted with permission.

FIGURE 15.17   A *Battlefield Vietnam* building with lightmaps. © Digital Illusions CE AB. 2004 Reprinted with permission.

One of the major drawbacks of lightmaps is that they require a high-resolution texture that takes up a lot of texture memory, even if we compress the texture or use 8-bit textures. If a too small texture is used for lightmapping, it will create leaking areas where the UV gets the wrong pixels at the wrong positions on the object. Figure 15.18 shows an example where the red area contains black dots that have leaked out due to a low-resolution texture.

FIGURE 15.18   Leaking lightmaps. © Digital Illusions CE AB. 2004 Reprinted with permission.

Light and shadows play an important role in how we visualize a game. Powerful lighting can do a lot for the content, both realistically and stylized. As we get more processing power, this will become more apparent. Programmers still work hard at getting GI rendering to work affordably in real-time. With increased processing power, real-time soft shadows will get a bit closer to reality, and we will not have to use lightmaps anymore.

Mesh Shadows

Some consoles still use faked shadows, where we place a single texture on an alpha plane under the object that we want to have shadowed. Although rarely used today, this can be a quick solution when a game lacks processing power to render shadows in code, split up an object for vertex shadows, or the memory to use the texture in the scene (see Figure 15.19).

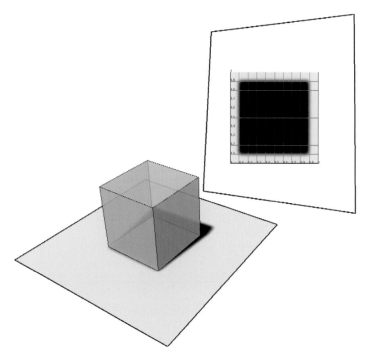

FIGURE 15.19   An Alpha texture masks out the shape on a polygon that simulates the shadow under the object.

IN PRODUCTION

We will create a lightmap for an object. We are going to create a GI-based lightmap to simulate the object being outdoors on a cloudy day. For this tutorial, we will use 3ds max 7 and its Bake to Texture function, although the same technique would be possible in other 3D programs that have similar functionalities.

The object we are going to create a lightmap for needs to have a unique UV set for the lightmaps. The default UV set where the textures are can contain tiling textures or overlaying UVs, which will corrupt the lightmap. Use the scene file for this tutorial Chapter15\3dsMax7\House_Raw.max on the companion CD-ROM.

ON THE CD

Apply an Unwrap UVW modifier to the mesh. Under Channel, make sure you work with an unused map channel; for this object, channel number two works fine (see Figure 15.20).

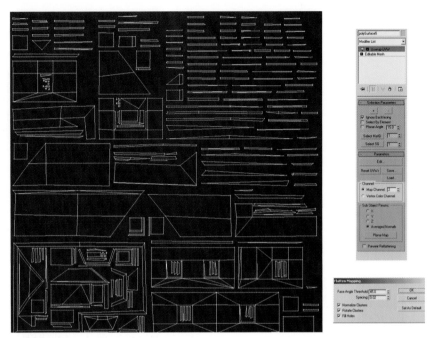

FIGURE 15.20   Left: Unwrap UVW window, Right: Unwrap UVW modifier with the UV channels set to two.

Open the Edit window where you can see the UVs. Now, select Mapping/Flatten Mapping (this is 3ds max Automatic Unwrapping). We want to unwrap the UVs so they cover as much as possible of the available UV layout. Face Angle Threshold determines at what angle the mesh will separate. We can go as low as zero to make sure we use as much of the available space in the UV as possible. The more we split up a model, the greater the risk that the lightmap will leak pixels. Leaking pixels happen when a polygon cuts in between a pixel and uses half of the pixel's light value on an area for which it is not meant. This is common when we are dealing with low-resolution lightmaps.

Face Angle Threshold at 27 and Spacing at 0.01 should do the trick. Close and collapse the modifier list. We now need a light. Create a Skylight under Create/Lights/Standard Lights/.

Place it anywhere in the scene. This light type represents a sky dome and gives us the sufficient quality we need for the lightmaps. Enter the skylight modifier and turn on Cast Shadows under its Render section.

Open Render to Texture under the Rendering Menu/ and set it up as follows (see Figure 15.21):

- Make sure that you Use Existing Channel and number two.
- Add a Lighting map Element under the Output Add button.

- Select Diffuse as Target Map.
- Adopt the lightmap size according to the pixel resolution required for the house. A size of 256 is good for this house.

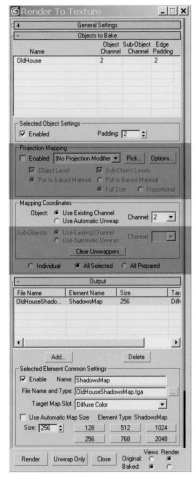

FIGURE 15.21   The setup in Render to Texture. Lightmap render.

Render. When finished, you will see your house with a GI lightmap on it. It has also saved the texture in the specified folder, ready for use within the game (see Figure 15.22).

By rendering a GI lightmap to multiply on our textured objects, we can add depth to our models, and it is a fast and easy way to give more shape to an object.

ON THE CD You can find the final UV scene in the Chapter15\3dsMax7\House_ Final.max folder on the companion CD-ROM.

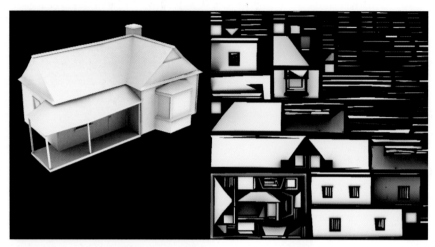

FIGURE 15.22   Final rendering, lightmap house.

SUMMARY

1. Vertices are the smallest part of a model, yet decide how we need to model our objects.
2. Per-vertex lighting needs many vertices to work correctly. If there are no vertices where the light hits the object, the object will remain dark.
3. Vertices can hold light, colors, and alpha values; these multiply together with the texture to add visual variations to the object.
4. We can bake the per-vertex intensity value into the mesh. This is useful for games that do not have light sources in the game.
5. Per-pixel lighting works on the texture pixels. Performance is dependent on the density of the UV ratio.
6. Code and artists can both create shadows, and we are moving toward more code-generated shadows. With more interactive shadows and light, we can change the way we create the art and games.
7. Dynamic objects use code shadows to be able to animate when objects move around in the game.
8. Lightmaps require substantial memory to use on all objects within a world, and is the best way to create smooth shadows baked into the objects.

16

HARDWARE AND GAME ENGINES

Game production is very hardware and software dependent. The technology behind the game and console dictates how we create art for the games. It is important, even for artists, to understand the technical parts within game development to use them to their full capacity.

Many machines are so technically special that it requires a very large set of thought-out workflows when we create art for them. Limitations on memory and processor power create several special cases. It is important for all parts of the system to be as integrated as possible. A computer is no faster than its slowest link. In this chapter, we concentrate on the graphics cards as they develop and add the unique features on which the games industry relies so heavily.

So far, this book has taught you the basic understanding of how to create art for games. Not all features mentioned are available on today's gaming consoles, making it important for you to know when and for what console the different processes should be used. Different graphics cards are capable of different things. For example, what we can do on an Xbox might not be available for us on a PlayStation 2 for performance or memory reasons.

PC TECHNOLOGY

PCs have the latest technology, in both hardware and software. The fourth part of this book relies on these various technologies, which are developed and used on the PC platform today. This makes some of the techniques unavailable or limited on the PlayStation 2 or Xbox.

Pc development and PC games are usually upgradeable by the release of a patch, thereby making the development process different because it is always easier to fine-tune gameplay and add features on a regular basis when everyone has access to updates over the Internet.

A good PC title can sell over a 1 million copies worldwide. PC development suffers from the "upgrading" possibilities. Although this is what drives the games forward, each game that the studio creates has to have new content with more detail. This process takes a long time, because you constantly have to redo the same objects with higher detail, learning new techniques and processes.

Graphics Cards

ATI and NVIDIA are continuing to create unique features in their hardware, where they develop new standards and methods. Many of the things we take for granted today once used software or the CPU to calculate. Today's graphics cards are processing most of the things that you see on the screen and have become extremely powerful.

The PC will most likely keep pushing the envelope and have the highest possible performance within games, as it is also the development platform for most games. Although the PC market share is small compared to consoles, it is where the latest technology, ideas, and the newest rendering technology show up.

We now have the ability to add details to meshes through normal maps, the use of more detailed texture maps, and detailed higher resolution meshes in larger more-content worlds. Not only has the demand of the graphics card's power increased, production has also started with graphics cards using as much as 512 MB of memory.

With the start of the NVIDIA TNT graphics cards, shaders were created. Each major new version of the graphics card extends the shader library functionalities. Older graphics cards, for instance, are still draw-call sensitive. Today's PC graphics cards support, among other things:

- Normal mapping, parallax mapping
- Latest shader techniques
- Per-pixel shader support
- Per-pixel dynamic lighting, soft GI lighting
- Support for soft stencil shadows
- Displacement mapping
- Support for Microsoft Direct Draw (DDS) compressed textures
- Multitexturing up to eight layers in one pass
- 4096 × 4096 textures, together with nonsquare textures

Gaming Consoles

Holding the largest market share, console machines are the platforms that sell the most amounts of games. A blockbuster console game can very well sell over 4 million copies worldwide.

Each game-console life span is a couple of years, a time span where its technology does not change. This lets the development team focus on new content and gives the team time to fine-tune processes. For each game created for a gaming platform, the team learns how to optimize and use the system better to create a more beautiful and better game than the earlier version. By the time the last games are created for an old game console, before being swapped out by the next generation, the console is pushed and used to its very limits. Games created for a game console cannot be patched or upgraded after the game is sold. This stresses the development to discover and correct faults and errors before shipment, making the testing time more important on a console game before it is released.

Gaming consoles are equipped with much less main memory compared to the PC, and although they use streaming processes to read data from CD-ROMs and hard drives to cache the information for larger worlds and faster loading times, they do not have the same advantages or large memories as the PC. New consoles are in development and games have started to be developed—expect release late 2005 to mid 2006. Xbox 2 and PlayStation 3 will support many of the graphical features that the PC is capable of today. With the same technology, they will set a new standard for gaming consoles.

Microsoft Xbox

The Xbox is a slimmed down PC. It contains a 933-MHz Pentium 3 with a Geforce 3+ graphics card. The Xbox holds a total of 64 MB of memory that it shares with the video memory. It has more memory than any other current release gaming console, and can therefore use more texture features. Running Windows CE, it is easy to integrate with a Windows production development.

With its memory and processor capacity, the Xbox supports many of the standard features that games use in today's PC industry, but as a limited scaled-down version:

- Normal mapping
- Dynamic lighting
- Per-pixel shader support
- Stencil shadows
- Draw calls sensitive
- Support for Microsoft Direct Draw (DDS) compressed textures
- Multitexturing up to four layers in one pass

Sony PlayStation 2

As the most popular gaming console, the PlayStation 2 holds over 60% of the market. PlayStation 2 is comparable with the PlayStation game console, and Sony developed its own hardware and tools to develop the games. Sony PlayStation 2 holds a total memory of 16 MB, which makes the workflow and processes unique in many ways, and makes game development for the artist very challenging to make things look good. The PlayStation 2 requires the system to use many small textures, tiled, and reused to achieve the best result. To create variation and lighting, vertex coloring is most commonly used.

PlayStation 2:

- Limited use of texture lightmaps due to limited memory available
- The use of layered texturing and detail maps
- Vertex lighting, and is commonly used with prelighting
- Painting vertex color and variations, mesh shadows
- Subdivision modeling with Tri-stripping for optimal performance
- Limited support for compressed textures; uses TGA—BMP
- Optimal texture sizes 64 × 64 to 128 × 128
- Multitexturing up to four layers in one pass

The PlayStation 2 does not support shaders, but allows programmers to write the material-specific features directly to the hardware to get high-speed materials, lighting, and effects.

Tomorrow's game consoles have today's PC graphics and power.

GAME EXPERIENCE

If you are not working in the industry and have an engine available to test your object that you have created, it is hard to learn all the specific functions and possibilities within game development. Although not required to create great art, it is important that you know as much as possible about the systems for which you create art. Luckily, there are several ways to learn with available engines and MOD tools, for the artists who thirst for playing with their objects inside a game.

License Engines

When studios create a game, not all develop their own in-house engine. Several game engines are available for licensing with full support and work processes worked out.

One of the largest supported engines available is Criterion Software® RenderWare suite. It supports all current platforms—PlayStation® 2, Xbox™, Nintendo® Gamecube™ and PC—together with tomorrow's Next-Gen gaming consoles. It also has a version that supports mobile consoles. RenderWare integrates a powerful physics, AI, audio, and graphics engine for developers to use when creating games. Many developers, after creating their game, offer their engine to be used to create your own game.

MOD

Many of today's PC games come with a MOD functionality, meaning that you can create your own game of the engine. They give you a perfect way to learn more about how you can implement the functionalities in this book. Each engine supports various techniques and has its own processes mentioned in this book. On the PC, several engines are using very similar methods to achieve the features inside the game. Therefore, if you can learn one very well, you will have a good understanding of how to move on and use another. Some of the games that offer good MOD editors and SDKs are id software with Doom 3, Valve's Half Life 2, Digital Extreme with Unreal 2, and Battlefield 2 with Mod Tools.

SUMMARY

1. To create the most efficient graphics for computer games, you need to understand the machine and the game engine.
2. Today's games require huge amounts of memory and processor power to achieve the latest standard quality of content and detail.
3. The PC platform sets the standard and develops the technologies, which later integrate into the game console.
4. Xbox is a scaled-down PC with much similar functionality.
5. The PlayStation 2's low memory dictates its techniques and use of textures and polygons; vertex coloring is most common on this machine.
6. The industry has many engines that developers can license for developing a game, and there are several in-house engines created to create unique games. One of the largest engines that support the most platforms is RenderWare.
7. MODs can help you test your object within a game and learn more about the import/export process within game development. It's also a good start to get more used to games and a way into the industry.

ADVANCED GAME ART PRODUCTION

As game content becomes more detailed, the workflows and techniques to create it tend to grow in complexity. It starts to take longer for each asset we add to the game, and requires artists to understand and be capable of using all the techniques and work processes to their maximum. With new gaming consoles coming and always being worked on, the entire industry is moving toward a new generation of quality and tool chains in development. New tools, new techniques—everything needs to upgraded.

Part IV introduces you to some complex workflows of new technology that work within the games industry; techniques used to create art that will become the standard of tomorrow's gaming platforms.

After learning Part IV and finishing the book, consider yourself a game artist. If you fully understand each part of this book, its technical side and the complex workflows, you are ready to produce the next AAA game in the industry.

IN PRODUCTION: MULTITEXTURING

As game techniques become more complex, we combine more of the keystones that the game techniques are built on that we learned in earlier parts of the book. In Chapters 8, "In Production: Model UV," and 9, "Texture Creation," we walked through a UV layout and texture-mapping tutorial where you learned how to texture an object with a single texture and fixed pixel ratio using diffuse and color maps. The object you created used a single UV set for all types of textures, color, specular, and alpha. While texturing using a single UV layout gives you the ability to create objects that look exactly the way you want them to, it also leaves something to be desired in memory expense and variation. When we create a texture as we did in Chapter 9, that contains both colors and structure (e.g., dirt, smudge, details), it becomes unique to the specific object. This is also true for a dirty brown brick wall as shown in Figure 17.1 that will look the same on all walls independent of their shape. If we would like to have a similar brick elsewhere with another color, or with other types of dirt, we need to create a new texture for these specific features—something that quickly becomes a memory issue.

FIGURE 17.1 A diffuse brick wall.

As the first of the more advanced chapters, we will combine the basic steps learned earlier in the book and learn how to use a more advanced color texture-mapping technique. The process will let you apply textures in layers with different blending modes, a method called *multitexturing*. You are able to separate the color texture into its various content color, detail, smudge, and dirt. Therefore, instead of having a single texture on an object, the system gives you millions of combinations for you to arrange the various textures together. To make sure we get the most out of each texture, we will combine the multitexturing layers with unique UV sets, one for each texture. Multitexturing is not a new process, and games have used similar techniques to add dirt and detail layers on their objects. However, we have separated the color from the specular and its light information, which separates the very foundation within the texture itself. Being the next step, as a technique it can become an important part of how we create textures in the future. Let's go through the different parts and learn about the process.

MULTIPLE TEXTURES

When using a multilayer texturing technique, our main artistic goal is to achieve as much variation as possible for the objects. The result of the blending gives us a system in which we have both the old diffuse and color maps mixed with the new blended possibilities. By having several dirt maps, detail, and color variations within an object, you can mix the texture sizes and positions and freely arrange the strength of the different parts to your liking. In contrast to a single texture system as in Figure 17.1, using a multitexture system to create the same wall, we would use the following four types of blending:

- Base texture
- Multiply blending one
- Multiply blending two
- Base texture/Alpha mask

These four textures (see Figure 17.2) combine a single texture with their stated blending modes.

To easier understand the process, we can rename the different blending modes to more proper names, according to what they will contain within the texture.

Base Texture—Color Map

The color map represents the very base colors of the material. In Figure 17.2, it shows as the color orange. To achieve a good result of a base

FIGURE 17.2   A multitexture layered brick wall split into four textures' base, multiply texture one, two, and one alpha.

color, we should keep the color map as neutral as possible, without shadows, light areas, or sharp details. We can, however, add color variations that help break the single color. The color map is the bottom layer and has no blending mode applied to it.

First Multiply Blending—Detail Map with Specular Map

The detail map acts like the original color map. In Figure 17.2, it contains the structure of the brick material. By using multiply with the detail map on top of the color map, we add structure to the texture. Keep the detail map clean from scratches, dirt, and tileable information; this way, it can easily become a very usable texture throughout the game. If we intend to use normal maps to the object, this is the part we base it on content wise. It is therefore important that the detail map does not contain any form of shadows or highlights, merely the information of the structure. As the layer representing the structure, it also contains the specular maps in its alpha channel.

Second Multiply Blending—Dirt Map

A dirt map adds the ability to add dirt at various places on the object. Represented as the scratches and bumps in Figure 17.2, it creates further variations and interesting details to the texture by being multiplied on top of the detail map.

Alpha Texture—Decal Map with Transparency

The decal map is a second color map, with the control of a masking alpha map you can control what, where, and how much of the texture should overlay on the underlying textures.

Using the decal map, you can add decals, cracks, and break up the original texture's tiling features.

Using the process of these four textures, we can build up an index of textures that we can use for the entire level. As we separate the texture-specific features, we are able to reuse them for more objects within each scene to create variations. When creating the first set of textures, we need to make sure they contain what can be useful later, or leave empty space in the texture for later use.

MULTIPLE UVS

By having a system where we can separate color into its various parts, the multitexturing system allows us to create a lot of variation within our textures. By adding multiple UV sets to the object, we can make the process even more useful. When setting up the different textures, it is important to know how you can mix them according to their size to achieve the best result.

The color map can be kept at an unspecified pixel ratio due to its clean and generic colors. Independent of resolution, the result will give further dynamic structure to the objects. It is important, however, that the map does not create seams of color between the UV borders.

As we multiply the detail map, we need to create this texture to the aspects required in the game, together with its correct pixel ratio. The dirt and decal layers UV can be of any resolution, as they represent the dirt and masked details of the objects. For example, a small poster close to the ground level on a building would use a larger area of the texture for higher resolution, while a high-up and faraway poster would use a less covered area, for lower resolution.

SETTING UP MULTITEXTURING BLEND IN 3D

To illustrate the technique better and make it possible for you to work with this process, we will set up a multiply blending system within Maya before doing the main tutorial for this chapter. The process is mainly a technique, so any 3D program with the supported functionalities should work. What you need to do is create a new UV set for each texture we want to blend. Then, connect the UV set to the right texture and blending method. To illustrate this shader, we will use Maya's Layered texture (see Figure 17.3).

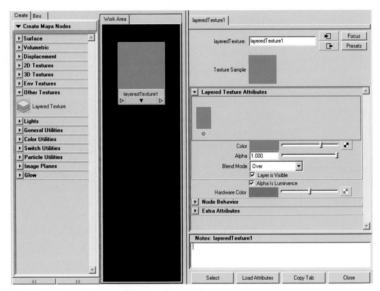

FIGURE 17.3   Maya's multilayered texturing tool.

Layered Texture Nodes and Textures

First, we need an object. Create a polygon cube. Open the Hypershade window and show the graph for the default Lambert shader in the "work area." Under Maya's Create Maya Nodes, open the 2D Textures tab and add two File nodes into the work area. Continue by opening the Other Textures tab and add a Layered Texture Node into the work area. These three nodes are the basics for what we need for the multiply texture blending (see Figure 17.4),

Double-click on the Layered Texture node. This brings up its attribute editor, and you will see a green rectangle as shown in Figure 17.3. Middle mouse click and drag in the texture file node from the work area next to the green rectangle. This adds them as new textures as layers, where each rectangle represents a texture connection and a layer; the rectangle furthest to the right represents the bottom layer.

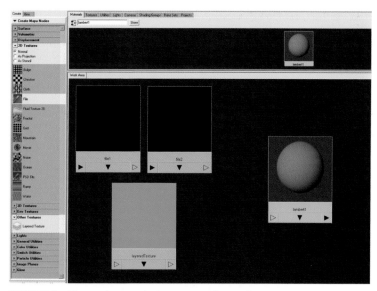

FIGURE 17.4   The nodes needed to create a layered texture.

Drag both the created file nodes into the layered texture window with the middle mouse button; two new rectangles will appear. Remove the green default layer by clicking on the small cross under the rectangle. Arrange the new texture nodes so the color file is located as the base layer, furthest to the right. Now, select the icon furthest to the left, which is going to be our detail texture, and change the blend mode to multiply as shown in Figure 17.5.

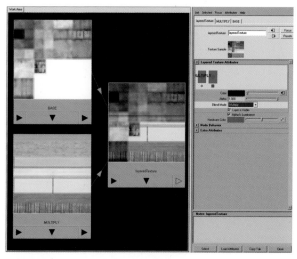

FIGURE 17.5   The textures added and layered with multiply.

Now all we have to do is connect this layered texture node to the color channel of the Lambert shader by holding Ctrl and middle mouse dragging the layered texture node into the Lambert shader through the Hypershade window.

Multiple Mesh UV Sets

Each object we create within a 3D scene comes with a default UV, and so does the cube we created. An object can, however, have several UV sets, which we can connect to the different textures in a layered texture. For this shader example, we are going to set up two UV sets, one for the base layer and one for the multiply. When working with the UV Texture Editor, you can switch between the active UV sets by selecting them under Image/UV Sets. We can create new UV sets by duplicating former sets and projecting polygons or empty UV sets. As we need to have one UV set for each texture assigned as a layer, create a new UV set by automatic projecting our cube, and enter a new name for the UV set. We now have two UV sets in the UV Texture Editor under Image/UV Sets as shown in Figure 17.6. Selecting one of them will swap the active set to the chosen one and tell Maya to work with only this set when cutting, moving, sewing, and projecting new UVs.

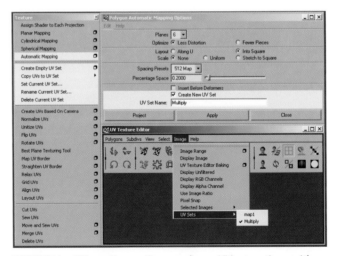

FIGURE 17.6   UV creation options, and new UV set options with Automatic Mapping.

Connect UV Sets to the Layers

We now have both the blending layers with the textures and two UV sets created. We need to connect them together and decide what UV to use for each layer. Maya lets you do this through the Relationship Editor. Select your object and open Windows/Relationships Editors/UV Linking/UV-centric. This brings up a window with two columns; the left column represents your layered textures, and the right represents the UV sets as shown in Figure 17.7.

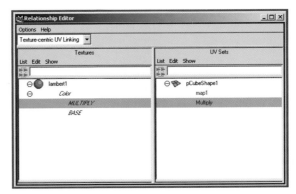

FIGURE 17.7   Connect the different layered textures to the created UV sets.

Selecting either Multiply or Base in the left column will highlight the map UV set in the right column because it is the default UV set. What we want is to connect the Multiply blending layer to the UV set we named Multiply. Left-click to select the texture Multiply in the left column, and then select the UV set Multiply in the right column.

This is the basic construction of a multilayered texture shader. They might look or work differently in a game environment depending on support, functionality, and implementation. Nevertheless, this setup should give you a good understanding and a head start on how things work.

IN PRODUCTION

We now know how to set up a multitexturing node, with multiply connected to a unique UV set for each texture. We are now ready to create a game object with these features.

This time, you are not building the model—the book provides one for you. However, the object needs a shader and UV sets with the different textures created for it. As done in Chapters 8 and 9, we will use Maya and Photoshop for this tutorial, but you should be able to use any other 3D or 2D program with similar functionalities.

ON THE CD

On the companion CD-ROM, open the file under Chapter17\Maya6\ OldHouse_Raw.mb.

Arranging Texturing

Before we start creating any textures, we need to look at the object we are mapping to decide how we want it to look (see Figure 17.8). This also determines what types of sizes and shapes we need for our textures.

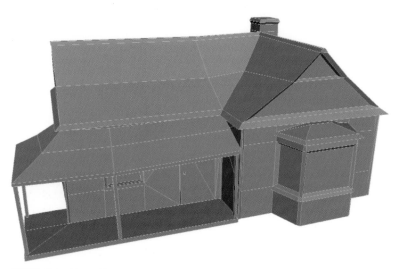

FIGURE 17.8   The object we are mapping.

Let's texture the house to look old, abandoned, and dirty. You can see that the house has sections modeled into the mesh. This will make it easier for us to map a tiling texture around it.

Visually, let's make the house look like a wooden cabin with gray-brown colors. The roof and walls are built with wood planks, the porch roof is made of metal, and the porch floor is older, worn and used wooden material. Finally, we need to have some specific textures for the windows for depth.

After deciding how we want the building to look, we need to calculate how large we want the textures to be. Remember that the textures we use with multitexturing act like indexes for more than one object. To save performance and memory, the game should use the same textures for all other objects within the same level. Let's start defining and creating each texture depending on what we need.

Color

Start by creating the index color map for the level. Because the color map contains no vital information other than the colors, you can use any UV pixel ratio when you map the objects. Depending on the size and capability of the graphics card, create it as large as the game system allows. The color information in our index texture will consist of various sizes due to the unspecified pixel ratio that we can use. Keeping the structure organized will allow us to fit more colors on the texture.

The texture should act like an index for the level, and the color within it as a palette. We want to have a good spectrum of colors and variations within the texture so we do not have to create another color map for the same level. Let's decide that the color texture should be a 1024 × 512. To make the texture as useful as possible, we should create blocks within the texture; we can give a higher resolution to some blocks that are used to a greater extent. Working in the 2D program, add smaller squares as blocks to the texture together with variation and dirt within the color as you did in Chapter 9. Adding dirt and variation at this stage will allow us to create more interesting texturing without using the dirt layer. As with a color map for a single texture/UV set, it is important that the texture does not have shadows or depth at this point. See the final color index texture in Figure 17.9.

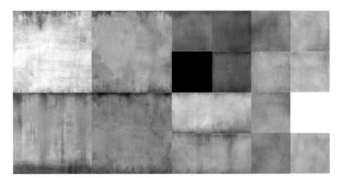

FIGURE 17.9   A color map, used as the index texture.

First Multiply—Detail

Although each multiply can contain various types of content, our first multiply will have the very simplest details, the very structure of the material. This texture will give the object its unique look depending on the material. A wooden barrel, a concrete block, an old rusty metallic barrel, or a window—it is all decided by this texture.

Because this layer is what gives the object its main structure, it needs to represent the correct size of the object. The information in the texture needs to have a pixel ratio that is equal to the rest of the objects within the game. As we learned earlier in the book, if the pixel ratio is 1 pixel/centimeter and a wall is 2.5 meters, it needs an area of 250 pixels in the texture. Since the pixel resolution within the texture needs to be kept high to maintain the detail, we will tile this texture, making the UVs appear outside the 0 to 1 coordinates. Tiling a texture for a building, we create it narrow but high. A $1024 \times 256 \times 1024$ will work fine, and represents $10.24m \times 2.56m$ pixels, with a current pixel resolution of 1 pixel/cm.

Collect photos and images of the different pieces that fit with the house and the level of the game. The detail map will also work as an index texture for the entire level, so it should contain structures that would be good for maximum reusability; for example, bricks, wood, concrete, canvas, and stucco as shown in Figure 17.10.

FIGURE 17.10   A detail map, the structure within the object materials.

As the detail map will multiply on top of the clean color map, we want to keep the details in the texture as sharp as possible. To use the basic structure of the system's full potential, the detail map should only contain grayscales for maximum reusability, so the color map decides the color of the wood or stones. The detail texture can contain colors as well, which lets us further change the variation of the object's structure with a higher resolution as shown in Figure 17.11.

Multiply works by adding the darkness and colors over the underlying layer. If you have a white color in the detail texture, it will not add anything. This way, we can use white to mask out transparent objects and dirt. The same works the other way around. If you have a completely white area on the object mapped with the color map, the detail map will become the dominant part and show the exact drawn texture. This is how we will map our single texture/one UV set texture to the objects. Creating the texture map with the correct pixel resolution directly within the detail map will require more total memory; as we will lose the benefits from using the color blending, we will need more textures in each level. We are going to use a part of the detail texture to add a window to map on our building (see Figure 17.12).

FIGURE 17.11   First multiply map can withhold colors to tweak the outcome of color map.

FIGURE 17.12   A detail index texture with a color detail part.

Second Multiply—Dirt

We will use the second multiply layer to add dirt to the objects. This layer creates the real variation possibilities for the artists. Every time we create objects in 3D, we need to give them character by adding dirt and variation to make them unique. Having the dirt map as a separate layer lets you overlay this on top of what you already have textured, in any size due to its own UV set. The result is that you can, with a single texture, map and dirty up an entire city with various unique objects.

We work with the dirt layer as if it is an index texture as well, create shapes, and add dirt and structures that easily can be reused in several places. Keep the dirt generic and blending into each other as shown in Figure 17.13. The texture can be both a tiling texture and a normal texture. When constructing tiling buildings, we want the dirt texture to be able to tile as well. Therefore, let's use the same size as the detail map uses, a 256 × 1024 format.

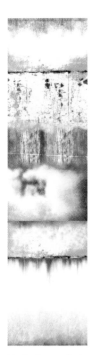

FIGURE 17.13   Variations of dirt and smudge.

 As with the detail map, the dirt map is layered as a multiply, making the object darker at places, just as dirt does. Giving the dirt a bit of color can add a lot of structure and variation to the objects.

Decals, Alpha

The decal texture is a base texture where we use the alpha channel to determine what is masked. This way, we can replace entire sections of a tiling wall with cracks to give it further structure. Because it uses the alpha to overlay its content on top of the other textures, the former map's content will disappear if the alpha is completely white. To maintain the visual aspect over the masked-out parts of the decal map, we should try to keep the same pixel ratio on this texture as we do on the detail map. For an easy transition from the detail map, we can create this texture with the same size for this tutorial, 256×1024 pixels. Figure 17.14 shows the decal map, where we have added some broken planks, a carpet, and some posters and plates.

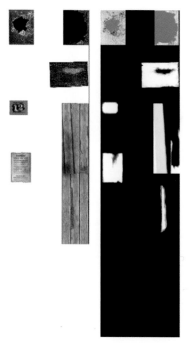

FIGURE 17.14   A decal map, text, and other alphas.

In this example, when we texture our house we will add a porch carpet, signs and posters on the wall, and variations to the broken windows, but leave parts of the texture white for further possibilities.

Layout UVs

We have now created the different index colors that we need for our scene and the object that we are about to map. We need to set up the multitexturing shader as mentioned earlier. Create a layered texture and add all four textures in the correct order. Now we are going to create the UV set for each layer, together with mapping the object correctly. Let's start with the Color UV set.

Color

As decided earlier, let's make the main part of the house gray-brown as a wooden ground color. The porch and supports around the house should be brown, and the roof a more grayish green. Let's use the default UV set for the color base, and create an automatic projection to lay out the UV coordinates (see Figure 17.15).

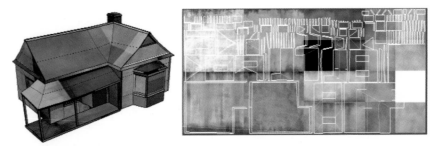

FIGURE 17.15   A color map with various colors together with the UV Automatic wrapped house.

Using Automatic unwrapping gives us a fast layout of the representative color that we want to have as the base. This is something that we can do freely without restricted pixel ratios and resolutions. We need to make sure that the UV border blends and matches in between the faces with no texture seams. Let's start by arranging the colors for the polygons that we want to represent the old and dirty white paint.

Select all the polygons from the sides and arrange them into the texture on the white color. Take some time arranging them so the structured dirt and color differences we created end up in an interesting and logical way over the object. After the white base is laid out, we continue with the other pieces of the house—darker window planks, supports, porch, and the doorknob. Go over the object to make sure everything has the color we want it to have.

Since we are going to use the detail texture to overlay the specific window texture, we need to arrange the windows' UVs inside the part of the color map that we created white. You can see the final image in Figure 17.16.

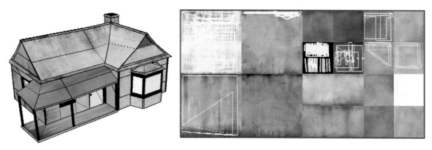

FIGURE 17.16   The entire house mapped with palette colors.

First Multiply—Detail

When adding the detail texture, the layer needs a new UV set, which we will create by doing a new Automatic unwrapping in a new UV set. Name the new UV set "Detail." We also need to connect the new UV set to the correct texture inside the relationship editor. After this is done, we should be able to see the multiply texture on top of the base color texture.

Make sure you are in the correct UV set when you continue working.

The detail texture is created to have a fixed pixel ratio. To make sure we get the pixels square, we use a test map to verify the ratio and resolution. Since the house is modeled in sections, we made the texture to tile from side to side, with a width of 256 pixels. To make all pieces tile horizontally, we need to sew the pieces together in this axis so they tile outside the 0 to 1 coordinates of the UV set as shown in Figure 17.17.

Continue to lay out all the various pieces and sew the different pieces together until the entire object is tiling with the correct pixel resolution tiling the UVs outside the 0 to 1 coordinates as shown in Figure 17.18.

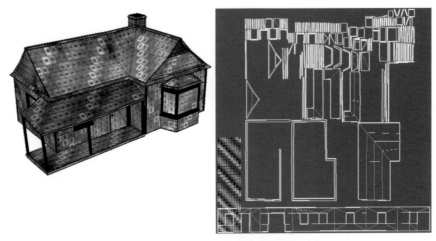

FIGURE 17.17   Laying out a tiling map with a detail test map.

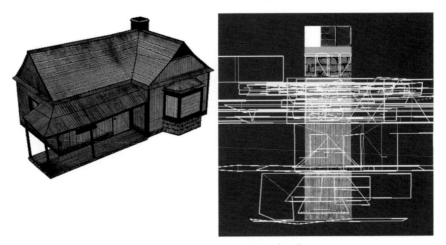

FIGURE 17.18   The completed UV layout with a correct detail texture.

To make the windows look more natural with painted reflections, we need to use a specific texture. Select the polygons that represent the windows and arrange them so they cover this part of the detail texture as shown in Figure 17.19.

After you create a new UV set with any of the projection modes, make sure you reset it to default for continuous projections.

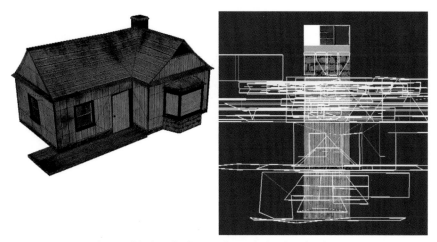

FIGURE 17.19   Windows added to the house through the detail index texture.

Second Multiply—Dirt

Looking at Figure 17.19, we can see that we already added some dirt and color variations to the house. We will break it up even further with another layer. The structure is already set within the detail map, so we are not limited by the resolution of the texture. As long as the dirt does not create seams between the UV borders, we are free to arrange the UVs to our liking.

To be able to do this, the dirt map needs a UV set of its own. We will create this by copying the first multiply layer. This way, we save a lot of time arranging the UVs, as the detail UV set already lines up as tiling.

With the detail map selected in the UV Texture Editor, select the Custom Box for the Copy into New UV Set under Edit polygons/Texture/ Copy UVs to UV set/. Here you will be able to enter the new name for the UV set. Name it "Dirt." Connect the UV set to the dirt texture in the relationship editor. Figure 17.20 shows the dirt map when applied with the detail UV map; it does not line up correctly.

When we set up the shader connection, we need to tweak the arrangement of the UVs on this UV set after we have copied it. Enter the UV Texture Editor, make sure you are in the dirt UV set, and spend some time arranging the dirt UVs to the positions where you want the dirt to be as shown in Figure 17.21.

Now we have a house textured with multitexturing and three different UV sets. As you can see, there are various options for how you combine the different textures together to get different results.

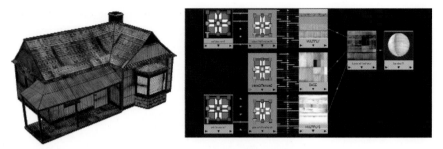

FIGURE 17.20 Dirt texture with copied UV set, needs tweaking.

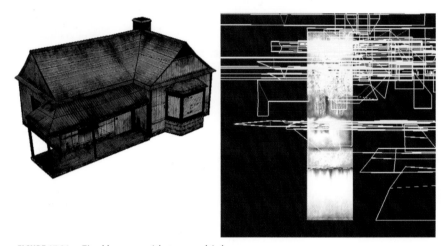

FIGURE 17.21 Final houses with two multiply.

Decals

As a final touch, we will add the alpha texture-blending mode as well. This requires a bit of a special setup, so we will go back to the shader to connect this one. Open the Hypershade and add another File node. Load the decal that has the included alpha in a 32-bit file. Drag this one in and place it as the top layer in the layered texture window. This connects the decal map to the default UV set, making the object appear as the decal map. We need to create a new UV set, and since we are going to use the decal map on limited areas for this mesh, we can start with an empty UV set and later project the polygons we would like it to affect. When we have the new UV set, we connect it to the decal texture in the Relationship Editor.

Using the UV Texture Editor, we can now copy UVs from specific polygons by choosing the UV set from which we want to copy. Select the face, change back to the Decal UV set, and paste. Alternatively, we can planar project or Automatic unwrap the specific polygons that we want to add the decal map to. Drag and arrange the new UVs so they get the position and color that you want them to have by using the decal map as shown in Figure 17.22.

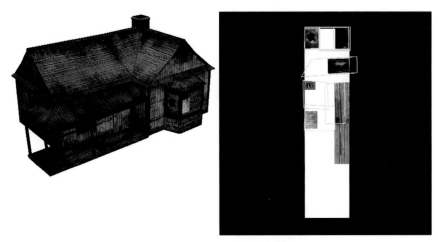

FIGURE 17.22   The final house with added decal and cracks.

On the house, we have added a carpet on the porch, broken windows, street number, signs, and a broken wooden plank in the door. Let's now look at the final house from several angles to see what our creation looks like in Figure 17.23.

FIGURE 17.23   The final house with all layers.

SUMMARY

In this chapter, you learned a rather complex construction and how a future process can combine various textures together in layers using multitexturing. The technique combines several textures into the same rendering call, together with using larger index textures throughout the level, which makes this technique very cost effective in both memory and performance. You further used the UV layout to set up a tiling texture on the tiling-prepared house, and learned how to set up and use several UV sets on an object. Let's review some points as a small reminder:

1. Multitexturing gives you the opportunity to separate each part of the color map into different layers, as color, detail, and dirt.
2. Using multitexturing, we can use fewer textures in the level as indexes, and map all objects with the same content.
3. By using multiply blending mode, the colors become darker with each layer. It is not possible to make something brighter.
4. You can use more than a single UV set per object.
5. You have the separation and freedom to UV map with different resolutions.
6. Color texture for this process has no texture ratio limitations.
7. Use details and dirt layers with tiling to maintain the highest possible resolution.
8. Decals uses alpha to overlay layers, and can remove former information in the layers.

18

HIGH-RESOLUTION MODELING

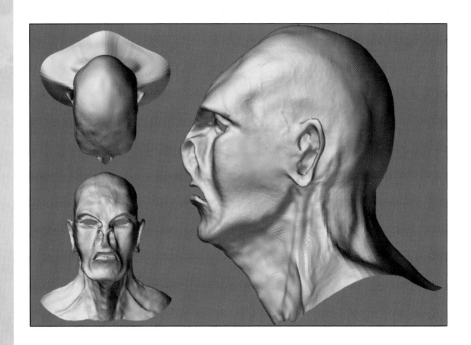

We are entering a new generation of gaming consoles, where objects contain considerably more details than they ever have. Added details look good, of course, and the consumer demands it, so the content becomes more complex for each new release of games. While the projects still have the same production length, adding detail to all assets multiplies the creation time of the entire project, which puts a lot of pressure on the techniques and procedures that we use to create our assets.

We are not yet able to use objects as heavy as a million-polygon animated character within a game, so we still use the low-polygon modeling techniques you learned in Part II in this book. The future will require us to change the workflow in many ways, for the objects created today in low-polygon will have to be in high-polygon resolution tomorrow.

To our advantage, there are existing tools accessible to the industry for these specific tasks that help us create these new assets within production time. Pixologic ZBrush and Nevercenters Silo have introduced the industry to techniques such as extracting a low-resolution mesh from a high-resolution mesh by artistically painting or constructing a cage around the higher resolution mesh.

This way, instead of creating the low-resolution mesh first, the artist would be able to concentrate on the visual quality of a high-polygon mesh that he can later use to extract a low-resolution mesh. Individual people have already tested this technique, but when entire teams need to learn new methods, it takes a long time to change workflows. With time, these techniques can become a standard in the future, and change the way we create game models.

Most 3D programs on the market have streamlined the workflow of how we create high-resolution meshes with the implementation of the techniques, edge modeling, smoothing, and SubD, something that will become crucial for us to know to be able to maintain production speed. Let's explain these techniques in more detail:

EDGE MODELING

Contrary to box modeling where you work with the object's faces to extrude, split, and scale to shape the model, the edge-modeling technique uses edges to move, scale, add, and shape the object by selecting edges as joining loops or rings, a workflow that has similarities working with nurbs, isoparms, and hulls (see Figure 18.1).

To work as seamlessly as possible with the edge-modeling technique, it is important that you keep the model in face (Quadrants) mode, which will make all edges loop automatically into each other. If a mesh has any Tri-gon or N-gon polygons, it can stop the loop selection or try to find the correct way back to the first selected edge.

FIGURE 18.1   3ds max edge
polygon mode—Editable Poly.

For selection, edit, and adding of edges, the technique has simple commands that speed up workflow operations. By selecting a single edge and using "loop" selection, it continues to select edges until it returns to the original selected edge (see Figure 18.2).

To split a face with a crossing edge, we can select two parallel edges and the command "connect." See Figure 18.3 where we have done this on the full loop selection.

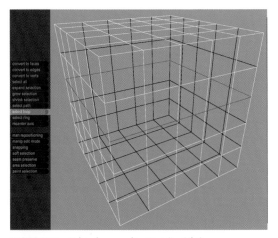

FIGURE 18.2   Edge loop selection (in Silo).

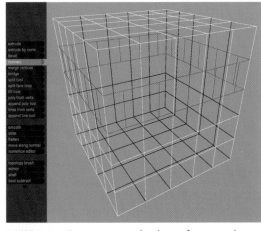

FIGURE 18.3   Connect two edge loops for new edges.

Edge modeling can also do "ring" selection. Instead of selecting the looping edges, it selects the parallel edges around the object until it returns to the first selected edge (see Figure 18.4).

To input a new edge that spans around the object, we can now "connect" these selected edge rings as shown in Figure 18.5.

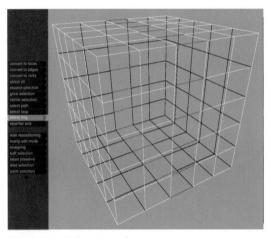

FIGURE 18.4   Edge ring selection.

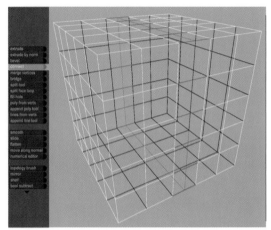

FIGURE 18.5   Connect ring for span of edges.

Using the edge-modeling technique, you are able to add a very high amount of polygons to the model, while easily being able to select and edit specific parts. For an example, see Figure 18.6, where the modeler uses edge modeling to maintain the structure and flow of the complexity.

Edge modeling can also help you get the best out of organic modeling, especially when it comes to mesh deformation. You can use edge modeling to place the edges so their flow represents muscles on an organic creature. When skinning and boning the object later, vertices and faces will react more naturally to the deformations.

Due to the structured way we model with edge modeling, we can combine the technique with smoothing. Smoothing subdivides the entire mesh globally for finer details and gives you control over divisions and level hardness. We can also use the SubD technique on the model, which gives us even finer details. Let's look at SubD next.

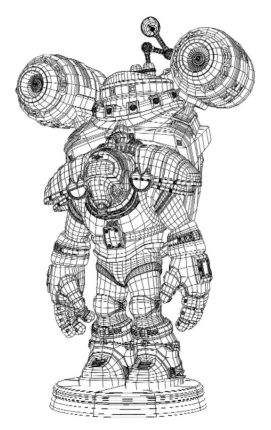

FIGURE 18.6   Character build with edge-modeling technique. ©2004 Ryan Love. Reprinted with permission.

SubD

SubD is a smoothing calculation technique that works in levels of detail. SubD also prefers the polygons to be of face (quadrant) mode. The lowest level gets its structure from the original polygon shape, working as a surrounding cage. Altering or adding polygons to the original mesh (the cage) changes the first level in the SubD model and adds additional shape to the SubD object as shown in Figure 18.7.

SubD and nurbs are based on a scalable resolution modeling technique, where you can select the level of detail in which you want to display or render the model. This means that SubD never subdivides the actual mesh with polygons to make the object smoother, like the similar techniques smoothing, mesh smooth, or subdividing (see Figure 18.8).

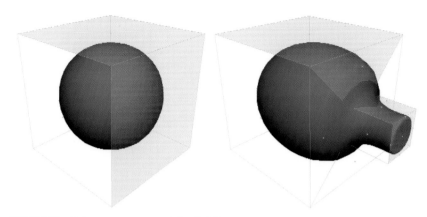

FIGURE 18.7 Polygon cage around the SubD.

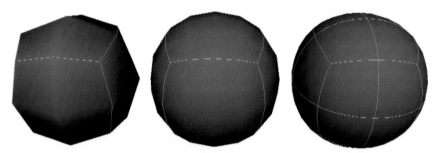

FIGURE 18.8 Scalable resolution, the same ball but with three different quality levels.

A SubD gets its form from a polygon object that determines the first level shape of the object.

You can then add divisions into the SubD object and create further details independent of the shape of the original polygonal object. With SubD you can add localized details into the mesh, by adding more vertices at selected areas.

Figure 18.9 shows this example, where we can see levels 1 to 4. Level 4 has altered and added geometry at specific areas, but the surrounding areas stay in the former SubD divisions.

Altering the courser subdivisions will keep the information of the finer detailed levels and affect them when changing the course shape.

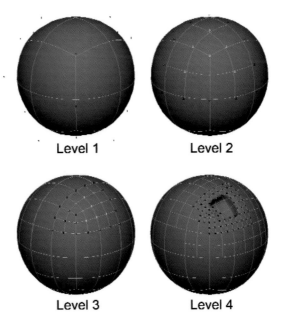

Level 1   Level 2

Level 3   Level 4

FIGURE 18.9   Different levels of detail.

There was thought that SubD (Sub Division modeling) should become the future of game meshes, as the system is very interactive and scalable. It would allow us to se-lect the quality depending on the hardware's performance. We will have to see if it happens in the future. Many interesting things happen with this technique as com-puters get faster and faster, and many programs are basing their new modeling techniques on similar functionalities.

THE NEXT STEP, PAINT IN 3D

The first 3D programs were command-line products, where we entered the positions and formulas to create objects that we could render. After this, we were pushing vertices within 3D space for years until recently when we were able to start painting our meshes fast and interactively. ZBrush, a program that is unique with its speed and interactive work-flow, has become an advanced 3D Photoshop and a key to creating life-like organic high-resolution models. ZBrush allows you to sculpt the 3D object by scale, push, pull, and move the shape with an adjustable brush size and falloff—all without being troubled with any of the traditional modeling techniques such as vertices, edges, and polygons. This has opened up a completely new scene of modelers.

ZBrush works similar to the SubD technique, where you can add details in various levels of detail. The technique allows you to freely traverse between the levels to add or refine the shape and detail of the model.

MODELING HI-RES FOR GAMES

We are still unable to use very high-polygon models within games but we can use the higher resolution to transfer the information from the detailed mesh into a texture as a normal map (see Chapter 19, "Normal Mapping"). After we transfer this information, there is no need for the high-resolution mesh, so from a production standpoint, it can seem like we spend many hours creating unused assets. From a quality standpoint, it gives us the ability to add extremely high polygon amounts onto our low-resolution meshes. Let's go over a workflow to see how we would create such a high-resolution object.

IN PRODUCTION

We are going to go over the procedure of creating a high-resolution mesh for our game. We will use it for the next chapter, where we will render normal maps and add shaders for it.

The process will simulate the process of creating a mesh for this purpose within game development. First, we will model a base mesh by using the edge-modeling technique; this mesh will be the object that the game will use. Importing this mesh in ZBrush as the second part of the tutorial, we will create the high-resolution mesh that we use to generate our normal map. Due to ZBrush's unique way of handling polygon information, you require this program for this tutorial. Pixologic offers the community a demo for download at their homepage at *www.zbrush.com*.

When this tutorial is completed, we need:

- One low-resolution model with the correct UV coordinates
- One high-resolution model

In theory, it does not matter if the high-resolution mesh has a UV set or not. You can either start by making the shape for the head in ZBrush, or choose to create your main shape within a 3D program and just use ZBrush for adding details.

Edge Modeling

First, you will need an idea of how the final mesh should look, following normal procedures of references and building an object.

For a game, we would want a whole creature to have normal mapping, but for this tutorial, we will concentrate on the head. Several people like to have different workflows for this purpose:

- Find your shape in ZBrush and build a low-polygon mesh around the high-polygon model, either in a normal 3D program or with the new programs discussed earlier in this chapter.
- Model a low-polygon mesh in your 3D program. Finish it with correct UVs, measurements, and proportions.

We find that the second process still works better. The faster we can finalize the low-polygon model within a game production, the quicker we can pass it to the animators and the texture artists for skinning, animating, and texturing. This way, we can finish several tasks while the modeler finishes the high-resolution mesh.

Many times, the actual shape of the character is limited so you would not want the character vertices to change too much from the point you enter ZBrush.

As always, when building the basic shape in game production it is important to concentrate on where you place the polygons for the best animation and detail in the game. Use your low-polygon knowledge together with edge modeling and muscle flow in this model to practice. In this case, the front of the character's face is the most important part, as the head will support facial animation. As we start to build the head that we want to use, we create the edges so they mimic the flow around the muscles by using quads. Figure 18.10 shown our final mesh with the loops representing the muscles and shapes that surround the eyes and mouth.

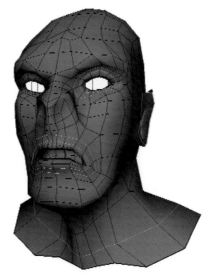

FIGURE 18.10   Edge looping with muscle flow on the creature's head.

We will also want to create a final UV layout for our object. Modeling a high-resolution mesh can take a long time, even if ZBrush is used, and we do not want people to sit and wait while you finalize the mesh. For the final UV, see Figure 18.11.

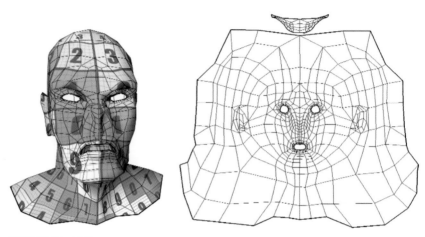

FIGURE 18.11 UV layout.

After you are finished with the mesh, let's export it, so we can import it into ZBrush. It is very important when importing your mesh that you have finalized it but not triangulated it. The quality you can expect from ZBrush is dependent on how you import your object. The program works best when objects are imported as Quads. Although ZBrush will allow you to import objects with N-gons (polygons with more than four vertices) and Tri-gons, the result can become distorted when you are subdividing and sculpting your model.

Export the mesh from your 3D program to an .OBJ with UVs. We have included the final head mesh as Creature_Head_raw on the companion CD-ROM under Chapter18\Maya6 or Chapter18\3dsMax7_OBJ.

ON THE CD

High-Polygon Modeling in ZBrush

ON THE CD

Import the file Chapter18\Exported_Final\CreatureHead_Final_Low.OBJ on the companion CD-ROM as an .Obj through the Tool/Import in ZBrush.

Select your mesh in the view. Move out in the working canvas view and click mouse button/hold to place the object on the canvas. While holding, move the mouse; this will determine its size. If you now click again, you will place another mesh into the canvas, something you do not want to do, since you can only work on one at a time. You want to make this object editable so you need to enter its edit mode (key shortcut T) to be able to start manipulating the mesh (see Figure 18.12).

FIGURE 18.12   Edit mode.

 Save the model in your 3D program, and rotate the objects so the front faces the minus Z-axis. This will make the object face toward you when importing it into ZBrush.

We now have the model in edit mode and are ready to start editing. However, it is important that we are able to return to the original mesh, should you want to re-export the original mesh for some reason later. One way to do it is to save a morph target under Tools/Morph Target/ Store MT (see Figure 18.13).

FIGURE 18.13   Store the morph target so you can export the main mesh back out again.

ZBrush uses subdivisions when it adds details to the mesh, which makes it possible for you to work in various resolutions of depth. You can freely move in between these resolutions and add or remove details; the more subdivisions you have, the heavier the model will become (more polygons), so it's good to start easy. We are now ready to start improving our model. Figure 18.14 shows the first subdivision level and the amount of detail you will have when the imported head was placed in the work area and you entered edit mode.

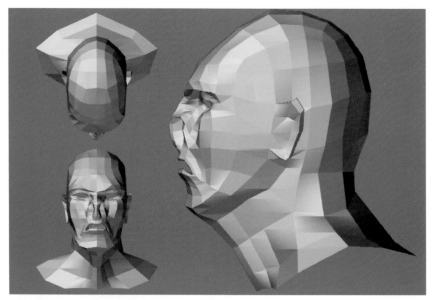

FIGURE 18.14   First edit of our head, from three directions.

The finer the detail you want to put into the mesh, the higher resolution you will need on the object. Remember to work from rough to detailed. Start by adding one or two subdivisions. The more you add, the slower the program will behave. Add divisions under Tools/Geometry/ with the Divide button as shown in Figure 18.15.

When painting in ZBrush, you can use a pressure-sensitive tablet to get an even stronger feeling of sculpting the mesh.

Working in ZBrush, you can let the program mirror your brushstrokes to the other side of the model. This requires your model to be identically modeled in the 3D program. You can turn this feature on and off during the workflow to create unique structures to each side. Use keyboard shortcuts x, y, and z to enable/disable this feature. Continue adding details to the mesh by painting with different strengths and brush sizes. Add detail to the areas you think are beneficial. We have added detail around the character's ear and eyes at this point, as shown in Figure 18.16.

FIGURE 18.15   Geometry control—divide to add subdivision

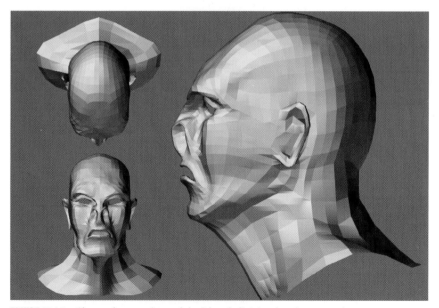

FIGURE 18.16   Shape the rough model with subdivision levels one and two.

In ZBrush, you have the option to add a masking selection, to decide on what area you want to paint. Click Ctrl and hold while you paint the selection mask as a dark shader over the object. To paint away the mask, hold Ctrl and Alt. Clicking in the empty workspace will invert the mask. See Figure 18.17 where we have applied the mask in the front of the face.

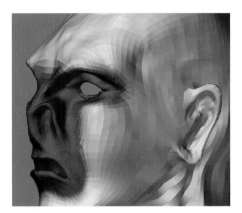

FIGURE 18.17   Selection masking.

Using selection masks makes it easier for you to make broad strokes over large areas without changing sensitive details in another by mistake. Let's continue to add detail to the object now that we finished the first two subdivision levels. To add much finer detail within the object, we need to add further divisions. In Figure 18.18, we have added more detail and it starts to take the shape we want it to have.

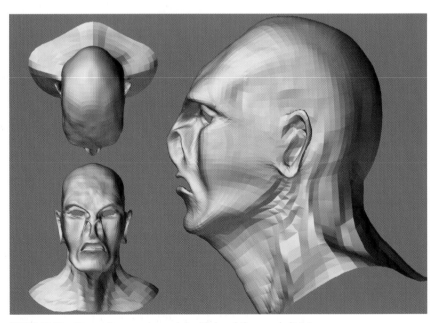

FIGURE 18.18   Shape the rough model with level three subdivisions.

When we start working in higher subdivision levels and adding finer details onto the object, the program can become rather slow, depending on the hardware you are using. ZBrush gives you the opportunity to hide the parts of the model that you are not working on for faster redraw. By pressing Ctrl and Shift, you enter the hide/show mode so you can select an area. Releasing the keyboard while still selecting inverts the selection tool. To unhide all again, Ctrl and Shift click the empty canvas (see Figure 18.19).

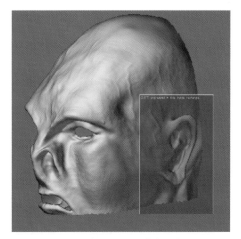

FIGURE 18.19   Hiding parts of the object.

Continue to work over the mesh, and add finer levels within the subdivisions. Normal maps cannot contain very small details, due to the restricted resolutions of the texture sizes used in today's games, so adding many small details can be unused work. Make sure you make the structures clear and exaggerate the shapes when you model in ZBrush (see Figure 18.20).

Finally, let's add some veins and smaller details to the forehead by using ZBrush's Projection Master. The Projection Master locks the object to work in a camera projection mode, where you use a texture connected as your brush to add further details such as veins, acne, wrinkles, and so forth (see Figure 18.21).

This is as much detail as the normal map will handle, so we wrap it up here. The mesh is ready for us to create a normal map in the next chapter. Make sure you save your Tool, since this is what contains all the subdivision information within ZBrush.

Export a high-resolution and a low-resolution .OBJ by moving to the level of detail that you want to export, and use Tools/Export/Export.

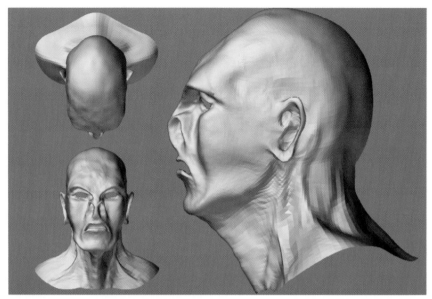

FIGURE 18.20   Finer details, division four.

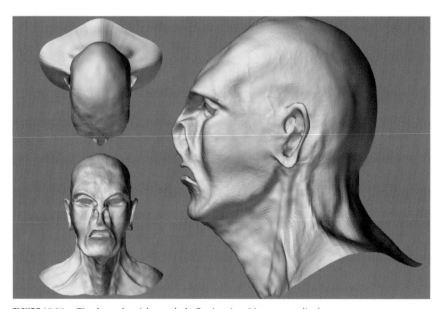

FIGURE 18.21   Final mesh with a subtle Projection Master applied.

ON THE CD

Now we have our meshes ready for the next chapter. You can see the final meshes under Chapter18\Exported_Final\ on the companion CD-ROM. The CD-ROM also includes the Final Tool for ZBrush for you to try under Chapter18\ZBrush2\CreatureHead_Final.ZTL.

SUMMARY

This chapter introduced you to two more modeling techniques, often used to work with high-resolution models. These will help you extend your modeling knowledge and improve your workflow. With the knowledge of high-resolution usage for games, you have learned how to produce a high-resolution mesh for use with normal mapping. By streamlining the process, we made it possible for the team to create the texture and animate the object while the modeler created the high-resolution mesh. We used ZBrush, a program that acts more like a 3D painting/sculpting tool, and has become a standard in many studios when they create organic shapes and characters. Let's look at some points to remember:

1. High-resolution modeling will adapt the way we create the objects in the future, due to the higher detail assets that the games will require.
2. Edge modeling maintains speed and control, even in large polygon meshes.
3. Edge modeling with edges constructed after how muscle flows, creates more natural deformations when skinning and moving characters in animations.
4. SubD is a level-based modeling technique with which you can add details in a lower level, and skin in a higher level.
5. We use high-resolution meshes for games to transfer the information from a detailed object into a texture as a normal map, mostly used for organic shapes.
6. The ZBrush method to handle object geometry is similar to the level detail of SubD, but it allows you to paint and sculpt the mesh with brushes and influence values.
7. Build and finalize your mesh for production speed, so other people can use the mesh while you are creating the high-resolution mesh to render the normal map.
8. When importing objects into ZBrush, make sure you have Quads.
9. Try to restrain from changing the final mesh's outer shape in ZBrush. Large changes will create skewed textures with the normal mapping.
10. Sculpt as much as possible with each level.
11. Normal mapping does not work well with too much information added into the texture, so the detail does not have to be overdone—production wise, it will just take up extra time.

NORMAL MAPPING

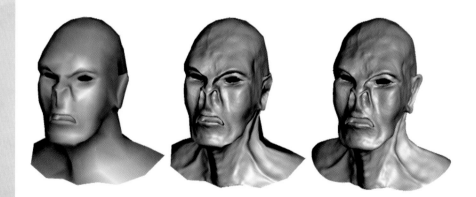

Imagine a wall made of bricks. In reality, the bricks and the masonry have different height levels. In game developing, we would create this brick wall as a flat plane. To model each brick would require too many polygons. Luckily, there are various techniques available to simulate more depth and information on an object.

The first technique to simulate this was bump mapping. This method uses a gray gradient texture to specify where the bumps appear, using different light intensity of the pixels, a result that we got by using multipass renderings. Bump mapping only works in one vector, however, and has limited information on where the light is coming in the scene.

We can consider normal maps the next step, a small evolution for game development. Normal mapping gives each pixel its own unique normal direction as defined by a particular color. This enables us to know what angle and direction the light is hitting an object on a per-pixel basis. Each texture can add structure to the object's shape by adding light and dark values, and we can get much more detailed objects within the scene. Normal maps become a very important part of creating highly realistic lighting within games.

To solve our earlier problem, by using normal maps, we can add the bricks on the wall to a texture that has directional light information. If the light moves, so will the structure of the bricks, giving us more true-to-life lighting.

It's important to know that normal maps only store the directions in the pixel normals; no height information is stored within the normal map. The normal maps are merely a simulation of how the light is viewed on the surface on the object. It does not alter the surface shape so it is a good idea to keep the normal information on the object's planar faces, and away from the object's silhouette.

As easy as it is to create bump maps using gradient gray textures, a normal map requires a unique process when created since it relies heavily on the correct light brightness and color value to get the correct normal direction.

ADOPTION COLOR MAP

The pixel normal gives the object the information of where the light is within the scene. Light and dark areas on the object are defined by the information in the normal map.

Adding a color map to the object that already has shadows and highlights would result in double transformation in light values. For instance, if we paint a brick wall with strong highlights and shadows on each brick, we can simulate that the light is coming from above. When we add the normal map and move the light under the brick, the engine tries to make the top of the brick dark and the bottom lit, reversed from the colors in our painted color map. The result will be that the light information blends with the color map and creates a gray, evenly lit area, erasing the feeling of light direction, depth, and shape (see Figure 19.1).

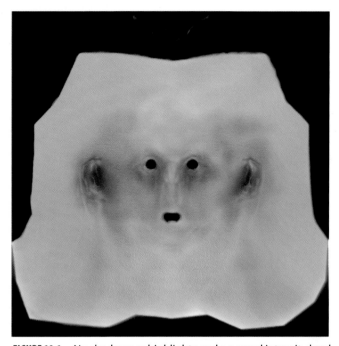

FIGURE 19.1   No shadows or highlights and a normal intensity level.

NORMAL MAP COLOR INFORMATION

Normal maps are stored in RGB image format. Each channel of R, G, and B represents X, Y, Z directions of the pixel vectors in relation to the UV direction of its vertex normals. Different colors indicate how the light direction is stored within a normal map, depending on how the object should use the normal. Artistically, there is a large difference between the different systems, making them hard to change from one to another by hand. Three main techniques are used within game development:

Tangent space: This method stores the alternation, compared to the tangent direction to the surface polygons.

Object space: This method replaces the surface information of the object shape.

World space: This method replaces the surface information dependent of the object's position in world space.

Each technique has its advantages and disadvantages. Tangent space normal map construction is easier and uses less blending of the colors than the Object (World) space technique. This makes it easier for us artists to paint in tangent space; however, it is possible to edit and paint all normal maps in a 2D program such as Photoshop after creation.

To get the desired results, normal maps require a lot of texture space. The also hold sensitive surface information that when compressed can be lost. To use them within a game production pipeline, the best solution could be to use small textures and keep the detail limited, relevant to the size of the texture.

Although it is possible to simulate depth with normal maps, it is not a bump map. The normals are the directional light information and cannot be altered after the normal map has been created. In addition, it is not possible to change the power of height within the texture.

TANGENT SPACE

Tangent space only stores the alternation of the directions in the texture, which means that no height information is stored within the normal map.

When creating a tangent space map, we use positive (1) and negative values (–1) of the X, Y, Z directions to represent the directional angle of the surface alternation. An RGB color of 0 will represent the vector at –1 (DOWN), 127 represents vector 0 (FLAT), and 255 represents vector 1 (UP) (see Figure 19.2).

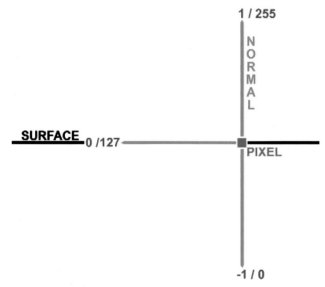

FIGURE 19.2   Directional –1 to 1 values.

Tangent space only stores the alternations of the normals in a texture using Red and Green to represent the X and Y directions. The Blue surface color represents the alignment to polygonal surfaces where the Z vector 1 is pointing straight (UP), making the color 127, 127, 255.

Translate these values into practical examples of a tangent map:

Y vector 1 (UP) is 127, 255, 127 shown as a green color.
Y vector −1 (DOWN) is 127, 0, 127 shown as a violet color.
X vector 1 (RIGHT) is 255, 127, 127 shown as a turquoise color.
X vector −1 (LEFT) is 0, 127, 127 shown as a peach color.

The directional orientation in the preceding examples is for the default values and in relation to what is up in your UV layout compared to your Y up in the texture. Some game engines have the Y negative as standard for their normal textures as they invert what is seen in the normal map inside the engine (see Figure 19.3).

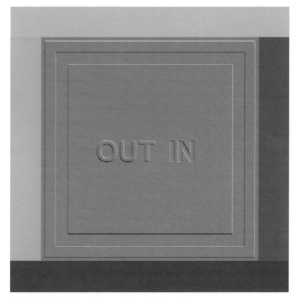

FIGURE 19.3   Tangent space RGB colors.

To get the illusion of height within the normal map, we need to include one up and one down value. If there is no alternation of normals, the texture will stay blue. To achieve different shapes, curves, and complex angles, the RGB values blend with each other to create variations of colors in the normal map (see Figure 19.4).

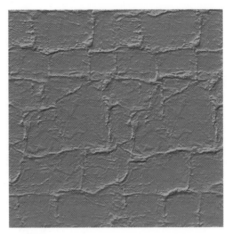

FIGURE 19.4 A tangent space normal map.
© Digital Illusions CE AB. 2004 Reprinted with permission.

We can create tangent space normal maps in three ways:

- A high-resolution mesh calibration
- A height map converts them from a colored image
- Paint them with the color representing the directional vectors

Tangent space has the big advantage that the same part of the UV can be reused on several objects, and within the same object, no matter what the light direction. Even overlapping UVs are allowed. It is also easy to paint your own tangent space textures.

OBJECT (WORLD) SPACE

Object and world space are different, but both have similar color versions. Both are more complex than the tangent space in their color values, since they replace all the surface information.

World space defines the world's coordinates and locks the normal map to the unique object rotation and position where you create the normal map in the scene. It does not support movement, animation, or instancing of the object.

Object space works in local space, where it is created and supports animation and moving objects.

Both of these techniques of normal mapping contain many more variations of colors compared to the tangent space. The values are unique to the shape of the object. Each color change is dependent on the shape and direction of each polygon's vector on the object. For example, the polygon facing X on an object is stored with a different color than the polygon that is facing Z (see Figure 19.5).

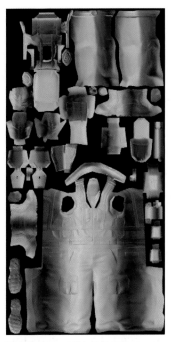

FIGURE 19.5   A World/object space normal map. © Digital Illusions CE AB. 2004 Reprinted with permission.

This makes an object space normal map unusable for tiling or UV overlapping, and what is on X cannot be used on Z since the light will be shown incorrectly. This type of normal map is also much more sensitive to texture compression due to all its colors. It is, however, less expensive than the tangent space, because it replaces the surface information, and calculation does not need to be done per-vertex.

The main techniques we create object space normal maps with are:

- A high-resolution mesh calibration
- Converting from tangent space maps

Since object space replaces the surface, it is possible to paint but hard to add information directly into the texture after the object has been created. It is, however, possible to do easier correction.

 The engine is replacing the surface normal with the normal map in object/world space.

NORMAL MAPS IN THE 3D VIEWPORT

Normal mapping has started to become an easy and accessible feature within 3D programs today—both Maya 6 and 3ds max 7 support normal map creation, viewing, and software render. Before we start creating the normal maps, we need to be able to know how we can see them in the viewport. Both programs use shaders to make this possible.

Maya

Maya uses its High Quality Rendering feature to be able to see the normal maps in the viewport, so make sure this is enabled in the viewport in which you are planning to see the object. It can be turned on and off under the Shading menu in the specific viewport when you are in shaded mode.

Open the Hypershade window. We are going to create a shader that can support the display of normal maps. Using the Work Area, add a shader and create a file node. Load the normal map into the file node. While holding Shift, click on the file node and drag it onto the shader. This brings up the Connection Editor. Find and click on the Out color in the left column and the Normal camera in the right column (see Figure 19.6).

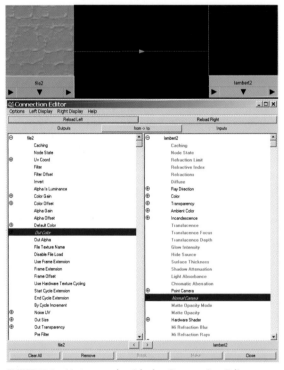

FIGURE 19.6   Hypergraph with the Connection Editor.

Rotate the object in the viewport; you should be able to see the normal map on the object.

3ds max 7

Normal maps were one of the main concentrations in this version. They have added many features to view and render normal maps within the program. To visualize the normal maps requires you to have DirectX drivers enabled.

Verify this by entering Customize/Preferences/Viewports/ where the display drivers should mention Direct3D 8.0 or 9.0.

All of these will need to use the Material manager (M).

3ds max 7 can display the normal map through DirectX shaders, Metal Bump9 Plug-ins, and within a normal Bump Node. Each gives us different options.

Standard Shader

Connect a normal Bump Shader to the Standard Shaders Bump map slot. Then, add a bitmap node to its normal Slot. In this bitmap, load your normal map (see Figure 19.7).

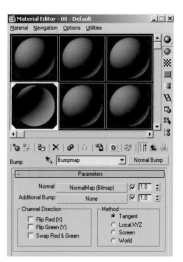

FIGURE 19.7   Using a normal bump inside the bump layer of a standard shader.

At the bottom of the standard shader is a tab called DirectX Manager. Open it, and enable DX Display of Standard Material. This makes the Show Map in Viewport icon turn pink, which you now enable.

With the bump map slots value you can now change the amount the texture should be visible on the model.

This technique makes it possible for you to get normal maps in software rendering.

Metal Bump9 Plug-In

At the bottom of the standard shader is a tab called DirectX Manager. Open it, and select and enable the Metal Bump9 in the Plugin Material option (see Figure 19.8).

FIGURE 19.8   Metal Bump9.

The Metal Bump9 shader works fine with tangent space; we have experienced inverted lights when a world/object space normal map was used.

DirectX9 Shader

3ds max 7 also supports direct use of DirectX9 shaders such as the HLSL shader RTTnormalMap.fx. With this shader, you get the option to load the different types of normal maps and specify what light to use (see Figure 19.9).

FIGURE 19.9   DirectX 9 with
RTTnormalMap.fx.

Creation

The process of creating normal maps has come a long way since it was first developed. With the latest additions to 3D programs, the process has become very efficient and easy.

When we create normal maps, a good idea is to exaggerate your details. Normal maps are very dependent on texture resolution. They are created for defining shapes, and light and dark areas. Large obvious shapes will work better than small complex shapes, which can become blurry when mapped with just a few pixels. Having a detailed object is dependent on the resolution of the texture and how many fine details we can add to a normal map.

Painting Normal Maps

World and object space maps are rarely painted. If there are some errors and miscalculations, they benefit from some touchups, using a smoothing or blur brush to even out the colors.

If we need to have object space normal maps, we can create tangent space normal maps, paint, change these, and when done, convert them to object space.

Therefore, we mainly work with tangent space, and as we have learned, tangent normal maps need two colors in one axis to work correctly, and the normals must have both an up color and down color to simulate an alternation on the surface. If we remove one of the two colors, the remaining line will try to act as both up (light) and down (dark) depending on the direction of the light.

Other things that are vital for the look of tangent space normal maps include:

- Line gradient and width
- Strength of color
- Blended colors
- Contrast in light values of height map

A thin line with a large contrast from the blue base color will make the edge very sharp (see Figure 19.10), while a smoothed gradient line (Figure 19.11) acts more like a ramp.

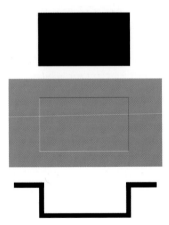

FIGURE 19.10   A short hard edge.

As you see in Figure 19.11, to get smooth round shapes you need to have a large space UV and texture space.

Since normal maps require large texture maps to look decent, it is important that you know how to make them as good as possible while keeping them small. The thinner the lines you can have to achieve the same result, the less texture space you will need to use for the object and the game.

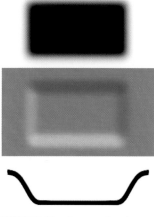

FIGURE 19.11   A smooth edge.

Making lines thin also makes them very sensitive in how we use them. If an object is mapped so the UV contains sharp diagonal UVs, they will create jagged and pixilated lines when viewed in the game. If we add extra antialiasing to make them less blocky, the lines become blurry and the sharpness is lost.

Antialiasing and smoothing become a problem with normal maps when UVs' borders and lines are mapped diagonally, so try to keep them straight in the UVs.

Tangent space is dependent on how you paint the texture before we convert it into the normal map.

The filter lets you put in negative scale numbers, for inverted colors. For example, if you convert a brick wall that has darker stones than the mortar, using a positive value on this area will make the stones go inward when you see them inside the game.

Photoshop Plug-In

NVIDIA developed a Photoshop plug-in that will create a tangent space normal map through a filter based on an RGB image. The plug-in is available from *developer.Nvidia.com* (see Figure 19.12).

We use the Photoshop filter together with our painted height map. It always creates blue color in Z-axis of the tangent world in standard RGB mode. If you flip or mirror the UV points inside the UV layout so they are angled in another way than the normal U and V, the normal map needs to be adapted to the orientation. This is adjustable by the check boxes invert X and Y options in the filter. To be sure of how it looks and that the light

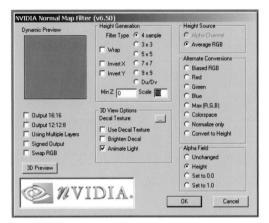

FIGURE 19.12 NVIDIA's Photoshop normal map tool.

works on the model that you have created, the most visual and correct way to verify is to create the texture and tweak it in the game for final quality.

By organizing the UVs so your layout does not use mirrored UV in your object and UV layout, you can restrain from using different tangent directions in your normal map creation.

When we paint and create a normal map from a height map, from a single drawn pixel line of black color, the tangent space will create three lines, two surrounding it and the surface in the middle:

- X-Up
- Z-Axis
- X-Down

This means, that if you paint a single dark line in the diffuse map as an indent, it would require three times the texture resolution for a normal map to get it to look correct. This single line will then look blurry in the game. To help it look sharper, we have to hand-paint the normal maps.

As you know, tangent normal needs an up and down angle, but does not need the middle flat Z-axis, so to make our lines extra thin and sharp in the textures, we would need to paint the lines manually in the final resolution, keeping them single line and with up and down next to each other. We can either sit a long time tweaking and updating the Photoshop filter output to get the correct result, or we can paint directly in the colors that we know the normal map is using.

Using high-scale values with the normal map tool can create banding and noise within the normals and when saved with the textures. Paint with large differences with the gray color intensities instead, and keep the values to a value lower than 20.

High-Resolution Mesh Calibration

Painting tangent normal maps or converting bump maps is fast. Although it is possible to enhance the shape by painting in normal maps, it is hard to get edges round and the shape exact. To get the best and most accurate result, high-resolution calibration is the most precise method available; it gives us the best results, although it is the most time-consuming process. All normal map techniques are supported when a normal map is created through a high-resolution mesh.

For high-resolution mesh calibration, you need to have two modeled meshes:

- One low-resolution polygon mesh with final UV
- One high-resolution polygon mesh

The computer does the process of creating the normal map. By placing the objects as close to each other as possible (intersecting each other is fine), it uses the low-resolution mesh as a base and offsets a projection depth, shooting out rays that search for the high-resolution polygon's angle and shape. When found, it transfers the results per pixel into the low-resolution UV layout and saves it as a normal map.

Both objects need to be very close to each other. If they are too far away, the rays can miss the object, thereby creating an empty result, or the normal map can become skewed and blurry. In some cases, lengthening the offset/depth of the ray fixes this, but it is best to keep the level difference of the objects to a minimum.

When you create very complex shapes such as large overhangs, object cave-ins, or where the polygons in the same mesh intersect or are too close to each other, it can be wise to split up the mesh and do projection in sections. For example, a human character can have problems on the limb intersections (creases), the mouth (cave-ins), and ears (overhangs).

Of the two meshes, only the low-resolution needs to have a UV map.

Maya 6

Maya uses Lighting/Shading/Transfer surface information in the Rendering module.

Select the source (high-polygon) as the first mesh and the target (low-polygon) as the second, and then run the command.

3ds max 7

3ds max uses the Rendering/Render to Texture feature to bake a texture with the normal information.

Select the low-resolution mesh and the high-resolution mesh as a projection. Add a Normalsmap Element.

Max supports world, screen, local XYZ (Object space) and tangent normal maps.

You can also change the direction of the X and Y of the tangent directions.

Max lets you use the traditional low-polygon offset between the two objects as well as a special cage projection mode. This cage mode extends the offset process with a controllable projection cage built from the low-polygon mesh. You have full control of how you want the projection done. Move it as close as possible to the high-resolution mesh for an optimal result.

ZBrush 2

ZBrush 2 supports the creation of Tangent and Object space normal maps.

If you imported the low-resolution mesh within ZBrush (2) as a base with correct UVs as we did in Chapter 18, "High-Resolution Modeling," you have the option to create normal maps within ZBrush (2).

When you've finished modeling the highest detailed subdivision level, go down to the coarsest detail level. Under Tools, open the Normal Mapping tab (see Figure 19.13).

FIGURE 19.13   Options for normal map creation within ZBrush.

ZBrush creates the normal map inverted in the Z-axis compared to your object's UVs. To use it in a game or in the 3D program, you need to flip it.

ATI and NVIDIA

Both of these graphic chip producers have their own normal map creating tools available for the public (see Figures 19.14 and 19.15).

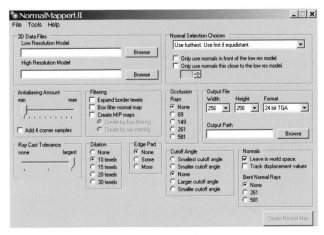

FIGURE 19.14   ATI normal mapping tools.

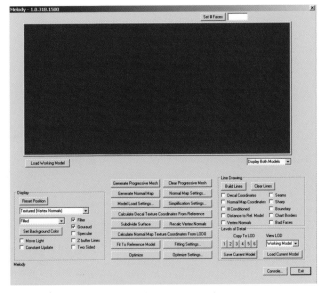

FIGURE 19.15   NVIDIA normal mapping tools.

They support both the same variations and their own file format. They are available to download through their developer homepages (*www.ati.com* and *developer.nvidia.com*), if this is something you want to examine further.

IN PRODUCTION

Since normal maps are becoming a future art asset, we need to create for the next-generation's consoles together with today's PC games. We will go over the objects we created throughout this book and add normal maps to them with the various techniques:

- Convert to tangent space normal maps from textures
- Paint tangent space normal maps
- Render object (world) space normal maps from a high-resolution mesh

Old House

This part of the tutorial files will only support Maya 6, but you can apply the theory and process with any 3D program. We will also use Photoshop with NVIDIA's Normal map filter to create the normal map textures. We are going to create the normal maps to be tangent space on the house that we created with multitexturing. Here we need to use the detail and decal maps information for its variations in height.

Let's look at the house again (see Figure 19.16).

FIGURE 19.16   Old house.

Load the file Chapter19\OldHouse\Maya\OldHouse_Raw.mb on the companion CD-ROM in Maya.

Load the detail map into Photoshop. We are going to use this as a base to create our normal map. The textures that we create from photographs are often noisy. This noise will create too much information in our normal maps and make it hard to reach a good quality (as we can see in Figure 19.17). We need to clean up the texture and make the lines between the planks very distinct and clear so they convert well with the normal map tool (see Figure 19.18).

Too much small detail within a low textured normal map makes it unreadable.

Flatten the layers to a single image, or Merge Down (Ctrl+E) if you only have two layers. Run the NVIDIA normal Map Filter. We want the alternation to really show, so set the Scale to 10 and check the box Invert Y (see Figure 19.19).

FIGURE 19.17 Detail texture with noise.

FIGURE 19.18 Detail texture cleaned up.

FIGURE 19.19 Normal map created from cleaned-up texture.

Now it's time to connect it to our object within the 3D program. Switch back to Maya and our Old house scene (see Figure 19.20).

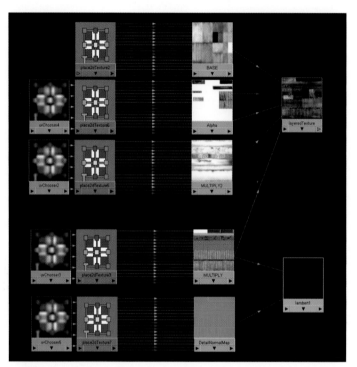

FIGURE 19.20   New connection in Hypershade.

The house is built with multitexturing, which does not work entirely together with the High-quality Rendering. We need to fix this and reconnect only the map with which we are working. By connecting the Out Color of the detail map into the Lambert color, we break the connection for the multitexturing node and will only see the detail map. We also need to add the normal map to the scene. Add a File Node, name it DetailNormalMap, and connect it to the Lambert camera.

We have added the normal map; however, it will not show up correctly before we tell the texture to use the correct UV map. With our house selected, enter the Relationship Editors/UV Linking/Texture-Centric and connect the DetailNormalMap in the left column to the Detail UV set in the right column by selecting them (see Figure 19.21).

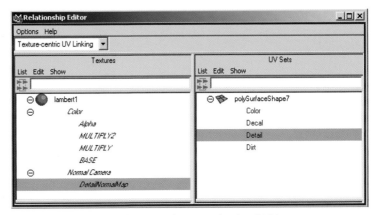

FIGURE 19.21   Connect the normal map to the detail UV.

You have now created the first normal map object. Rotate a directional light within the scene to see how the normals on the pixels update according to the light source (see Figure 19.22).

You can find the final setup OldHouse_Final.mb together with a scene with only the shader OldHouse_Shader_Setup.mb under Chapter19\OldHouse\Maya\ on the companion CD-ROM.

ON THE CD

FIGURE 19.22   Final detail map house.

AK-47

Let's look at the AK-47 that we textured in Chapter 9, "Texture Creation." It is time to add normal maps for it on the things that we did not model—the large divot on the side, on the magazine, and the small bolts and scratches. Time is of the essence, so we are going to paint a height map that we use NVIDIA's Photoshop filter on to get the correct information into the object and a tangent space normal map (see Figure 19.23).

FIGURE 19.23   AK-47, adding more detail into the surface.

Open Photoshop and load in the texture for the AK-47. Make sure you have a correct UV set inside the texture so you can see where you are going to add the divots and information (see Figure 19.24).

Create a new layer above the UV layer with a 50% Opacity. Fill it with a gray 128, 128, 128. This will become our base layer. Now create another layer over the base layer. This one will include our normal map information. Remember that the darker the colors you paint close to the bright ones, the stronger the angle will become. Painting with different values of grayscales gives you different height/depth variations on things like bolt and divots. Painting inside the top layer creates higher and lower alternations of the main surface, depending on the gray intensity you use.

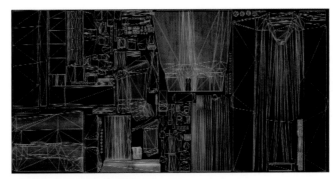

FIGURE 19.24   Texture with UV.

We have flipped some of the AK-47 UV directions. The magazine and the wooden handles are mapped horizontally (same axis both in texture and on object), while the stock and barrel are mapped vertically (rotated UVs compared to the object). The UVs' direction in the object is dependent on the normal maps that you generate. Always check your work; this will affect the lighting so we are going to create the normal map for this gun in two passes (see Figure 19.25).

FIGURE 19.25   The AK-47 has rotated and flipped UVs compared to what is UP of the normal.

You will notice that since we straightened out all the UVs in the weapons layout, it becomes very easy to draw the normal map structure into the texture. Let's start by painting in the horizontal parts of the object.

The magazine has hard bevels outward, so let's paint these white. We'll paint the divots black (see Figure 19.26).

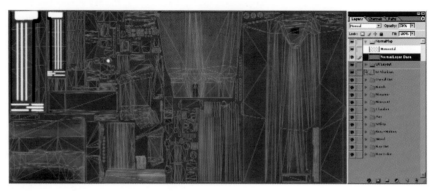

FIGURE 19.26   Horizontal information.

Let's start with the Vertical information. This part has a lot of interesting structure we can add. Painting in the shape of the top screw of the stock, bolts, and divots, we add more structure to the stock and the barrels. We can also paint in a small darkness, and add a lighter color to the areas that we want to simulate rounder or harder shapes within the mesh (see Figure 19.27).

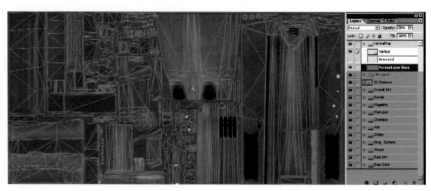

FIGURE 19.27   Vertical information.

By changing the brush hardness level, you can create rounder and harder edges on the normal map.

Now let's see how this looks in our 3D program. We needed to separate and create the normal map in several passes, as the AK-47 Layout has several UP directions. Let's create a merged texture from the two passes.

Change back the Base layer Opacity to 100% so the background is gray. For this, we are going to use NVIDIA's normal map tool (see Figure 19.28).

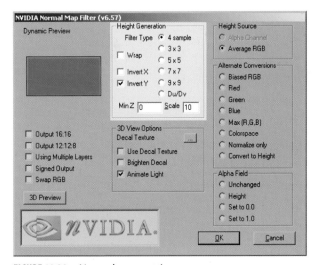

FIGURE 19.28   Normal map settings.

First pass—Horizontal UV:

- Hide the vertical layer.
- Select the horizontal layer.
- Select/All (Ctrl+A).
- Edit/Copy Merged (Shift+Ctrl+C).
- Create a New RGB Document (Ctrl+N).
- Paste in the information. (Ctrl+P).
- Flatten the layers to a single image, or Merge Down (Ctrl+E) if you only have two layers.
- Run the NVIDIA normal Map Filter.
- We want the alternation to really show, so set the Scale to 10 and check the box Invert Y.

(See Figure 19.29.)

FIGURE 19.29   Horizontal normal map information.

Second pass—Vertical UV:

- Hide the horizontal layer.
- Select the vertical layer.
- Select/All (Ctrl-A).
- Edit/Copy Merged (Shift+Ctrl+C).
- Create a new RGB document (Ctrl+N).
- Paste in the information (Ctrl+P).
- Flatten the layers to a single image, or Merge Down (CTRL+E) if you only have two layers.
- Run the NVIDIA normal Map Filter. We want the same alternation as the first pass.
- Scale to 10. Leave the Invert Y checked, but also check the box Invert X.

(See Figure 19.30.)

FIGURE 19.30   Vertical normal map information.

We need to combine these two textures. Hold Shift while dragging one into the other; this places the texture at its correct position. Cut out the parts that are covering the bottom layer so they merge into one texture. Flatten and save as a JPG (see Figure 19.31).

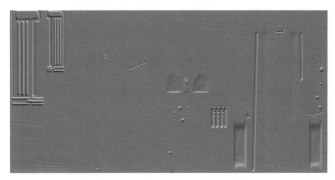

FIGURE 19.31   Final normal map.

Open Maya. Create and apply a File node. Attach your normal map texture to the normal camera so we can get updated information on our AK-47 (see Figure 19.32).

FIGURE 19.32   AK-47 without and with normal maps.

Finally, make sure you update the diffuse texture to work as a color texture. Reduce the highlights and hard shadows within the AK-47 texture (see Figure 19.33).

FIGURE 19.33   The final gun with texture.

Creature Head

For this example, we are using 3ds max 7; however, other programs are available with similar functions. In Chapter 17, "In Production: Multitexturing," we modeled a head with high-polygon modeling.

The character will use animations in the game, so we are going to create the object with an object space normal map. This will save us performance when we do vertex skinning. 3ds max calls it object space Local XZY. We are going to create the map using the low- and the high-resolution mesh technique (see Figure 19.34).

Import both the low-resolution and the high-resolution .OBJ files into the program. Scale them if needed. Make sure the UVs for the low-resolution mesh are unfolded properly with a good pixel ratio. The process will sample the high-resolution's surface from how it looks. Smoothing groups and hard/soft edges will alter how the surface looks when transferred onto the low-resolution mesh. It is important that the high-resolution mesh have smooth edges (groups) where it needs them. If it has hard smoothed edges when we transfer the information onto the low-resolution mesh, the information within the normal map will also

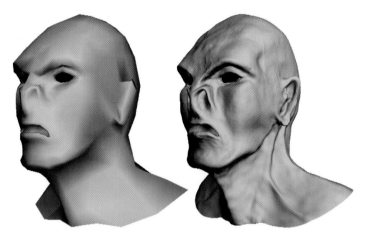

FIGURE 19.34   Low- and high-resolution modeled meshes.

become hard and faceted. If you are importing an .OBJ from ZBrush, the object has no smoothing groups, so make sure to add one. Select the entire mesh and add it to smoothing group 1, or remove them all.

Time to bake the normal map. Make sure that both objects are at the exact same position and that both objects' rotation and scale values are reset (see Figure 19.35).

FIGURE 19.35   Exact same position, size, and
rotation on the objects.

Open Rendering/Render to Texture (O). Here you will see all the controls that you need to bake a normal map to the low-polygon mesh from the high-polygon mesh (see Figure 19.36).

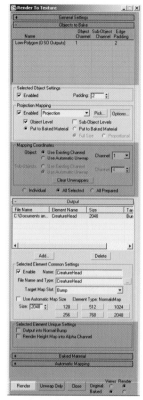

FIGURE 19.36   Render to texture view.

Under Object to Bake, you will find the projection tools.

1. Make sure that the checkbox under Selected Object Settings is enabled.
2. Under Projection Mapping, enable the projection modifier and choose the high-polygon face by clicking the Pick button.
3. Uncheck the use of Sub-Object Levels.

Enter Options, where you will find the various normal map techniques.

1. The Cage is great if you want to adapt the projection of the low-resolution mesh; for this head, it is enough for us to use the Offset technique, so uncheck Use Cage.
2. Under normal Map Space, choose Local XYZ, which is 3ds max 7's equivalent to object space (see Figure 19.37).

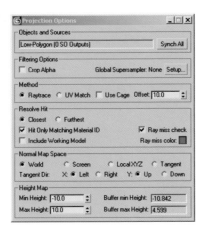

FIGURE 19.37   Projection options.

Close this option window and return to Render to Texture. Under Mapping Coordinates, make sure that you are using the UV channel that your object uses; in this case, channel 1.

Under Output, we have the options of choosing what elements we want to bake into the texture.

1. Add a Normalsmap as an element.
2. Enable and name the texture under Selected Element Common Settings.
3. Uncheck the Use Automatic Map Size box; we have spent time to create a good and useful UV for our object.
4. Choose the size in which you want to render the normal map.

We are all set to render at this stage, but we are going to let the program connect the rendered texture to our normal Bump Shader. For this, we need to select the Target map, and let it know that we are going to use the normal map node.

1. Check the Bump as the Target Map Slot.
2. Under the Selected Element Unique Settings, check the Output into normal Bump box.
3. Render. Make sure you look at the saved normal map; the render view does not show the correct output (see Figure 19.38).

Notice the small rendering errors behind the ears. This is something that we can fix with Photoshop by color correcting the affected area. Since we connected the shader directly to the object, hide the high-resolution model and rotate the object with or without added light sources (see Figure 19.39).

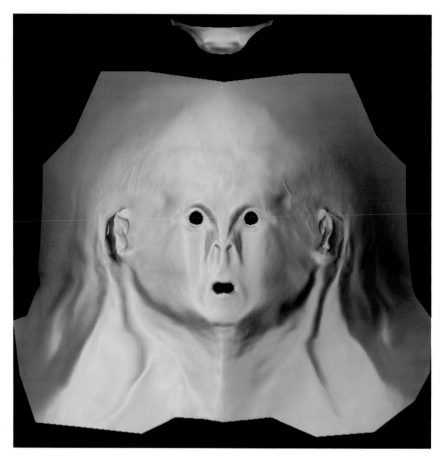

FIGURE 19.38 The rendered normal object space map.

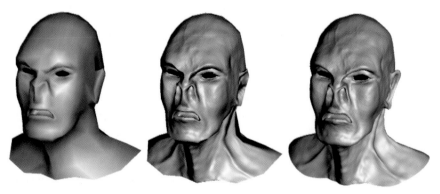

FIGURE 19.39 The low-resolution mesh, low-resolution mesh with normal map applied, and the high-resolution object next to each other.

We now have a head consisting of 1050 triangles that has the details of a 320,000-triangles head. As we can see, the result is rather good. In Chapter 20, "Shaders," we'll build the different components to our new head and take a closer look at it with color, specular, and normal maps.

PARALLAX DISPLACEMENT MAPPING

Normal mapping is a very powerful technique where the normals of the pixels decide the angle of the light that hits them. Although they simulate depth, normal maps do not include a depth value. We can use Parallax Displacement mapping, by combining a height map with a normal map, we get both the depth control and the directional light information. Parallax Displacement mapping gives stunning results and can be the final step to use if we ever want to create a realistic brick wall within game development.

SUMMARY

A normal map is a hot topic, it has evolved, and the major 3D programs have started to integrate the feature. You probably noticed that normal maps are also rather complex. By reading and understanding this chapter, you learned the technical side behind tangent, world, and object space normal maps, and learned how to create normal maps by painting, converting, and transferring from a high resolution. You also learned to use the tools that we use within game production today. There was a lot to keep track of, so let's sum up the most important parts:

1. A normal map stores the direction of the pixel and shows this as a color, dependent on direction.
2. Normal maps have no height value to them, but simulate a 3D feeling.
3. There are three main types of normal maps used in game development, world, object, and tangent.
4. Each of the various types has different color calculations and looks different from the others.
5. Tangent space supports all types of objects, although it is the most expensive method because it needs the vertex information to determine the shape of the object and then alter the pixel normals from this.
6. Object/world space is the least expensive, and replaces the complete surface information. World space fixes the texture to the unique object in the world. Object space allows objects to change position and deform in games, commonly used for animated characters.

7. Tangent information creates three values of a single line when created: up, flat, and down. This makes the same thin line in a color map become much thicker when the same resolution is used for the normal map.

8. A single line in a normal map uses a minimum of two lines to get a single line. This makes the texture use a higher-resolution texture to simulate a single line in a color texture and can create a mismatch in the texture.

9. Getting high and sharp textures with normal maps requires very large textures. Too many small details within a low-textured normal map make it unreadable due to the resolution required.

10. Normal maps are very texture compression sensitive, so it is important that they be saved correctly to keep quality, and save memory.

11. When converting a photo or painted diffuse texture with the Photoshop Normal Map Filter, it is important to clean up the texture so it has very little noise. Make sure that black goes in and white goes out.

12. When painting normal maps and converting them using the Photoshop Normal Map Filter, paint on a 127,127,127 as a midlevel color, representing the surface height. Black causes the normal to bump in, and white causes the normal to bump out.

13. Different engines calculate their tangent normal map differently; tangent space supports flipping in Y and X, and should be matched up with the UVs on the object.

14. When transferring a high-resolution mesh to a normal map, the two meshes should be as close as possible. The low-polygon mesh needs to have a correctly setup UV layout.

15. The program samples the surfaces and transfers the angles from the high-resolution mesh into the UV of the low-polygon mesh.

SHADERS

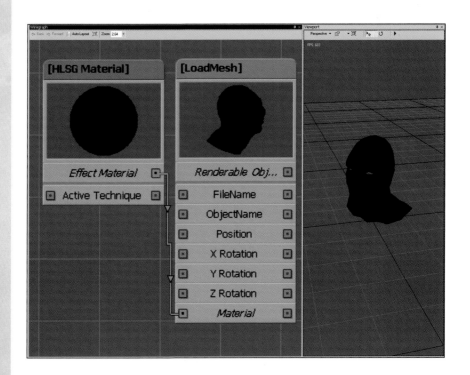

Think of shaders as the 3D rendering program's surface materials; however, shaders for games can do so much more. A shader is a set of instructions created with a high-level programming language. When combined, they create new features and functions to provide rendering-related computations. A shader works like a small plug-in/script that we can update in real time while the main program is running. A shader does not need to compile before it is used, as it is simply a script. Shaders require the graphics card or the console to be shader-capable and have the necessary instruction sets available. If the hardware does not have this feature, the shader needs to be hard-coded into the game engine.

Each new generation of graphics hardware has allowed the complexity of the shaders to advance further. This makes the shader hardware-dependent and needs to be adapted for architecture. If the shader uses unsupported instructions in old hardware, the shader will malfunction. For full functionality, the shader needs to be scaleable. This makes the shaders very useable, since as plug-ins they allow us to transfer and reuse the technology in other games and between platforms. In addition, it's possible for artists to use shaders within 3D programs to visually experience the objects the way they would appear in the game.

Programmers have been writing shaders for games for a long time, both in assembly and as plug-ins. Recently, the industry has started to release intuitive shader programs that allow the artist to create shaders to achieve the best visual experience, a power that comes with great responsibility and a required understanding of gaming performance and architecture.

A shader operates on the smallest components in the mesh and the texture, per-vertex and per-pixel, controlling light, colors, and animation, among other things. Shaders have changed the way we create art for games, and will continue to do so.

VERTEX SHADERS

Vertices are the smallest components of an object. Letting the shaders control them will let you manipulate their transformation, lighting, colors, and, to a limited extent, texture coordinate transformation. With a vertex shader, you can manipulate the vertices to achieve moving water, cloth-simulation, waving grass, and so forth. They also allow you to control animated features such as character skinning, morph targeting, facial expression, and animations.

A vertex shader cannot create or remove vertices, only manipulate them within the mesh.

PIXEL SHADERS

Pixel shaders give full control over the shade, intensity, and color for each individual pixel. They make it possible to create different blending variations between colors and textures, creating features such as specular light, normal mapping, nonstandardized lighting, and cartoon shading. Pixel shaders have limited or no knowledge of neighboring pixels and lights (numbers, kind, color, etc.), which must be specified within the shader.

When working with pixel shaders, we need to learn that everything is taking place in render passes. The fewer render passes we can use, the more speed we can achieve. Newer PS versions in the graphics card support instructions that enable more textures and features in fewer passes, making the content and features faster.

To achieve the visual goal, using a combination of both vertex and pixel shaders is common. For example, when a pixel shader calculates per-pixel lighting, it needs the information of the polygon orientation that it gets from the vertex shader.

SHADERS FOR PROGRAMMERS

There are two main standards for graphic rendering APIs: SGI's OpenGL and Microsoft's DirectX. Each API has its own instruction sets for the shader code base.

DirectX, Microsoft

In the mid-1990s, Microsoft created the first version of DirectX as a stand-alone interface for programmers. Today, DirectX is part of the Windows operating system and has become one of the standard APIs to create games.

Direct X comes with the High Level Shader Language (HLSL).

OpenGL

SGI created the OpenGL standard in the early 1990s. OpenGL is compatible with Windows, Mac, Linux, Unix, and BeOS, among other operating systems, consoles, and hardware. It has become the most widely supported API for interactive 2D and 3D graphics applications.

OpenGL comes with the OpenGL Shader Language (OGSL).

NVIDIA CG Shaders

NVIDIA has developed a shader version that integrates run scripts for both OpenGL and DirectX, making it possible to seamlessly use both technologies in the hardware.

NVIDIA has also worked together with Alias and Discreet to integrate the ability to view and use CGFX inside 3D programs. It comes as a standard shader with both Maya 6.01 (Bonus Tools) and 3ds max 6. If you are using an older version of Maya or 3ds max, plug-in shaders are available at *developer.nvidia.com*. There is also the ability to have the real game shaders work within Maya or 3ds max while you are modeling, so you can see how it will look inside the game.

This implementation lets you create your own shader effects and try them out on your objects.

SHADERS FOR ARTISTS

Artists generally do not care much for numbers and hard algorithms, so programs have been developed for closing the bridge between the programmer and the artist. ATI and NVIDIA have created Rendermonkey and FX composer. Although good, they give limited intuitive options to the artists, and you would need to view and edit code to get the best results.

RtZen Rt/Shader and Mad Software Inc.'s Shaderworks are two programs that set the standard for the next generation of shader creation. They both use graph systems and icons to represent the instruction sets and functions. Their construction is to use connecting nodes rather than write code.

IN PRODUCTION

We are going to build simple shaders that we can bring into 3ds studio max or Maya. This tutorial describes how to create a shader in Rt/Shader, something that will teach you more of how shaders link and use textures.

ON THE CD

For this tutorial, you will need a copy of Rt/Shader. Install it from the Programs\RtShaderGinza\Setup.exe folder on the companion CD-ROM.

Rt/Shader uses something they call the High Level Shader Graph (HLSG) and Low Level Shader Graph (LLSG). These are graph extensions of the code-based GLSL/HLSL. The LLSG is the most advanced and technical of the supported graph techniques. Rt/Shader can be unfamiliar to many, so we will start with a brief introduction to explain the basic structure of how the program works. If you have worked with Maya's Hypergraph or 3ds max's Particle View, you should understand the connection and the workflow.

After starting the program, you will see a large grid working area called the Wiregraph. This is the program's primary tool for creating the nodes for the various wire connections. This is where we are going to build our shader (see Figure 20.1).

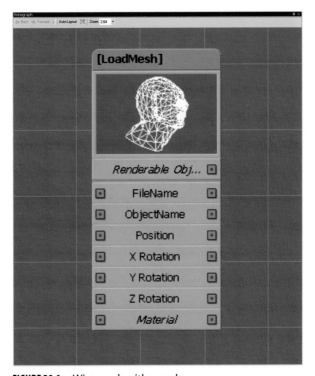

FIGURE 20.1   Wiregraph with a node.

Click the right mouse button in the Wiregraph. This will give you a selection of commands and functions that you can add to the shader, this is a good and fast way to work. Each node has one or two function slots. These work as the connection points to other sockets and functions in other nodes. A left socket means data input while a right side socket means data output as seen in Figure 20.2.

FIGURE 20.2   A node's Slot functions and its Socket connection.

For a better understanding of how to operate Rt/Shader, please refer to the program's help.

Color, Specular, and Normal Maps

Let's now focus on the shader creation.

1. In Wiregraph, right mouse click and select Objects/Create LoadMesh Assembly. This will create a standard mesh node, which by default is occupied by a teapot. We want to exchange this teapot for the creature head we created in Chapter 18, "High-Resolution Modeling." Open the file Chapter20\Rt-Shader_Objects\CreatureHead_Low. ASE on the companion CD-ROM.

ON THE CD

2. Click on the Input socket of the FileName slot on the LoadMesh node. It will let you load in the correct 3ds max format file.

Once loaded, you will see it in the Viewport as a wireframe model. To see it as shaded, we need to create a material for it. For this, we are going to use the HLSG node.

3. In Wiregraph, right mouse click and select Materials/HLSG Material. This is the base shader that we are going to connect to our model.
4. Click hold left mouse, on the output socket for the Effect Material slot for the HLSG Material, drag, and release to the Input socket of the Material slot of the LoadMesh node (see Figure 20.3).

The socket color turns green when the connection is permitted; otherwise, it is a red cross.

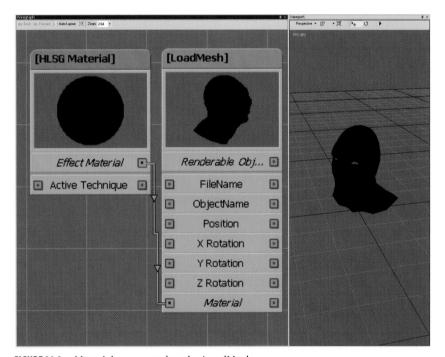

FIGURE 20.3   Material connected to the LoadMesh.

This made our object black. As a standard material, it has no color or values assigned to it. Now, enter the Shader with which we will work.

5. Double-click on the HLSG node.
6. This will enter the material node and its hierarchy, changing the wiregraph. This is where the main connections between the nodes are taking place and the shader is being built. The material includes new nodes that you can combine to create your shaders. We are in-

terested in adding a normal map, specular map, and a color map to our head. To do this, we need to create some new nodes.
- In Wiregraph, right mouse click and add a Lighting node.
- Add three Texture nodes, one for each texture we are going to use in the shader.
- Add two Composite nodes.

7. That might have clouded up the wiregraph, so we are going to name the different nodes.
- Name the Texture nodes Specular Map, Color Map, and Normal Map.
- Name the Composite nodes Texture Blend and Final Blend.

8. Let's load the textures and connect this shader together. The two texture nodes will blend by a multiply in one of the composite nodes.
- Click on the socket Texture input in the Node Color Map, and select the color map.
- Connect Color Map, Output output to Color Blend, Color 1 input.
- Click on the socket Texture input in the Node Specular Map, and select the specular map.
- Connect Specular Map, Output output to Color Blend, Color 2 input.
- Connect Color Blend, Output output to Final Blend, Color 1 input.

9. We are now going to load the Normal Map texture and change the light to be "single source."
- Click on the socket Texture input in the Node Normal Map, and select the normal map.
- Connect Node Normal Map, Output output to Node Lighting, Normal Map input.
- Lighting Node, Diffuse output to Final Blend, Color 2 input.

10. Finally, we are going to connect our whole setup to the Pass node (see Figure 20.4).
- Connect Final Blend, Output output to Pass, Color input.

11. If you plan to use you new shader with 3ds max or Maya, they only support a single light source, so we need to change the Light Node.

12. Click on socket input on Light Mode in Node lighting and select Single.

13. To export the shader, right-click in the wiregraph and select Export Shader to FX File.

There, you have now created and saved an HLSL shader, ready for your 3D program and your game.

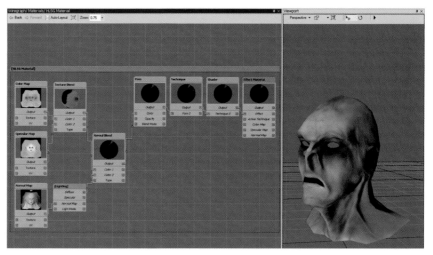

FIGURE 20.4 Final connection schematic.

Multitexturing House Shader

Let's do something more advanced by setting up a multitexturing shader. Earlier in the book, we created a house with textures, UVs, and normal map shadows. Let's also create a shader that supports our building.

We are going to use HLSG for this example as well, together with a LoadMesh, so create both of them.

ON THE CD

1. Load Chapter20\Rt-Shader_Objects\OldHouse_MultiTexturing.ASE through Objects/Create LoadMesh Assembly from the companion CD-ROM.
2. Create a Materials/HLSG Material, connect it to the LoadMesh Material socket, and then enter the HLSG Material.

Our house has six textures that use five unique UV sets, which is more than Xbox and PlayStation2 support in one pass. Therefore, an object like this would need two passes, or only be used in a PC game. Here is the setup that we need to create:

UV Set 0, Color Map
UV Set 1, Detail Map, Normal Map
UV Set 2, Dirt Map
UV Set 3, Decal Map
UV Set 4, Light Map

This shader is much larger than the former normal mapping, specular, color map tutorial, so we want to keep the wiregraph organized. We will therefore not create everything at once, but rather make the shader in steps.

Start by creating these nodes:

- Two Vertex UV
- Two Texture
- One Composite

UV Sets 0, 1, 2, and 4 are multiply, so we can group these together. This will be our first task. The Node Vertex UV is where you decide the UV set. We need one for each texture. Let's start with the color map and detail map.

1. Rename Texture Nodes, Color and Detail.
2. Connect the Output output of the Vertex UV to the Texture UV input on both nodes.
3. Click on the UV Set input socket and set the node that is connected to the Texture Color 0 and Texture Detail 1.
4. Load the textures within the sockets for the Texture nodes.
5. Connect the Texture Nodes Output sockets to the Color 1 and 2 inputs of the Composite. Name this node "Composite 1." (See Figure 20.5.)

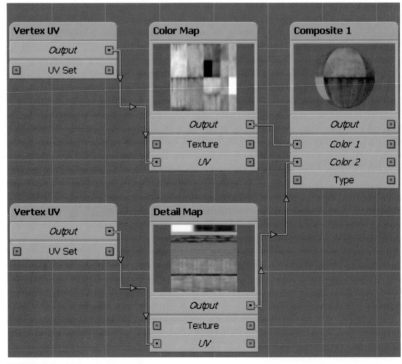

FIGURE 20.5   UV set connection.

Now we are going to do the same thing for the dirt and lightmap. Instead of recreating these, do a marquee select over what you have created and right mouse click on an empty area in the wiregraph.

1. Create a template through the command Save Selected as Template. Name the template "UV setup."
2. Add a new UV setup by right mouse clicking in the empty wiregraph.
3. Update the UV to the correct set, load the correct textures, and name them. The dirt map has UV set 2, and the lightmap has UV set 4.
4. Name this Composite "Composite 2."

Now we are going to add the decal map. It uses an alpha, so it needs a specific setup to work. For this, we need:

- One vertex UV
- One texture
- One select component
- One composite

Since the decal is not a multiply, we need to split the texture that has a transparency in its alpha to a different node.

1. Connect the vertex UV to the texture and rename the Texture "Decal Map."
2. Connect the output from the texture to the Selected Components Color 1 input.
3. Through the socket, change the Select Component to Alpha in the Type Slot.
4. Connect Select Components Output to the Composite Color 2 input and rename it "Composite 4." (See Figure 20.6.)

We now have each of the pieces separate, but let's start to connect these values first and look at the result before we connect the normal map. To do so, we need to connect all our Composite nodes to our Single Pass node. Composites 1 and 2 need a new Composite node to blend with each other, and then a final Composite node to blend the rest

1. Make two Composites, and name them "Composite 1&2" and "Composite 3."
2. Connect the Output from the Composite 1&2 to Composite 3 Color 1 input.
3. Connect the Output from the Composite 4 to Composite 3 Color 2 input.
4. Change the Type of Composite 3 Node to Alpha2.
5. Connect Composite 3 output to Single Pass Node Color input socket.

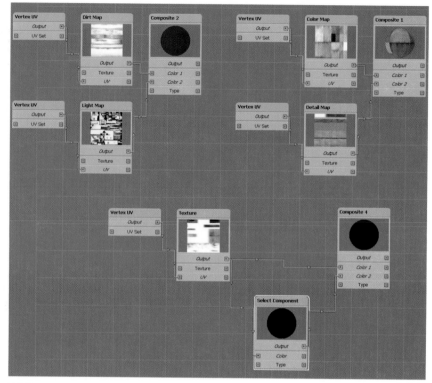

FIGURE 20.6   Three sets of UV setup connections.

Rotating your model, you will see all the different layers of textures together with the final lightmap. An added normal map will try to override the lightmap values and we will most likely experience some strange results. Nevertheless, let's do it (see Figure 20.7).

It is very important how we blend the normal map together with where we place it in the hierarchy. Building up the lighting and the normal map, they will share UV Set number 3, so for this we need:

1. One Vertex UV, One Lighting node, One Texture node, One Composite.
2. Load normal map, rename node, and connect it to the Normal Map socket of the Lighting node.
3. Set Vertex UV to 1, as the normal map shares the detail map's UV set.

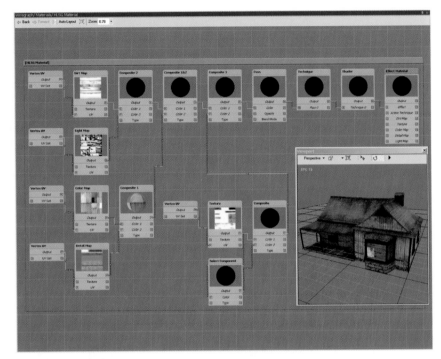

FIGURE 20.7   Connection without a normal map.

We are going to add the Composite next to the detail map with the same UV set. Make it shine a bit more so we can clearly see the result.

1. Remove the connection between Composite 1 Output and the Composite 1&2 Color2 input.
2. Connect the Diffuse socket output from the Lighting node into Color 2 on the newly created Composite. Name this node "Composite 5."
3. Change the Type of Composite 5 to Add, for added light within the object.
4. Connect Composite 1 Output output to Composite 5 Color 1 input.
5. Reconnect the Composite 1&2 color 2 slot input by using the Composite 5 Output. (See Figure 20.8.)

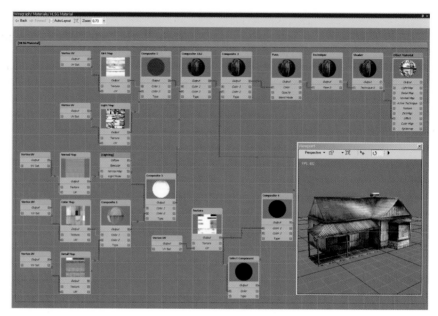

FIGURE 20.8   Final connection with the normal map.

SUMMARY

Artists will be more involved with the next generation of shaders and creating materials for next-generation gaming consoles and games. We are moving toward what will become a standard in the industry.

This chapter afforded you an introduction and an understanding of what shaders are and how you can create them. You also learned how to use Rt/Shader, a program specialized to be very intuitive for artists. Let's sum up the chapter:

1. Shaders are small scripts that execute within the graphics card hardware.
2. Shaders are dependent on the version of code that the graphics card supports.
3. PC games support scaleable shaders, so they work on all different cards on the market.
4. NVIDIA has created a shader language (Cgfx shaders) that combines the functionality for the two main shader languages: OpenGL and DirectX shaders.

5. There are two main shader types: Pixel and Vertex shaders.
6. Vertex shaders let you control movements and vertex colors, and we use them to control skinning and animating of vertices.
7. Vertex shades cannot delete or create vertices, only control them.
8. Using textures within Pixel shaders, graphics cards are limited to the number of textures they can use in each render pass. This is different for each console and Pixel shader version.
9. Rt/Shader and Shaderworks are two new programs that have taken a step toward an easier user interface for programmers and for artists to use and understand shaders better and create them faster.

ABOUT THE CD-ROM

The companion CD-ROM to *Game Art: Creation, Direction, and Careers* contains all art assets necessary to follow the tutorials and exercises in the book. Feel free to use these models and the content as starting points for your own game art.

Chapter Folder Content

Chapter 8   Modeling—Contains reference images, max and Maya files for modeling the weapon.

Chapter 9   Texturing—Contains Photoshop files for the tutorial, Maya and max files for the 3D object, and the example Photoshop image with layers for the Scratch map example.

Chapter 15   GI Lightmaps—Contains 3ds max Setup and Final scenes together with a lightmap.

Chapter 17   Multitexturing—Contains 3ds max and Maya scenes with images for the tutorial.

Chapter 18   Hi-Resolution Modeling—Contains the file needed for tutorial, 3ds max, Maya, and Zbrush scene, and tool files. It also contains the final exported meshes.

Chapter 19   Normal Mapping—Contains textures and 3d meshes needed for Normalmap texturing.

Chapter 20   Shaders—Contains Models, texture for use with Rt/Shader and Chapter 20.

Extras   Contains a testmap so you can test and verify your mapping on objects.

Images   Contains all images used within the book, for higher detail.

Programs   Contains the tryout version of Rt/Shader—Internet connection is required for registration.

USE OF SCENE FILES

Maya

To use the scenes on the CD-ROM:
Set the Project to the specific Chapter (Scene) on the CD by the command File/Project/Set/

3ds max

To use the scenes on the CD-ROM:
Load scenes from folders.

Recommended System Requirements

In order to make use of the CD-ROM and follow the tutorials fully, the following system is recommended:

- AMD Athlon™ or Intel Pentium® 4 processor
- Windows XP or Microsoft Windows 2000
- 512 MB RAM
- 1 GB of available hard-disk space
- Geforce 4 or ATI 8500 or greater video card
- 1280 × 1024 or greater resolution
- CD-ROM drive
- Internet or phone connection required for product activation
- Photoshop and a commercial 3D product to use the tutorial files (such as Maya, 3ds max, etc.)

Software on the CD-ROM

Rt/Shader—GINZA
Graph Shader program used for creating shaders in Chapter 20.

SYSTEM REQUIREMENTS FOR GINZA

- Windows XP
- 300 MB of available hard-disk space
- Microsoft NET Framework 1.1
- Geforce FX or ATI 9500 or greater video card
- DirectX 9.0c
- Requires a trial license key (Internet required)

Further information on installation can be read in the file: Release-Notes.txt in program folder on the CD-ROM or can be found at:

www.rtzen.com
RTzen, Inc.
601 108th Ave NE
19th Floor
Bellevue, WA 98004
Inside the US: 1 (800) 73-RTzen
Outside the US: +1 (425) 943-3893
Main FAX: +1 (425) 696-0620

INDEX